PROJECT MANAGEMENT STUDY GUIDE

Study questions for certification and college exams
based on the *PMBOK® Guide – Sixth Edition*

Tom Schoen

1411Consulting, LLC

ContactUs@1411Consulting.com

6 5 4 3 2 1

Contents

ACKNOWLEDGMENTS

Too many friends to mention everyone. This effort is a result of many great project teams, discussions with experienced project leaders with demonstrated success and college undergraduate project management students. Each led to a better understanding. And still, do today.

I would like to recognize one friend who directly influenced this study guide. Jed's project management experience and our discussions about project management are incorporated in this study guide. When I needed someone to review the study guide I reached out to Jed. Jed's feedback was invaluable. The result is a much better study guide. Thanks, Jed!

This book would also not be possible without the support of the PMI® Central Illinois Chapter (PMI®-CIC). I became PMP® certified after graduating from the PMI®-CIC Project Management Professional (PMP)® prep course. The chapter and its members continue their support today.

Thanks everyone!

Tom

PREFACE

The purpose of this study guide is to aid the student who is taking a project management course in college or preparing for the Project Management Professional (PMP)® or Certified Associate in Project Management (CAPM)® exams.

Additional learning source
You will find free online learning materials to help prepare you for the (PMP)® and (PMI-ACP)® exams at 1411Consulting.com.

How to use this guide
Studying practice questions is a proven technique to pass exams successfully. To maximize learning, the key to using this guide is to understand each answer to a question. Not just memorizing the question's correct answer. It is just as critical to understanding why the other answers were incorrect.

There are different ways to leverage these questions. The first is to answer all the questions and then check the answers. This method simulates an exam "like" scenario where you complete the questions before checking the number answered correctly.

The second method is to answer one question and then check the answer. This approach enables studying the topic of each question for understanding before moving on to the next question.

A third option is to read the answers. Answers provide an understanding of each topic plus a reference for further understanding. This approach may be best when starting to learn the material.

Exam tips
Incorporate into your workday
To help learn the processes, tools and techniques, inputs, and outputs, it is a good practice to start incorporating them into your daily activities. For example, you just attended a kick-off meeting where the charter was approved? Think – we just finished Develop Project Charter. Working today on a deliverable for your project? Think – Direct and Manage Project Work.

It would help if you also incorporated the terminology into daily language. "Where may I access lessons learned to develop this new project charter?" "We need to Perform Integrated Change Control to understand the impact of this change request."

These tips can be especially beneficial if you and another person in your group are both preparing for the exam.

Thanks for the tip, Jed!

"The best next step is…"
For exam questions that ask "the BEST next step is…?" determine where the question is in the PDCA process to determine which answer is correct.

Plan-Do-Check-Act (PDCA) underlies many project management processes. Each knowledge area has a "Plan" process in the planning process group to create a knowledge area plan. The executing process group ("Do") follows for each knowledge area. After producing the process output or outputs, they are typically "Checked" by a Monitoring and Control group process. If the results match expectations, the project team continues to "Act" by performing the verified process using the same tools and techniques to produce more. If the results do not match expectations, then the team starts over beginning with the planning step.

Multiple-choice tests
I recommend searching the internet for tips on taking multiple-choice question exams. It is essential to practice these techniques when preparing for an exam.

A common multiple-choice question exam technique is to eliminate answers that you know are incorrect. For example, are you able to eliminate two of the four answers as incorrect? This technique lets you focus on just the remaining answers.

Now that you have eliminated the known incorrect answers, apply the basics. What answer is the most ethical choice? What answer best demonstrates servant leadership? What answer is the next step to Perform Integrated Change Control? What is the next step in producing the deliverable?

Additional resources

There are many resources available to prepare for a project management exam. A student should confirm any resource is the correct edition based on the targeted exam. Some resources may be for prior editions. Using obsolete resources may result in the student preparing for the exam with missing or outdated terms and definitions.

Project Management Institute (PMI)®

The Project Management Institute (PMI)® web site provides many resources. If preparing for a PMI certification, you may wish to join PMI to receive applicable discounts.

AGILE

The purpose of this section is to link the *PMBOK® Guide* processes and concepts with Agile roles, tools, and processes. This section, plus the suggested reading, will help prepare a student for Agile questions on the exam.

In practice, leaders should draw from all concepts and approaches, along with their knowledge and experiences. Leverages these is beneficial regardless of the methodology, predictive, Agile, or hybrid, that is implemented on the project.

Changes

The *PMBOK® Guide – Sixth Edition* contains more references to the Agile methodology than prior editions. In some cases, the *PMBOK® Guide* identifies the concepts or terms as Agile. In other cases, they are not identified. This second case may make it difficult for a student with no previous Agile work experience or education to recognize these references to Agile.

Agile frameworks

There are many different Agile frameworks. These include the Scaled Agile Framework (SAFe), Crystal, and eXtreme Programming (XP). Experienced Agile teams may draw from more than one framework, using the applicable concepts from each, on a single project.

Scrum is another Agile framework that has enjoyed popularity for many years. Scrum is an excellent framework to study as the approach aligns with common Agile values and principles that may be on the exam.

The Scrum Guide

Often organizations and teams customize methodologies and frameworks. This customization is common. The downside is someone might have Scrum experience but never been on a team that thoroughly implemented the Scrum methodology and framework.

This experience may lead to being poorly prepared for the exam. It is essential in your preparation to "return to" or learn the methodology as defined without customizations. There is no better place to start learning Scrum, and Agile processes in general, than *The Scrum Guide* (Scrum.org, 2019).

Linking Agile with the *PMBOK® Guide – Sixth Edition*
User Story

An individual requirement or feature. Initially, user stories briefly describe a requirement and may include acceptance criteria.

The team progressively elaborates on a user story. Progressive elaboration occurs by decomposing or further defining each user story. Progressive elaboration, along with decomposition, support many of the topics in the *PMBOK® Guide – Sixth Edition*.

Product Backlog

A list of all user stories for the project and product. One key difference between Agile and traditional projects is the Agile methodology embraces changing requirements. If the organization, product owner, or customer identifies a new requirement at any time, the user story (requirement) is modified or added to the product backlog.

In the *PMBOK® Guide – Sixth Edition*, the product backlog activities are aligned with the Collect Requirements process. At this point, the user story may or may not be in-scope for the project. Whether the user story will be in-scope or implemented occurs next in Agile frameworks.

The product owner reviews all the user stories in the product backlog to determine the user stories that provide the highest business value. This frequent assessment of the relative business value of each user story results in the reprioritization of all user stories. The product owner is performing the *PMBOK® Guide – Sixth Edition* Define Scope process to determine which user stories will be in-scope or included in the next sprint. This reassessment is performed just before each sprint planning session.

One must keep in mind that the implementation of some user stories in the product backlog may never occur. Those user stories are out-of-scope. By definition, these out-of-scope user stories have less relative business value than the chosen user stories.

Sprint or Iteration Planning

Estimate Activity Resources, Identify Risks, Plan Risk Responses, Estimate Cost, Plan Procurement Management (make-buy decisions), etc. Agile projects execute these processes each sprint or iteration during sprint planning. In traditional methodology projects, these processes may only be performed once during the planning phase for the entire project.

The team compares the estimate of all user stories to the sprint capacity of the development team. Only those user stories, whose estimated sum equals the team's capacity per sprint, are chosen for this sprint. These selected user stories are the in-scope user stories. Any additional estimated user stories are "returned" to the product backlog for consideration in a future sprint.

Another key Agile concept defined during sprint planning is the definition of completed or "done." When is the user story "done?" When the screen refreshes in less than two seconds? One second? The ability to measure done is critical for the team to verify and the customer to validate the completion of the user story. The definition of done and the metrics to measure done align with the quality and requirements knowledge areas of the *PMBOK® Guide – Sixth Edition.*

Product Increment

A product increment is a useable version of the product, service, or result built during the sprint and prior sprints. The user stories selected from the product backlog during sprint planning further define the product increment.

Agile concepts embrace progressively elaborating on everything – requirements, design, estimates, etc. An example of progressive elaboration is the core Agile concept of incrementally creating a deliverable each iteration that provides more and more business value.

Sprint or Iteration

A sprint is a brief, typically two to four weeks long, period where the development team produces an increment of the product. Sprint is a Scrum specific term. Other Agile frameworks may use the term iteration. On the exam, sprint and iteration should be considered the same.

A sprint aligns with the *PMBOK® Guide – Sixth Edition* Direct and Manage Project Work process. During a sprint, the team produces a product increment or deliverable. Each product increment must produce and demonstrate what is known as either a Minimal Viable Product (MVP) or Minimal Marketable Product (MMP). In other words, each product increment must add business value by producing a working version, perhaps with just the minimum features of a viable deliverable.

.

Daily Scrum or Daily Standup

This Agile event is a daily meeting for the project team directly responsible for creating the product increment during the iteration. Some teams may refer to this event as the "standup meeting" since daily is assumed.

Each team member answers three questions during a standup. "What did they do since the last standup?" "What do they plan to complete before the next standup?" "Is there anything impeding their progress?" Daily standups are time-boxed to fifteen minutes. Follow up to anything brought up during the standup is done after the meeting with only the necessary required team members.

Standup meetings are part of the project's communication management plan, as defined in the PMBOK® Guide – Sixth Edition. Daily standups also provide frequent work performance data – "What did I do since the last standup?" This data is quickly transformed into work performance information by asking – "Is there anything impeding my progress?" The scrum master immediately knows the task status (work performance data) and if the task is on, behind or ahead of schedule (work performance information)

Daily standups are an excellent example of an Agile event that may provide significant benefits even to teams using traditional project methodology. Leaders should consider tools and techniques from all methodologies when leading projects.

Sprint or Iteration Reviews

At the end of each sprint, the project team demonstrates the product increment in a sprint review meeting. The team is seeking customer validation that the deliverable meets the customer's requirements.

Sprint reviews are a critical review step. The development team previously verified they produced what was asked for by the customer in a user story. But now that the customer sees the results, the customer may not validate or accept the results. Not accepting the results may be due to several reasons. These reasons include changing business needs, now that the customer sees the outcome, realizes it is not acceptable, etc. The team may reference the Control Quality and Validate Scope processes in the *PMBOK® Guide – Sixth Edition* for inputs, tools, techniques, and outputs to complete the verification and validation of product increments.

In traditional methodologies, when the customer requests a change, the result is one or more formal change requests. These change requests are then assessed for impact and require approval. The result is these changes may not be well received by the team due to the effect on the project schedule.

Agile frameworks anticipate the customer may change requirements. Anticipating changes even late in the development is one of the Agile core principles. Agile handles changes by modifying existing or creating new user stories. The product owner then selects from all user stories those with the highest business value for the team to work on during the next iteration. In Agile, this occurs without creating change requests and following a more rigid change process common to traditional methodologies.

Agile projects may still require formal change procedures. Leveraging the *PMBOK® Guide – Sixth Edition* Perform Integrated Change Control process may be necessary, for example, to request services and support outside of the Agile project.

Sprint Retrospective or Introspective

At the end of each sprint or iteration, the development team meets to review the just completed sprint. What went well, and the team should continue? What didn't go well, and the team should stop? What could have gone better if the team did more of or less of something?

The goal of a retrospective is for the team to reflect and recommend improvements to increase the efficiency and effectiveness of the processes, tools, and techniques. By improving productivity, the team will be able to complete more user stories and, in turn, deliver more business value quicker to the customer and organization.

Retrospective commonly refers to this review when done at specific intervals, such as the end of a sprint. The term introspective may be used instead of retrospective. However, the term introspective commonly describes a review meeting to improve whenever the team determines one is needed.

Retrospectives align with processes, tools, and techniques such as quality management plan, Monitor Quality, etc. as defined in the *PMBOK® Guide – Sixth Edition*. Retrospectives also align directly with the Plan-Do-Check-Act (PDCA) concept. The PDCA concept underlies all quality improvement concepts and processes defined in the *PMBOK® Guide – Sixth Edition*.

Product Owner or Customer
The product owner prioritizes the user stories in the product backlog. The highest priority user stories are the ones that will be worked on next by the development team. This person is responsible for delivering the highest business value as quickly as possible.

In traditional methodologies, the project manager often prioritizes the project team's work. In Agile, the product owner or customer prioritizes the work.

The product backlog contains all the project requirements or work. These requirements include not only project or product requirements but all the work that the team must complete. Need to implement a risk response plan? Those plans are prioritized by business value in the product backlog by the product owner. Complete stakeholder communication or documentation? These communications are prioritized by business value in the product backlog by the product owner. Implement a process improvement activity? These improvements are prioritized by business value in the product backlog by the product owner.

Scrum Master, Coach or Team Leader
Agile methodologies emphasize servant leadership. This emphasis contrasts with the perception of traditional methodology leadership were the project manager is directive. Traditionally the project manager tells project team members exactly what to do, when to do it, etc. based on the approved schedule, cost, and scope baselines. I propose the directive

leadership approach is inappropriate for leading any project today regardless of the methodology.

Where's the project manager? An Agile project may have a project manager that performs some of the traditional responsibilities. In other cases, either the scrum master, product owner, or the project development team will perform traditional project manager responsibilities.

For example, the scrum master ensures the project team has what they need. The scrum master does this by removing project team impediments, protecting the project team from nonvalue-added interruptions, being a project vision champion, and educating the project team on Agile methodology usage. Today, all and more is expected from a project manager, scrum master, coach, or team leader regardless of the methodology.

Project Development or Delivery Team
The project team members directly responsible for delivering the product, service, or result. Agile teams typically have twelve or fewer members.

In Agile, the team self-organizes by collaboratively working together. The team estimates the effort to complete user stories. The product owner and scrum master accept these estimates. The result is an empowered team motivated to complete the user stories in the sprint.

References

Agile Alliance
Agilealliance.org. 2019. Agile Alliance. [Online]. [28 September 2019]. Available at: https://www.agilealliance.org/

Agile Manifesto
Agilemanifesto.org. 2019. Agile Manifesto. [Online]. [26 December 2019]. Available at: https://agilemanifesto.org/

Agilemanifesto.org. 2019. Agile Principles. [Online]. [26 December 2019]. Available at: https://agilemanifesto.org/principles.html

The Agile Practice Guide
Project Management Institute and Agile Alliance. 2017. The Agile Practice Guide. United States: Project Management Institute, Inc.

The Scrum Guide
Scrum.org. 2019. The Scrum Guide. [Online]. [2 September 2019]. Available at: https://www.scrum.org/resources/scrum-guide

Questions

1. The team is evaluating the deliverables from the last sprint. The evaluation includes how well the team worked together and the processes used to produce the deliverables. What is the team performing?
   A. Root cause
   B. Retrospective
   C. Assessment
   D. Review

2. The sponsor anticipates new requirements throughout the project. Which of the following from the Agile Manifesto BEST aligns with changing requirements?
   A. Individual and interactions over processes and tools
   B. Working software over comprehensive documentation
   C. Customer collaboration over contract negotiations
   A. Responding to change over following a plan

3. The customer wants to understand how much work remains before completing the project. What chart would provide this information?
   A. Burndown chart
   B. Burnup chart
   C. Completion chart
   D. Sprint chart

4. The project team is evaluating different alternatives. Each team member shows their level of support for an alternative by either raising a closed hand or up to five fingers. What BEST describes this technique?
   A. Decision making
   B. Fist of five
   C. Voting
   D. Participation

5. An Agile team member has deep expertise in security programming. However, the team member's skills are much more limited in creating test cases and other needed skills on the team. What BEST describes this person's skill set?
   A. I-shaped
   B. T-shaped
   C. Limited
   D. Focused

6. What is the highest priority on Agile projects?
    A. Early and continuous delivery of valuable software
    B. Welcome changing requirements
    C. Working software
    D. Continuous attention to technical excellence

7. An Agile team is estimating effort to complete a requirement. The team considers the relative work, risk, and complexity compared to other requirements. Which of the following is the team using?
    A. Analogous estimating
    B. Predictive estimating
    C. Bottom-up estimating
    D. Story point estimating

8. There was great concern that the customer would be frustrated with the project changes. As a result, the team embedded the customer into the team. Often incorporating their suggestions in the deliverables. What BEST describes this approach?
    A. Partnering
    B. Co-creation
    C. Co-production
    D. Collaboration

9. A complex technical project is about to begin. The team expects frequent changes while the organization learns about technology. What life cycle is BEST?
    A. Agile
    B. Predictive
    C. Iterative
    D. Incremental

10. The team is reviewing with the customer the deliverable from the latest sprint. The customer is pleased with the demonstration and accepts the deliverable. What BEST describes this review?
    A. Retrospective
    B. Sprint review
    C. Deliverable review
    D. Customer review

11. The customer wants to know how long it will take the team to produce a deliverable. What BEST describes this?
    A. Response time
    B. Cycle time
    C. Lead time
    D. Production time

12. Which role promotes listening, mentoring team members to achieve personal growth, coaching versus controlling, trust, and respect?
    A. Servant leader
    B. Project manager
    C. Sponsor
    D. Key stakeholder

13. Each day the team gathers to discuss what they worked on yesterday, what they will work on today, and if there are any blockers to their progress. What is this discussion called?
    A. Daily retrospective
    B. Daily updates
    C. Daily status
    D. Daily standups

14. The team doesn't have a complete understanding of a requirement. So the team will produce and review a prototype with the customer. What type of risk is this?
    A. Event risk
    B. Ambiguity risk
    C. Unknown risk
    D. Variability risk

15. Before each sprint, all the outstanding work is re-prioritized. Who prioritizes this work?
    A. Sponsor
    B. Customer
    C. Product owner
    D. Team

Answers

The *PMBOK® Guide – Sixth Edition* contains many references to Agile. The purpose of this section is to provide additional background to common Agile concepts and practices.

It is essential to prepare for exam questions about Agile. Sources for additional study include *The Scrum Guide* (https://www.scrum.org/resources/scrum-guide), the *Agile Practice Guide* published by the Project Management Institute, Inc., and many online sites.

Unlike all other sections, this section's answers may not contain *PMBOK® Guide – Sixth Edition* page references. This lack of page references is due to the brevity of Agile information contained within the *PMBOK® Guide – Sixth Edition*. Regardless, one may expect Agile questions on the exam.

1. B. Retrospective
   - The team is reviewing their work to determine what went right and what could have gone better. The team is learning. This learning event is known as a retrospective. A retrospective, or introspective, may be done at any time by the team. In other cases, retrospectives occur at specific intervals. For example, a retrospective done at the end of the sprint is known as a Sprint Retrospective. Retrospectives are one of the agile principles – *"At regular intervals, the team reflects on how to become more effective, then tunes and adjusts its behavior accordingly."*
   - (*PMBOK® Guide – Sixth Edition*, page 276)
2. D. Responding to change over following the plan
   - t is essential to understand and apply the Agile Manifesto to exam questions. This is critical. In this question, the sponsor anticipates new requirements throughout the project. As a result, the sponsor realizes the team will need to quickly, and willingly, reprioritize work to meet these new or changing requirements. Agile is well suited for this.
   - Is there no planning in Agile projects? No. Be sure to understand the Agile Manifesto values. The preference is for what's on the left side "over" the right side. It should not be interpreted that what is on the left side replaces what is on the right side. Agile projects are, by definition,

responsive to changing requirements and willing to change the plan to do so. Predictive or waterfall projects, on the other hand, focus on executing the approved schedule baseline (i.e., schedule). Therefore predictive projects are reluctant to accommodate changing requirements that impact the schedule.

- Is Agile better than the waterfall project life-cycle? No. Understanding which life cycle is best for the project is a crucial early decision. Applying the wrong life cycle to a project ensures at a minimum greater difficulty in achieving the business objectives.
- Agilemanifesto.org. 2019. Agile Manifesto. [Online]. [26 December 2019]. Available at: https://agilemanifesto.org/

3. A. Burndown chart

- A burndown chart shows how much work is left to complete the stories (requirements) in the backlog. The burndown chart duration maybe for a day, sprint, an iteration, or the entire project. The burndown chart may show the ideal or original, actual and forecasted remaining work. (*PMBOK® Guide – Sixth Edition*, page 226)

4. B. Fist of five

- Also known as "fist to five." The fist of five is a voting decision-making technique. Each team member may hold from zero (closed fist) to five fingers to show support for an alternative or decision. Any team member holding up less than three fingers is allowed to share the reason for their lack of support. The voting continues until all team members hold up three or more fingers. (*PMBOK® Guide – Sixth Edition*, page 203)

5. A. I-shaped

- Sometimes when a person is a subject matter expert, they are classified based on their skill as I-shaped. Meaning they have in-depth knowledge in a single subject or skill set. However, they may not be able to assist the team in other areas.
- While expertise may be critical to the project's success, often in Agile projects, T-shaped people are more desirable. T-shaped people can perform competently at more than one skill. For example, a senior software developer may also be able to write and execute test scripts. This flexibility is critical to keeping the sprint deliverables on schedule. The Agile concept of self-

organizing teams depends on having T-shaped people. (*PMBOK® Guide – Sixth Edition*, page 310)

6.   A. Early and continuous delivery of valuable software

- One of the Agile principles is, "*Our highest priority is to satisfy the customer through early and continuous delivery of valuable software.*" Agile projects focus on producing software that provides business value in the eyes of the customer. Understanding the Agile Manifesto and principles may help in choosing the best exam question answer.
- Agilemanifesto.org. 2019. Agile Principles. [Online]. [26 December 2019]. Available at: https://agilemanifesto.org/principles.html

7.   D. User story estimating

- Agile teams use story points to estimate and plan work to complete requirements (stories). This estimation is relative to other work on the project, as noted in the question. It is essential to understand that user story points are unique to each team. This uniqueness is due to the individual project requirements and team member skills. Therefore, one cannot compare the performance of two Agile teams based on completed story points per sprint.
- Over time the team's velocity is determined by the number of story points completed each sprint. Velocity enables estimating how many story points the team may complete in future sprints. The highest priority stories, whose combined story point total is less than or equal to the velocity, is planned for the next sprint.
- (*PMBOK® Guide – Sixth Edition*, page 203)

8.   B. Co-creation

- Co-creation incorporates, or embeds, affected customers with the project team. To the point where those customers are partners in the creation of the project deliverables. (*PMBOK® Guide – Sixth Edition*, page 505)

9.   C. Iterative

- Determining a solution, certainly for complex solutions, often benefits from prototyping, which is common in the iterative life cycle. Prototyping may be done during the analysis and design phase to demonstrate and reach consensus. The team further refines the solution during the build and test phases before deployment.
- It is essential to realize a project may benefit from values, principles, or characteristics of more than one life cycle.

For example, the project may leverage the iterative approach during design. While leveraging the waterfall life cycle during the development and deployment phases. Applying the benefits of more than one life cycle is referred to as a hybrid life cycle.

- (PMBOK® Guide – Sixth Edition, page 151)

10. B. Sprint review

- After each sprint, the team conducts a sprint review with the customer. Before the review, the team has verified the sprint deliverables (i.e., performed Control Quality). The customer then validates (i.e., performs Validate Scope) the demonstrated deliverable during the review. The team may incorporate feedback from the customer in future sprints.

- It is important to note how Agile may use processes in *PMBOK® Guide – Sixth Edition*. Some sources of Agile describe sprint reviews as the team demonstrating the sprint deliverable to the customer for acceptance — little more. Therefore, Agile teams may gain insight from Control Quality and Validate Scope on how to prepare and conduct sprint reviews.

- Scrum.org. 2019. The Scrum Guide. [Online]. [2 September 2019]. Available at:
  https://www.scrum.org/resources/scrum-guide

11. C. Lead time

- Lead time is a measurement of time from once a story is ready until delivery to the customer. Placing a story on the Kanban board indicates the story is ready to be worked.

- Teams use a Kanban board to track story progress from ready to design, develop, and test until the story is available for delivery to the customer. After completing a task, the story is moved to the next task, a column on the board.

- The time to process a task is known as cycle time. While response time is the time, a story waits before being started.

- (*PMBOK® Guide – Sixth Edition*, page 177)

12. A. Servant leader

- The best answer. While associated with Agile, servant leadership is now expected regardless of the project life cycle. Today's most successful project managers, sponsors, and key stakeholders all demonstrate servant leadership principles.

13. C. Daily standups
   - Agile teams gather each day, typically time-box for fifteen minutes. These discussions are called daily standups. Each team member answers three questions. What did they do yesterday? What will they do today? Are there any blockers hindering their progress? Typically the product owner, scrum master, and others do not speak during these standups. Only the team members speak. (*PMBOK® Guide – Sixth Edition*, page 364)

14. B. Ambiguity risk
   - Sometimes customers don't know what they want. Even if they are confident, once they see the deliverable, customers may only then realize that they need something else.
   - Another example is will a new unproven technology satisfy the project needs? The Agile life cycle supports teams that must deal with the risk of ambiguity.
   - (*PMBOK® Guide – Sixth Edition*, page 398)

15. C. Product owner
   - It is the product owner's responsibility to prioritize the development team's work based on business value. The product owner determines the business value with input from the customer and other stakeholders.
   - The list of all outstanding work, in priority order, is kept in the product backlog. Based on the Agile Manifesto of *"responding to change over following a plan,"* the work in the product backlog is reprioritized before each sprint. Work is then selected from the product backlog, based on priority, for the development team to produce during the next sprint.
   - (*PMBOK® Guide – Sixth Edition*, page 177)

INTRODUCTION, PROJECT LIFE-CYCLES AND PROJECT MANAGER ROLE

This section covers the first three chapters of the *PMBOK® Guide – Sixth Edition*. These chapters cover many critical terms and topics that build the foundation for understanding project management.

Ethics

Always demonstrate the highest standards when it comes to ethics and professional conduct.

The PMI® Code of Ethics and Professional Conduct (https://www.pmi.org/about/ethics/code) clearly defines expectations. Both for the exam and professionally while you are a member of the Professional Management Institute (PMI)®.

Some may find this topic more difficult since personal conduct and ethical norms vary across organizational cultures. All should take the time to understand the PMI® expectations.

Most exam questions focus on "how" you work. Where in the process is the project? What is the best activity to do next? What is the benefit of control charts?

Professional conduct and ethics are about the "way" you work. The result is ethics and professional conduct expectations underlie all exam questions. For example, on the exam, you may be able to reduce the question's potential correct answers to two of the listed answers. In analyzing the remaining two answers for correctness, you should choose the answer that best supports expected ethical and professional conduct behaviors.

What's a project?
"A temporary endeavor undertaken to create a unique product, service or result." (PMBOK® Guide – Sixth Edition)

This definition seems clear. However, you must apply some context and understanding.

- Is a 10-year effort temporary? Yes. Many projects span years (e.g., building a power plant).
- Is assembling a car unique because of the different colors and options? No. Assembling a car is repetitive and on-going, so it is considered operations.
- Is building a new software application a project? Yes. Is supporting that application's distribution from an app store a project? No.

Project Life Cycles
Are predictive or adaptive. If a life cycle has both predictive and adaptive characteristics, it is known as a hybrid.

The most common predictive life cycle is known as traditional or waterfall. Predictive life cycle projects determine the scope, schedule, and cost of the project early in the life cycle. These projects focus on maintaining the scope throughout the project.

Agile projects are adaptive life cycle projects. Agile projects embrace changing scope right up to just before an iteration. These projects tend to focus on controlling the cost and time constraints throughout the project.

More on Agile
The *PMBOK® Guide – Sixth Edition* contains more references to the Agile life-cycle than prior editions. In some cases, explicitly calling out Agile. In other cases, just referencing Agile concepts and terms. This second case may make it difficult for a student with limited previous Agile work experience or education to recognize these Agile references.

The exam preparer is encouraged to read Annex A3 – Overview of Agile and Lean Frameworks (*PMBOK® Guide – Sixth Edition*) for a minimum understanding of Agile for the exam.

Often organizations and teams customize methodologies and frameworks. The downside is that perhaps you have experience with Scrum or another Agile framework. But you have never worked on a team that fully implemented the Agile methodology and framework as defined.

If this is your experience, it may result in being poorly prepared for an exam. It is essential in your preparation to learn the methodology as defined initially without customizations. A great place to start learning Scrum, and Agile processes in general, is *The Scrum Guide* (https://www.scrum.org/resources/scrum-guide).

Another reference source is the *Agile Practice Guide* (Agile Practice Guide (2017). The Project Management Institute and the Agile Alliance® (https://www.agilealliance.org) published this guide.

Can we change that?
No. If "that" is enterprise environmental factors.
Enterprise environmental factors (EEFs) are outside the control of the project team. Examples include the organization's culture, infrastructure (e.g., computer network capabilities), location of offices, the skills of the people within the organization, etc. The project team can change none of these.

EEFs are inputs to many processes. Rather than memorize all possible EEFs, remember the project team cannot change or influence them. For example, you are the project manager of a team chartered to improve the organization's culture. Yet your team must operate under the current culture until the project completes. At that time, the new culture will be an EEF for all active and future projects.

Can we change these?
Yes. If "these" are organizational process assets.

The team modifies organizational process assets (OPAs) to the needs of their project. Have you ever asked someone for a copy of their PowerPoint presentation so yours would have the same "look and feel"? Ask them for a copy of a project charter so you could quickly create a charter for your project? Ask someone to send you a spreadsheet so you can track your project's budget the way accounting wants? All are examples of organizational process assets. Like EEFs, don't memorize all the possible organizational process assets. Just remember that templates, life cycles, guidelines, etc. may be changed by the project team to suit the project's needs better.

A quick web search produces many good examples of organizational process assets. For example, the state of Maryland provides several templates. This web site is an excellent example of a repository of organizational process assets that a project team can leverage and tailor to their project's needs. (See http://doit.maryland.gov/sdlc/Pages/Templates.aspx)

Project manager

Someone who is accountable for achieving the project's objectives. In this case, the definition of accountable means the one who must justify decisions and explain the results.

A project manager may ask other stakeholders to be responsible for different deliverables on the project. But the project manager remains accountable for all project results.

The project's sponsor and key senior stakeholders are going to ask the project manager to explain the project results. Good or bad. They will not ask a team member, who may have been responsible for doing the work that produced the results, to explain the results.

Successful project managers demonstrate the following skills.

- Leadership. Through the development of the project team members who deliver business value to accomplish the organization's strategy.
- Technical project management. The efficient and effective application of project management techniques and tools.

References
Life cycles

Wikipedia.org. 2019. Incremental Build Model. [Online]. [2 September 2019]. Available at:
https://en.wikipedia.org/wiki/Incremental_build_model

Wikipedia.org. 2019. Iterative and Incremental Development. [Online]. [2 September 2019]. Available at:
https://en.wikipedia.org/wiki/Iterative_and_incremental_development

Questions

1. A project team member wants to apply for a new job posting. This new position would be a promotion. However, the project team member doesn't have experience with the technology listed in the job posting. However, the team member has demonstrated the ability to learn new technologies quickly. What should the team member do?
   - A. Apply for the job, based on demonstrated ability to learn new technologies
   - B. Don't apply for the job, since they are not qualified
   - C. Apply for the job, but clearly state the lack of experience
   - D. Apply for the job, and quickly complete an on-line course for the required technology

2. A product owner determined their organization did not meet terms of an agreement. The seller had not complained. When should the product owner address this issue?
   - A. At the moment of non-compliance
   - B. After project closure
   - C. During the close procurement process
   - D. Only after the seller complains

3. You are a new project manager and look forward to finally controlling everything that influences a project. You meet with an experienced project manager who shares with you the organizational hierarchy and culture, government regulations that will impact the project, and the skills and talents of potential project team members. These are all considered?
   - A. Constraints
   - B. Assumptions
   - C. Enterprise environmental factors
   - D. Organizational process assets

4. Product life-cycle costing includes which costs?
   - A. Deployment costs
   - B. Design through testing costs
   - C. Startup through testing costs
   - D. Concept through retirement costs

5. What is a "statement about uncertainty?"
    A. Risk
    B. Risk event
    C. Assumption
    D. Constraint
6. What is a project? (choose all that apply)
    A. On-going
    B. Identical outputs
    C. Temporary
    D. Unique outputs
7. The project manager identified a need for a stakeholder role. This person would set up the metrics, create a breakdown structure, and track results in a register. Which of the following BEST describes this role?
    A. Sponsor
    B. Product owner
    C. Benefits champion
    D. Program manager
8. A senior project manager was mentoring an inexperienced project manager on organizational change management. What is the purpose of OCM?
    A. Explain why a change is being made
    B. Explain how a change is being made
    C. Change process for Agile projects
    D. Replaces predictive change management
9. What BEST describes the organization's culture?
    A. Organizational Process Asset
    B. Enterprise Environmental Factor
    C. Constraint
    D. Assumption
10. The manager has authority over several projects and activities or work that are related. What BEST describes this situation?
    A. Program
    B. Portfolio
    C. Project
    D. Operations

11. The project manager and team were identifying risks. The project would need to ensure adherence to various personal identity information compliance laws. Which risk strategy or strategies is best?
    A. Avoid and mitigate
    B. Avoid
    C. Avoid, transfer and mitigate
    D. Avoid, transfer, mitigate and accept

12. The product owner was working with a subject matter expert (SME) to create personas. One persona for each of the identified user groups who would be impacted by the next release. The product owner and sponsor are working on which of the following processes?
    A. Change management
    B. Integrated change management
    C. Organizational change management
    D. Stakeholder identification

13. A project manager offered a friend's son an open position on the team. The son had just graduated from college and barely met the grade point average specified in job requirements. Other candidates were better qualified. The project manager was not expecting anything in return from their friend for hiring their son. Did the project manager violate any professional conduct?
    A. Fairness
    B. Honesty
    C. Responsibility
    D. Respect

14. A project manager and product owner were discussing how to determine the success of projects. Which of the following BEST describes the success of a project?
    A. Completed on time
    B. Completed under cost
    C. Realized business value
    D. All scope delivered

15. What is the role of the project manager? (choose all that apply)
    A. Project management knowledge
    B. Interpersonal skills
    C. Accountable for results
    D. Project funding

16. What is the hierarchy from highest to the lowest level?
    A. Portfolio, Program, Project
    B. Project, Portfolio, Program
    C. Portfolio, Project, Program
    D. Program, Project, Portfolio

17. The product owner became aware of a change to emission compliance laws. Since the project already started, which action should the product owner take?
    A. None. The change occurred after the project started
    B. None. The accept risk strategy will be used
    C. Adjust the product backlog
    D. Perform integrated change control

18. A senior manager has created a project charter and is now seeking a project manager. The senior manager contacts the Project Management Office (PMO). The PMO organization will assign a project manager and ensure the project meets organizational expectations. What BEST describes this type of PMO structure?
    A. Supportive
    B. Directive
    C. Controlling
    D. Functional

19. The project manager engaged a subject matter expert (SME) to help with change management. The SME has experience influencing, facilitating, and coaching up and down the organizational hierarchy. What BEST describes this role?
    A. Change sponsor
    B. Change manager
    C. Change agent
    D. Change champion

20. A business recently purchased another business. Part of the business case was savings from implementing efficiencies across both businesses. What BEST describes this business case driver?
    A. Market demand
    B. Organizational need
    C. Customer request
    D. Technological advance

21. Project phases or releases generate which type of business value?
    A. Planned
    B. Expected
    C. Realized
    D. Anticipated

22. The organization provides guidelines, templates, and lessons learned. The project manager and project team are reviewing these items to determine which one to leverage on your project. All these are examples of what?
    A. Enterprise environmental factors
    B. Artifacts
    C. Organizational process assets
    D. Documentation

23. The project manager is discussing the project needs with a functional manager. Specifically, the project manager is asking for the Subject Matter Expert (SME) on a new technology to be part of the project team. The functional manager agrees but states the person cannot start for two months. What BEST describes this condition?
    A. Assumption
    B. Constraint
    C. Commitment
    D. Expert judgment

24. The project manager realizes the project stakeholders will progressively define the deliverables during the project. Changing the deliverable requirements during the project will lead to many changes before the delivery of the final product. What life-cycle would be BEST for this project?
    A. Predictive
    B. Agile
    C. DevOps
    D. Matrix

25. The project team member reported they completed 50% of their assigned project task. Which of the following BEST describes this statement?
    A. Work performance report
    B. Work performance information
    C. Work performance status
    D. Work performance data.

26. A leader wanted to show a leadership video on the Harvard Business Review web site during a presentation. While preparing for the presentation, the leader was never able to get the video to play for its entirety from the web site. The leader shared their frustration with a technical support team member. The team member offered to "rip" the video and email the leader a copy. What should the leader do?
    A. Accept the offer as the leader was only going to show the video anyway
    B. Decline the offer and continue to work on it
    C. Accept the offer and ask they delete the copy after sending it
    D. Accept the offer because the exposure only benefits the Harvard Business Review

27. A senior project manager mentored others on how to implement risk management on their projects. The project manager was certified and was known for developing creative and effective risk response plans. What type of power BEST describes this project manager?
    A. Positional
    B. Informational
    C. Referent
    D. Expert

28. The project team decided to have an electrical contractor wire the new office space. The procurement manager suggested three contractors the project team should consider. The organization has prior experience with each of the contractors. What BEST describes this list of contractors?
    A. Enterprise environmental factors
    B. Constraints
    C. Organizational process asset
    D. Resources

29. The project manager was continually communicating amongst the sponsor, key stakeholders, and the project team. The project manager often discussed project risks. The stakeholders often gave the project manager feedback, and in turn, the project manager provided feedback. What BEST describes this project manager's skills?
    A. Leadership
    B. Technical project management
    C. Professional
    D. Business management

30. The product owner is planning for the introduction of a new product feature at the next release. The product owner is concerned about the acceptance of this change. Which of the following would be BEST to leverage?
    A. Integrated change control
    B. Organizational change management
    C. Surveys
    D. Communication management

31. The organization just re-organized.. resulting in an existing project having a new sponsor. The new sponsor re-assessed the business value of each major project deliverables. Some deliverables now will produce greater business value than others. What should the product owner do next?
    A. Nothing. The project will deliver the same total value
    B. Nothing. The product backlog is set
    C. Nothing. The sprint backlog is set
    D. Re-prioritize the product backlog

32. The scrum master asked for an audit of the lab testing equipment. The purpose was to ensure the accuracy of the equipment. Which of the following BEST describes the reason for this audit?
    A. Measure compliance risk
    B. Measure if project is in compliance
    C. Assess noncompliance
    D. Confirm compliance

33. The sponsor and project manager were discussing a new project. Some of the tools and techniques to produce the deliverables were well known. But in a couple of cases, how to build the other deliverables was not known. What life cycle is the BEST choice?
    A. Predictive
    B. Agile
    C. Hybrid
    D. Adaptive

34. The product owner was attending a conference where she learned about a new data retention policy. Implementing this policy must be done in two months. Which of the following is the BEST choice?
    A. Ask the scrum master to make the appropriate changes
    B. Review and adjust product backlog
    C. Empower the team to address this change
    D. Review and adjust the sprint backlog

35. An external business environment change will impact the project. What of the following is the BEST action by a product owner or project manager?
    A. Recommend options to minimize the impact
    B. Identify the impact and update the product backlog or scope baseline
    C. Update the risk register
    D. Update the schedule and cost baselines

Answers

1. C. Apply for the job, but clearly, state the lack of experience
   - Being honest is one of the expectations of all people, not just leaders, in all their interactions. The team member must share the lack of experience in all interactions about this opportunity. The hiring organization may still offer the team member the job based on other demonstrated skills and knowledge. One of those may well be honesty.. (The *PMI® Code of Ethics and Professional Conduct* https://www.pmi.org/about/ethics/code)
2. A. At the moment of non-compliance
   - Compliance requirements include complying with the terms and conditions of all legal agreements. The product owner must bring this non-compliance issue to the immediate attention of the seller. Doing so often results in both the buyer, the product owner's organization, and seller organizations quickly reaching a mutually acceptable solution. The solution may be to correct the issue per the original terms and conditions.
   - Does this question address another topic? Yes, ethics. Recalling the expected ethics of a project manager alone enables you to answer this question. The only ethical answer is to bring this issue to the immediate attention of the seller. The PMP® and CAPM® exams include the project manager code of ethics and professional conduct expectations. One may trust those same expectations apply to product owners and others associated with any project.
   - (The *PMI® Code of Ethics and Professional Conduct* https://www.pmi.org/about/ethics/code and references in the business environment section)
3. C. Enterprise environmental factors
   - The project manager, even in a projectized organization, does not control all influences on a project. These influences and factors that the project manager and team do not control are enterprise environmental factors. The question lists some of these factors. (*PMBOK® Guide – Sixth Edition*, page 38)

4. D. Concept through retirement costs
    - Caution. Product life cycle costing references the entire life of the product, service, or result. Product life cycle costing is different than the project life-cycle.
    - When evaluating solutions, it is crucial to assess all costs from concept through retirement. This assessment is essential because one solution may be less costly to deploy, but over time due to high maintenance or other costs have higher product life cycle costs than alternative solutions.
    - (*PMBOK® Guide – Sixth Edition*, page 245)
5. C. Assumption
    - Assumptions are "statements about uncertainty." Typically accepted as true and stated with certainty without any proof.
    - Senior managers may state assumptions that further lends credibility that the assumption is a statement of fact. "The cost will not exceed $10,000."
    - A project manager should never accept assumptions. Instead, the project manager must remove all uncertainty of the assumption or create a risk response plan to address the probability and impact of the assumption.
    - (*PMBOK® Guide – Sixth Edition*, page 38)
6. C. Temporary and D Unique outputs
    - Projects are temporary and produce a unique output (product, service, or result). Temporary may be confusing as some projects may last many years. Yet once the output is delivered, the project ends.
    - Likewise, a unique output may be confusing. Building data centers across a region may seem like identical outputs. Yet each data center must be tailored to specific needs of the geographical location, regulations, etc. resulting in a unique data center. (*PMBOK® Guide – Sixth Edition*, page 4)
    - Operations are an on-going effort that produces identical outputs (product, service, or result). A service desk that answers customer's application questions, deployment of a software package version, etc. are all examples of operations.

7. C. Benefits champion

- The benefits champion focuses on ensuring the project's business value is realized and communicated within the organization.
- One responsibility is to create a benefits breakdown structure. This hierarchical chart identifies tangible and intangible benefits at each level within the hierarchy. Additional benefits champion responsibilities include maintaining a benefits register to track benefits, creating metrics, and communicating the realized business value throughout the organization.
- (See references (Levin, 2015) in the business environment section)

8. A. Explain why a change is being made

- Organizational change management (OCM) addresses why a change is being made. The "why" for the change is essential, especially for changes that will generate emotional responses. OCM focuses on the human impact from the change - whether that impact is perceived or real. A critical component of any OCM effort is empathy.
- For example, a project will introduce a change to the culture of the organization. As expected, some people like the existing culture. Some did not. Some will be in the middle. An OCM plan must be created and delivered to address each of these audiences.
- Perform integrated change control is still essential. It describes the steps and who will perform those steps to implement the change.
- How well stakeholders accept a change will significantly impact the project's success. For changes perceived by stakeholders to affect them personally, well-executed OCM is critical to the successful implementation of the change.
- OCM and perform integrated change control applies to all projects. Agile, predictive, and hybrid.
- (PMBOK® Guide – Sixth Edition, page 113 and references in the business environment section)

9. B. Enterprise Environmental Factor

- The organization's culture consists of shared visions, practices, beliefs, risk appetite, and many other factors.

Sometimes referred to "as the way we work" or "the way we do things." Understanding an organization's culture enables to project team to anticipate expected responses to situations by the organization. Often there is a formally stated culture and an informal culture that may more accurately reflect reality.

- As an Enterprise Environmental Factor, the organization's culture influences the project team. And the project team cannot change that culture. Even if the project's objective is to change the culture, that project team still operates under the existing culture until the implementation of the project deliverables to change the culture.
- (*PMBOK® Guide – Sixth Edition*, page 38)

10. A. Program

- Program is a related collection of projects and may include related work or activities. For example, a medical division may have active projects to update the existing web site, create a mobile app, and to implement data analytics package. The medical division may also provide the expertise to analyze the data (e.g., related work). (*PMBOK® Guide – Sixth Edition*, page 14)

11. D. Avoid, transfer, mitigate and accept

- It is easy to assume a team should apply only the avoid or mitigate risk strategies to any compliance requirement. This approach would result in excess cost and time – waste.
- The use of a compliance classification scheme (CCS) will help the team determine the correct risk strategy and response plan. CCS identifies the level of compliance. Which, in turn, may correlate to the penalty for non-compliance. For example, an organization may have to pay a hefty fine for a significant compliance issue. They would want to apply the avoid risk strategy in this case. On the other hand, a minor compliance infraction may only result in a warning to change. In this case, the team may implement the accept risk strategy.
- The cost of quality is part of determining the risk strategy. Balancing the cost of conformance (preventative and appraisal) against the cost of non-conformance (failure).

The amount of this difference will impact the chosen risk strategy.

- (*PMBOK® Guide – Sixth Edition*, page 282 and 443)

12. C. Organizational change management

- Organizational change management (OCM) helps people make a change. OCM focuses on why a change is occurring. Explaining why, especially to stakeholders who perceive the change will negatively impact them, is critical to the success of a project.

- Creating personas is one technique to ensure OCM addresses all stakeholder groups. A persona is a fictional character representing the needs, likes and dislikes, background, desires, etc. of a specific stakeholder group. OCM efforts are targeted to each persona to address specific concerns about the change. To convince those stakeholders described by the persona to accept the change.

- (See (Sanchez, 2018) in the business environment section)

13. A. Fairness

- The project manager did not demonstrate fairness. While the son met the requirements, other candidates were better qualified. The project manager did not act impartial, one of the key characteristics of fairness. (*The PMI® Code of Ethics and Professional Conduct* https://www.pmi.org/about/ethics/code).

14. C. Realized business value

- Delivering all the scope on time and cost is only part of the criteria to determine the success of the project. A project must deliver the expected realized business value first and foremost to be successful.

- A project is chosen based on the business value identified in the project charter. Next, the project team creates project plans to deliver that value. Otherwise, the organization may have benefited more by allocating the project resources to other initiatives.

- (See (Phillipy, 2014) in the business environment section)

15. A. Project management knowledge, B. Interpersonal skills, and C. Accountable for results.

- A project manager is accountable for results by applying their technical project management, leadership, and strategic and business management skills. (*PMBOK® Guide – Sixth Edition*, page 56)
- Project funding. While a project manager will need to determine the project budget and cost baseline, typically the sponsor is accountable for ensuring sufficient project funding.

16. A. Portfolio, Program, Project

- A portfolio is an organizational-wide initiative to achieve an organization's strategic objective and typically includes more than one program.
- A program coordinates the delivery of a significant benefit to the organization across multiple projects or activities.
- A project delivers a specific set of capabilities. These capabilities may be related to the deliverables of other projects and activities.
- (*PMBOK® Guide – Sixth Edition*, page 44)

17. C. Adjust the product backlog

- There is a hint in the question. A product owner is an Agile project role. Therefore, the project is an Agile project which handles changes by adding the change to the product backlog.
- The team must further elaborate on the story to understand the requirement and assign a business value. The relative business value of the story determines the prioritization of the story in the backlog. With the highest prioritized stories worked before lower priority stories.
- The business value may be positive or negative. Typically the business value of compliance requirements is negative. Since the project backlog includes both positive and negative business values, prioritization of stories is by the absolute business value of each story. For example, a story to address compliance may have a negative business value of -$1M. Another story may have a positive business value of $500K. The first story would be prioritized over the

second story in the product backlog since it has a larger impact on the business value of the project.

- Including stories to address risks in the backlog produces what is known as a risk-adjusted product backlog.
- (*PMBOK® Guide – Sixth Edition*, page 131 and references in the business environment section)

18. B. Directive

- Directive PMOs provide all project management responsibilities by providing the project manager. Directive PMOs have the highest control over the project alignment with organizational project management expectations. (*PMBOK® Guide – Sixth Edition*, page 48)

19. B. Change manager

- The question describes the role of organizational change management (OCM) change manager. This manager uses expert judgment to mentor and coach others across the organization with a focus on the development and support of the change sponsor and change agents.
- A change sponsor or champion spans the impacted or perceived to be impacted, organization. They are typically a senior leader. However, just because the change champion is a senior leader, they may not have extensive experience leading changes. Likewise, change agents may have little or no experience leading organizational change. Therefore, the change manager must be a respected and trusted expert throughout the organization.
- (See references in the business environment section)

20. B. Organizational need

- The organization must become more efficient to remain competitive in the market. When two businesses combine to form one business, often projects are begun to lower the resulting overhead cost.
- (*PMBOK® Guide – Sixth Edition*, page 78)

21. C. Realized

- Projects must produce realized business value and benefits over the project's deliverable life cycle. In other words, real, measurable results. With someone responsible for tracking the deliverable life-cycle benefits based on agreed to methods. For example, in the USA, the business value may be monitored and reported according to generally accepted accounting principles (GAAP). In other cases, the organization may have internal methods to track and report the realized business value.

- Your professional experience may be different. Your organization may not track realized business value and benefits. Or perhaps your projects have been small and not required to monitor deliverable business value. Remember on the exam projects are large and expected to produce deliverables that produce real business value and benefits - realized business value and benefits.
- (See references in the business environment section)

22. C. Organizational process assets

- Organizational process assets are lessons learned, templates, documents, etc. that are available to the project manager and team. The project team reviews and confirms that the project team can leverage these assets. Either as is or after modifying the asset for their project.

- In reality, your organization may not have a well-defined and maintained organizational process asset repository. However, for any exam, the best practice of an organization process asset repository is assumed unless otherwise stated.

- (*PMBOK® Guide – Sixth Edition*, page 79)

23. B. Constraint

- A constraint, by definition, is a limit or restriction. In this case, the SME is not available for two months. This constraint will result in one or more "cannot start before" schedule tasks delaying the project. (*PMBOK® Guide – Sixth Edition*, page 28)

- Different sources may propose different "groupings" of constraints. A common grouping of constraints is scope, time, and cost, which is known as the triple constraints. In other contexts and questions, additional constraints, quality, risk, etc. will be included in a grouping. The result is you must understand the context to determine what is considered a constraint. As a starting point for understanding, always start with the triple constraints. These three constraints may be inclusive of all other types of constraints. The significance of these triple constraints is acknowledged as only these constraints are monitored and controlled with an approved baseline.

24. B. Agile

- The Agile life-cycle facilitates producing deliverables that are acceptable to the customer. During an Agile project, the deliverables are progressively defined, produced, and validated by the customer. The team may produce deliverables on a consistent cycle (e.g., every two weeks). The customer then defines the next group of capabilities, and the cycle repeats. (*PMBOK® Guide – Sixth Edition*, page 19)

25. D. Work performance data

- Work performance data is raw data without context. The project team member stated they completed 50% of their assigned project task. Is that good? Bad? On schedule? Without context, a project manager cannot answer this question. If the plan were for the project team member to complete 40% (ahead of schedule), 50% (on schedule), or 60% (behind schedule) during this period, the answer would vary significantly. (*PMBOK® Guide – Sixth Edition*, page 26)
- Work performance information is the result of applying context to work performance data. Context is defined in the planning process group and is found in the schedule, cost, or scope baselines and other planning process group outputs. In this question, if the project plan called for the project team member to complete 50% of their work, and they reported completing 50%, the task is on schedule. Since the question does not provide context, you cannot determine work performance information that shows the project is on schedule or not.
- Work performance reports communicate work performance information to stakeholders. The purpose of work performance reports is to generate awareness or action from the receiving stakeholders. For example, a schedule work performance report that shows the project is behind schedule may include a request for additional resources resulting in a functional manager assigning additional people to the project.

26. B. Decline the offer and continue to work on it
    - The leader must demonstrate responsibility. One may assume, based on USA copyright law, that the Harvard Business Review posted the video to be viewed only from the web site. HBR did not explicitly grant permission to download. Responsibility includes adhering to copyrights, agreement terms and conditions, and commitments.
    - As a leader, project manager, it is critical to demonstrate this behavior to others. In this case, explaining to the technical team member that copying this video without permission was not acceptable.
    - (*The PMI® Code of Ethics and Professional Conduct* https://www.pmi.org/about/ethics/code)

27. D. Expert
    - The question describes a person who is considered an expert. Leaders, team members, and organizations often possess or demonstrate more than one form of power. For example, the other answers are possible choices but the best answer, in this case, is Expert. (*PMBOK® Guide – Sixth Edition*, page 63)

28. C. Organizational process asset
    - Having a preapproved list of electrical contractors, sellers is an example of an organizational process asset. The project team may choose any one of the contractors based on which contractor best fits the needs (e.g., when they start and finish the job, cost, contract terms, etc.) of the project. (*PMBOK® Guide – Sixth Edition*, page 40)

29. A. Leadership
    - Project managers spend almost all their time communicating with stakeholders. Often the underlying topic is risks as projects are very dynamic.
    - For example, the common occurrence of a team member telling the project manager they will be going on vacation alters the project's immediate risk profile. What is the impact on the schedule? Does the team need to transfer knowledge before the member leaves for vacation?
    - Another example is a stakeholder asking for a new project requirement. This requirement may change the project

scope. What is the impact and risk of this new requirement on finishing the project at the currently approved cost and schedule baseline?

- (PMBOK® Guide – Sixth Edition, page 61)

30. B. Organizational change management

- Why? OCM process provides tools and techniques to address the "why" a change will occur — addressing the human emotions of the change. Predictive and Agile projects may gain benefits from OCM.
- The product owner was concerned with the acceptance of the change. There are typically three audience groups for any change. Early adopters. They are willing to try the change as soon as it is available. Resistors. This audience group is reluctant to change. They do not see any value in changing. The group between early adapters and resistors may be the largest. This group is undecided as to when to change or to change at all. Using empathy and targeted messaging, the "why" is shared with each target audience group. The result is a higher acceptance rate of the change.
- How? Perform integrated change management defines "how" a change will occur by identifying all the impacted plans and baselines. Although associated with predictive projects, perform integrated change management also applies to Agile projects. Integrated change management is performed on Agile projects whenever story planning identifies an impact to other stories or implemented product features.
- (See references in the business environment section)

31. D. Re-prioritize the product backlog

- The product owner is responsible for prioritizing the product backlog based on business value. The story or stories delivering the most significant business value prioritized the highest.
- This impact on the project is a result of a change in the business environment. In this case, internal to the organization. In other cases, the impact may be external to the organization (e.g., a competitor introduces new product

or features to an existing product, changes to regulation and laws, etc.)

- *"Welcome changing requirements, even late in development. Agile processes harness change for the customer's competitive advantage"* is an agile principle. Changing business value drove this re-prioritization and may be considered new requirements. Remember, if the change to requirements is significant, the team will stop working even during a sprint. The team will then begin working on the new requirement.
- (See references in Agile section (Scrum.org, 2019))

32. A. Measure compliance risk

- Quality audits measure the effectiveness and efficiency of tools and techniques. In this case, lab tools used to test deliverables. The miscalibration of these tools may increase the risk of compliance.
- If this testing equipment is not performing as expected, products may pass when they should fail. The deliverables are non-compliant. Or the products may be deemed non-compliant when, in fact, they are compliant. Resulting in waste.
- (PMBOK® Guide – Sixth Edition, page 290)

33. C. Hybrid

- The hybrid life cycle integrates predictive with adaptive life cycles, leveraging the strengths of each.
- When the deliverable scope, and how to deliver that scope, is known, it is best to use the predictive life cycle. Also, the inputs, tools and techniques, and outputs to produce the scope are known.
- For the deliverables where that is not the case, an adaptive life cycle is the better choice. Adaptive life cycles include incremental and iterative life cycles. These may be known as the Agile life cycle.
- The incremental life cycle decomposes the product scope into increments. With each increment designed, built, and delivered once completed. The benefit of the incremental

life cycle is the risk reduction of providing a full solution all at once.

- The iterative life cycle refines the product deliverables with each iteration. This life cycle produces interim deliverables through a cycle of prototyping, feedback, and refinement. Repeating this cycle, starting each time with the previous refinement, results in the final scope of the deliverable.
- (See references and PMBOK® Guide – Sixth Edition, page 19)

34. B. Review and adjust product backlog
   - Use good multiple-choice exam techniques and Agile knowledge to answer this question.
   - Who prioritizes work? The product owner. They would not delegate this responsibility to the scrum master or the team. Knowing this eliminates two of the answers.
   - How long is a sprint? Typically two to four weeks. This policy doesn't go into effect for two months. Be sure you don't read more into the question and imply assumptions on your part. The question does not state an urgency that would require reviewing or adjusting the current sprint backlog. Therefore, this eliminates another answer.
   - The product backlog includes both product and project scope. Being compliant with document retention policies is a project requirement. The product owner should review and adjust the product backlog.
   - (See references in Agile section (Scrum.org, 2019))

35. A. Recommend options to minimize the impact
   - Yes, the project must address this change. If, for example, this is a compliance change, the project must be compliant.
   - However, as a project manager, product owner, or anyone for that matter, you do not just accept the impact of implementing a change. You must understand the change and seek options to reduce the schedule and cost impact on the project. While still meeting the requirements.
   - This effort to reduce impact may be part of continuous improvement. Everyone should always be seeking ways to be more effective and efficient. Continuous improvement is part of every monitoring and controlling process.

Specifically, in this case, to control the project scope, cost, and schedule while meeting this new requirement.

- (PMBOK® Guide – Sixth Edition, page 671)

INTEGRATION MANAGEMENT

Integration, by definition, is to "form, coordinate, or blend into a functioning or unified whole." For project management, the Integration Knowledge Area is responsible for coordinating a whole unified set of tailored processes to produce the project objectives successfully.

The Integration knowledge area processes produce outputs that have a significant impact on any project. These processes authorize the project manager to consume the organization's resources (e.g., people, money). Plus, it is this knowledge area that produces the deliverables to create the business value the project promised.

Is this an approved project? (Develop Project Charter) The approved project charter defines the project scope, deliverables, start and end dates, plus many other critical factors that set the boundaries for the project. Although project management begins with the Develop Project Charter process, the project itself does not start until the project charter is approved. The sponsor, key stakeholders, project manager, and perhaps other stakeholders signify approval by signing the project charter. An approved project charter authorizes the project manager to expend the organization's resources to achieve the project objectives.

How will the project objectives be accomplished? (Develop Project Management Plan) The project management plan is an umbrella project plan than integrates all other knowledge area plans, schedule, scope, and cost baselines, plus additional plans such as the configuration management plan.

Where are the deliverables produced? (Direct and Manage Project Work) This process directs and manages the actual work that results in the production of the project deliverables. If the project is to deliver a software app, this is where the development work occurs. If the project is to construct a building, this is where the construction work occurs.

Where is the source of knowledge? (Manage Project Knowledge) Leveraging previous experience from lessons learned is critical to every project. The ability to leverage prior experience eliminates redundant experimentation and discovery by each project. Does every project team need to create a unique project charter from scratch? Develop a new procedure to mitigate a common risk to all projects? In turn, each project must add to the organizational knowledge to be leverage by future projects.

How are we doing? (Monitor and Control Project Work) This process produces work performance reports. The purpose of these reports is for stakeholder awareness of the project's status. These status reports may also generate decisions and actions by stakeholders. The work performance information produced by the monitoring and controlling process group is the basis for these reports.

What is the impact? (Perform Integrated Change Control) This process ensures the assessment of proposed changes across the entire project before implementing the change. For example, a change to the schedule task start date may impact more than this single schedule task. This change may affect numerous downstream schedule tasks, resource calendars, cost, or other factors. The change control process will approve or deny the change after completing an integrated assessment. The team will only implement approved changes.

May I have the deliverable? (Close Project or Phase) A project is not completed until the project is closed. Likewise, each phase within a project is completed only after the closing of that phase. Once closed, the process transitions the deliverable to the customer or operations organization. It is only after this transition that the original business value promised in the approved project charter begins to be realized.

Integration by definition is to "form, coordinate, or blend into a functioning or unified whole." For project management, the Integration Knowledge Area is responsible for coordinating a unified whole set of tailored processes to successfully produce the project objectives.

Questions

1. The sponsor has provided the project manager with a description of the project and how and when the benefits will be realized. The project manager is now documenting the project's scope, business case, existing agreements, and other organizational process assets. What BEST describes the document provided by the sponsor?
    A. Benefits management plan
    B. Project charter
    C. Project description
    D. Project management plan

2. The project manager created a spreadsheet to track information. This spreadsheet describes the situation, actions taken, and the result of those actions. The team uses this spreadsheet to research possible solutions during the project for the same or similar situations. What BEST describes this spreadsheet?
    A. Issues log
    B. Change log
    C. Lessons learned register
    D. Solutions log

3. The project team is currently implementing an approved change. Which process describes what the project team is executing?
    A. Develop project charter
    B. Direct and manage project work
    C. Perform integrated change control
    D. Monitor and control project work

4. A project manager just closed the project. In total, the project manager executed the Close Project or Phase process five (5) times on this multi-phase project. How many phases did this project have?
    A. 0
    B. 1
    C. 4
    D. 5

5. Market demand, an organizational need, customer request, and regulatory or legal requirements are all examples of what?
    A. Project deliverables
    B. Organizational process assets
    C. Business case
    D. Business need

6. The project manager just received authorization to add people to the project. The project manager is also acquiring office space and other resources to begin the project. Which document provides this authorization?
    A. Project charter
    B. Business case
    C. Business documents
    D. Agreements

7. You are a new project manager and have just been assigned to your first project. The Project Management Office (PMO) has provided you with initial training on project management. Your good friend has been a project manager for a number of successful projects and has offered to be available if you have any questions. What BEST describes your friend?
    A. Stakeholder
    B. Subject Matter Expert (SME)
    C. PMO
    D. Sponsor

8. Information is created and analyzed by many processes. Which of the following is produced by the Direct and Manage Project Work process?
    A. Work performance information
    B. Work performance data
    C. Work performance reports
    D. Work performance status

9. The stakeholders approved the project charter. The project manager begins to prepare the project plan that will provide a complete integrated project plan for the project. What BEST describes this plan?
   A. Project schedule
   B. Project plan
   C. Project management plan
   D. Scope baseline

10. Each project manager and the team is responsible for advancing the maturity of their organization. This responsibility includes improving existing knowledge and creating new knowledge within their project. Which process focuses on this responsibility?
    A. Perform integrated change control
    B. Manage project knowledge
    C. Develop project charter
    D. Plan communication management

11. The project manager assessed the current state of the project. As part of the assessment, the project manager confirms the schedule and budget forecasts are still valid. The project manager is now reporting these results. What BEST describes this process?
    A. Direct and manage project work
    B. Perform status
    C. Monitor and control project work
    D. Project management plan

12. The project manager has compared work performance data to the schedule baseline. The project is behind schedule. The project team assesses the situation and determines they can reduce an activity duration by using a different technology solution. This decision will enable the project to get back on schedule. The project manager receives approval for this change. What BEST describes this type of change?
    A. Corrective
    B. Preventative
    C. Defect repair
    D. Update

13. A project team member implemented a change to the approved requirements after talking with the customer. Who is responsible for this change?
    A. Customer
    B. Team member
    C. Project manager
    D. Sponsor

14. Two project managers are discussing which document provides the business need, objectives, and information to justify starting a project. This document describes the scope of the work to be done if the project is selected to proceed. What BEST describes this document?
    A. Benefits management plan
    B. Business case
    C. Scope document
    D. Project document

15. The project manager received a proposed change to the project scope baseline. What process must the team execute?
    A. Create WBS
    B. Collect requirements
    C. Perform integrated change control
    D. Change control

16. The project manager just presented the project update to the sponsor and key stakeholders. The update wholly and accurately described the current state of the project. Yet the sponsor and key stakeholders were not satisfied. What may be the BEST cause of their dissatisfaction?
    A. Lack of forecasts
    B. Project is behind schedule
    C. Project is over budget
    D. Forecasts were negative

17. The project team is identifying roles and responsibilities for all the knowledge areas. A project team member has offered to lead the scope management knowledge area. Another project team member, with communication experience, volunteered to lead the communication knowledge area. Who is BEST suited to lead the project integration efforts?
    A. Sponsor
    B. Project Manager
    C. Project team member
    D. Key stakeholder

18. A new project manager begins working on an existing project. The new project manager wants to understand the plan to address project risks, the approved project funding, and the approved scope. Which document should the project manager begin with to gain understanding?
    A. Scope baseline
    B. Cost baseline
    C. Project management plan
    D. Risk management plan

19. The procurement manager notified the seller of the completion of the project contract. The project manager and procurement manager are now updating systems to archive the final results of this contract. What process are they performing?
    A. Close procurement
    B. Close project or phase
    C. Control procurement
    D. Monitor and control project work

20. What knowledge area is responsible for ensuring meeting schedule dates, project benefits align with efforts, knowledge is created and shared, and progress toward the objectives is sufficient?
    A. Project integration management
    B. Project scope management
    C. Project schedule management
    D. Project stakeholder management

21. The project manager and team have created a project plan that includes multiple project phases. The project team is transitioning the phase's deliverable, or product increment, to the customer. What process group BEST describes what the project team is performing?
    A. Planning
    B. Initiating
    C. Executing
    D. Closing

22. The sponsor has completed a project charter and selected the project manager. Has the project started?
    A. No. The project starts after the project charter is signed.
    B. Yes. The project charter and an assigned project manager marks the start of a project.
    C. No. A budget must be approved.
    D. No. A budget and scheduled must be approved.

23. The project team is currently spending considerable time in this phase. The project team will spend most of the team's time and other project resources during this phase. What phase is the project time currently performing?
    A. Initiating
    B. Planning
    C. Executing
    D. Monitoring and Controlling

24. The project manager is reviewing the meeting minutes from the last planning meeting with the team. One team member questions the minutes regarding the project management plan timeline. The project manager reviews how the timeline was determined, developed, and the business needs to complete as planned. The team member is satisfied with the explanation. What BEST describes what occurred?
    A. Conflict management
    B. Facilitation
    C. Meeting management
    D. Best practice

25. The project manager will hod a stakeholder discussion at the end of planning. The agenda is to communicate the project objectives, explain stakeholder roles, and gain commitment to proceed to the executing phase. What BEST describes this discussion?
    A. Update meeting
    B. Status meeting
    C. Kick-off meeting
    D. Stakeholder meeting

Answers

1. A. Benefits management plan
   - The creation of a benefits management plan occurs before a project charter. The benefits management plan describes how and when the realized project's benefits will occur. This approach is beneficial because the project manager must understand the magnitude and timing of all expected project benefits. The benefits management plan includes assumptions, constraints, risks, strategic alignment, and other sections specific to the benefits. The project does not start until the project charter is approved, not the benefits management plan, by the sponsor, key stakeholders, project manager, and perhaps other stakeholders. (*PMBOK® Guide – Sixth Edition*, page 77)

2. C. Lessons learned register
   - The project manager created the lessons learned register. This register will log and update the knowledge gained by the team. Keep in mind knowledge includes not just what worked, but also what didn't work for the team to achieve an objective or overcome a challenge. The team shared this knowledge with the organization throughout the project and at the end of the project. (*PMBOK® Guide – Sixth Edition*, page 104)
   - It is important to recall your previous project experiences. Registers and project documents are created and maintained in spreadsheets or other common business tools. Existing templates, registers, and other project documents are good examples of organizational process assets.

3. B. Direct and manage project work
   - Project deliverables are significant outputs that result from the work done during the Direct and Manage Project Work process. Work includes implementing approved changes to those deliverables.
   - It is essential to understand in this question the team is implementing an approved change. Since the change is

approved, the team has already completed the perform integrated change control process. Therefore this answer may be eliminated from potential correct answers.

- One must be able to trace key project artifacts (deliverables, documents) across knowledge areas and individual processes. In this case, the Direct and Manage Project Work process produces deliverables for the entire project. No other process creates project deliverables. To complete this recommendation, one should be able to trace deliverables from requirements gathering through verification and validation of, and finally handing over the deliverable to the customer.
- (PMBOK® Guide – Sixth Edition, page 90)

4. C. 4

- The project manager must execute the Close Project or Phase process at the end of each project. Completing this process is valid for all projects, even projects that were stopped regardless of the reason before producing the project deliverables.
- Since the project manager executed the Close Project or Phase process five (5) times and must perform it once at the end of the project, this project had four (4) phases.
- It is common to split large projects into phases. At the end of each phase, the project manager must execute the Close Project or Phase process. The end of a phase is a critical junction for any project as the sponsor, project manager, and other key stakeholders assess the project and determine if the project should proceed to the next phase.
- (PMBOK® Guide – Sixth Edition, page 121)

5. C. Business case

- Why should a project be started? Why should this project be selected versus another project? Because of the business case.
- The sponsor, project manager, and perhaps other stakeholders must complete a cost-benefit or other analysis to determine if the organization should start the project. In some cases, whether to start one or another project is

based primarily on the cost-benefit of each. In other cases, regulatory requirements or a customer request may be sufficient to justify the project.

- Keep in mind, an organization only has a finite amount of resources (e.g., cash, people, facilities, etc.), so not all projects will be started.
- (*PMBOK® Guide – Sixth Edition*, page 78)

6. A. Project charter

- A signed project charter is required before the project manager starts gathering and applying all the necessary organization's resources to achieving the project's objectives. Having an approved project charter enables the on-boarding of the project team.
- The business documents, business case, and benefits management plan, plus other documents support the justification of the project. But until the sponsor and other key stakeholders approve the project charter, often by formally signing the project charter, the project has not begun.
- When a project starts may be confusing as before the signing, the project manager and a small number of subject matter experts and team members have been drafting the project charter. It appears from these efforts that the project has started. That is not the case. The application of these resources is strictly limited in scope to just the creation of the project charter.
- (*PMBOK® Guide – Sixth Edition*, page 75)

7. B. Subject matter expert (SME)

- A Subject matter expert (SME) is a standard industry term for an individual or group with valuable prior experience and knowledge. This best describes the friend in the question. In the PMBOK® Guide, SMEs are called expert judgment. (*PMBOK® Guide – Sixth Edition*, page 94)

8. B. Work performance data

- The Direct and Manage Project Work produces work performance data (e.g., the team produced how many deliverables in the last hour, day, month). Work performance data does not have a context. In other words, the team produced one deliverable today. Did that meet expectations? Exceed? Disappoint?

- Work performance data is input to Monitoring and Controlling processes that will assess the data against the plan, baseline, or expectation for context. The result is work performance information. The project team now knowns they met, exceeded, or under-produced based on expectations or plans. Work performance information is input to work performance reports that are shared with stakeholders to communicate the project status or to drive action.
- (*PMBOK® Guide – Sixth Edition*, page 95)

9. C. Project management plan

- The project management plan provides a complete and integrated plan for the entire project. The project management plan describes how the project will be planned, executed, monitored, controlled, and closed. Because of the magnitude of this plan, the project management plan is broken into integrated sub-plans for each knowledge area, includes major baselines, and may contain other project information. (*PMBOK® Guide – Sixth Edition*, page 82)

10. B. Manage project knowledge

- One basic expectation of a project manager is they are a champion for continuous improvement during the project. Continuous improvement by nature improves existing knowledge or creates new knowledge within the team. The project manager is responsible for sharing this knowledge throughout the organization by performing the Manage Project Knowledge process. (*PMBOK® Guide – Sixth Edition*, page 98)

11. C. Monitor and control project work

- An output of the Monitor and Control Project Work process is work performance reports. These reports are communicate project status to stakeholders either for awareness or to trigger action. (*PMBOK® Guide – Sixth Edition*, page 112)

- The Direct and Manage Project Work process creates work performance information. Processes within the Monitoring and Controlling process group take work performance data and compares that data to plans and baselines to produce work performance information. Monitor and Control Project Work process creates work performance reports from the work performance information. These reports as distributed by communication knowledge area processes.

12. A. Corrective

- A corrective action change request reenables the project, product, service, or result to achieve the original expected or planned outcome. The question is a good example. By implementing new or different technology, the team will be able to recover lost schedule time. (*PMBOK® Guide – Sixth Edition*, page 96)

13. C. Project manager

- The project manager is responsible for all Project Integration Management processes. The project manager may not delegate this responsibility to any other person or group.

- It is essential to note the question does not mention approving the change before implementation nor the project manager's involvement. Both are serious issues. The impact of the change on the project's schedule and cost baselines, schedule, risks, etc. are assessed in the Perform Integrated Change Control process. Lack of awareness of this change does not reduce or remove the project manager's responsibilities. As the responsible person for Perform Integrated Change Control, the project manager must address these issues. (*PMBOK® Guide – Sixth Edition*, page 115)

14. B. Business case

- The project's business documents, the business case, and benefits management plan, are created before starting the project charter. The business case identifies causes for the problem to be addressed or drivers to achieve an opportunity, risks, etc. A project's business documents are assessed based on business needs, relative business value compared to other organizational projects, and initiatives. If the project is selected, these business documents are inputs to creating the project charter. (*PMBOK® Guide – Sixth Edition*, page 77)

15. C. Perform integrated change control

- A request to change to the project scope baseline was received. If this scope change request were before the approval of the scope baseline, then it would not be necessary to execute the change process.
- However, the question states a scope baseline exists. This statement confirms the project scope baseline is approved, and therefore the project manager must execute the Perform Integrated Change Control process.
- By executing Perform Integrated Change Control, the project manager verifies the impact of this change across all knowledge areas for the entire project. Did this change cause the schedule baseline to change? Cost baseline? Quality management plan? Or other components of the project management plan?
- (*PMBOK® Guide – Sixth Edition*, page 113)

16. A. Lack of forecasts

- Forecasts are vital components of any update. A forecast is a current estimate to complete (ETC) the project.
- While sponsors and key stakeholders are very interested in the current project status, they are just as, or more so, interested in the future anticipated project performance. This interest is primarily on the project schedule and cost forecasts.
- Why? The schedule and cost forecast impact not only the project but the organization as a whole. If the schedule forecast indicates the project will finish later than the baseline states, resources will not be released back into the organization until later than currently planned. This delay will delay other organizational initiatives. If the cost

forecast indicates, the project will complete under budget, that savings can be applied to other projects in the organization enabling the organization to create additional business value

- *(PMBOK® Guide – Sixth Edition*, page 113)

17. B. Project manager

- The project manager does not need to lead all project activities, whether this leadership is across one or more knowledge areas or a specific single issue in the issue log.
- The project manager, however, must lead the integration processes. The project manager may not delegate this leadership role. These processes "integrate" all other knowledge area processes. By leading the integration processes, the project manager fulfills their accountability for the success of the project.
- *(PMBOK® Guide – Sixth Edition*, page 72)

18. C. Project management plan

- The project management plan provides a complete and integrated view of the entire project. All knowledge area plans, constraint baselines (time, cost, scope), etc. are considered to be part of the project management plan. As a result, the project management plan describes how the project's deliverables will be produced (executed), validated, verified (monitoring and controlling), and how to close the project.
- Additional project documents are also critical to the successful completion of the project but are outside the scope of the project management plan.
- *(PMBOK® Guide – Sixth Edition*, pages 86-89)

19. B. Close project or phase

- After notifying the seller in the Control Procurement process that the contract is complete, the project manager and team must complete additional activities. These Close Project or Phase process activities include updating the buyer's organization records, archiving data, etc. *(PMBOK® Guide – Sixth Edition*, page 123)

- In previous versions of the *PMBOK® Guide*, there was a Close Procurement process. Many of those process activities now reside in the Close Project or Phase process.

20. A. Project integration management
    - The list of expectations in the question is just some of the expectations. Who on the team must be responsible for delivering these expectations? There can only be one person. The project manager. The project manager personally performs these responsibilities as each directly impacts the project outcomes.
    - The project manager does not need to personally do all the project work or assume all the project responsibilities. The project manager may delegate risk assessment, issue tracking, schedule maintenance, and other project responsibilities to other project team members. However, the project manager does, at all times, remain accountable for the project outcomes. Being responsible for the Project Integration Management processes links directly to this accountability.
    - (*PMBOK® Guide – Sixth Edition*, page 123)

21. D. Closing
    - Transitioning the deliverable to the customer occurs at the end of the phase or project. This transition is a critical step as the project's deliverable begins to create business value through usage by the customer. (*PMBOK® Guide – Sixth Edition*, page 127)
    - The question uses the term product increment. A product increment is functionality added at the end of an iteration. Agile projects commonly use the term increment while traditional projects use the term phase. The product increment may be used immediately by the customer n to start realizing business value.

22. A. No. The project is not started until the project charter is signed.
    - The project is in the initiating process phase since the sponsor has created a project charter and selected the project manager. However, the project has NOT started.

- In reality, the project manager must verify, clarify, and often improves on the sponsor's project charter. The signing of the project charter occurs once the project manager understands the project charter and, in turn, the objectives of the project.
- The sponsor signs or authorizes the project charter. Additional key stakeholders may also sign the project charter. The signing of the project charter ensures conscious awareness by the signers that they are committing the organization's resources to the project.
- The approved project charter marks the start of the project. The project manager may now expend organizational resources, including assigning people to the project team to achieve the project's objectives.
- (The *PMBOK® Guide – Sixth Edition*, page 81)

23. C. Executing

- Although the complexity and duration of projects vary, project teams spend most of their time and resources during the executing phase. During the executing phase, the team produces the actual project deliverable(s). (*PMBOK® Guide – Sixth Edition*, page 90)

24. B. Facilitation

- Achieving buy-in is one outcome of facilitation. Successful facilitation ensures the participation of all team members and reaching mutual agreement on decisions. The ability to facilitate discussions is one essential characteristic of successful project managers. (*PMBOK® Guide – Sixth Edition*, page 86)

25. C. Kick-off meeting

- A kick-off meeting may occur throughout the project. The most common reference to a kick-off meeting occurs between completing planning and beginning the executing phases.
- Keep in mind the project has already started when this kick-off meeting occurs. The project began with the signing of the project charter. This kick-off meeting shares

the results of the planning phase and clarifies to all stakeholders the team is starting the executing phase.

- Completing or beginning other phases or milestones may also merit a kick-off meeting with stakeholders.
- (*PMBOK® Guide – Sixth Edition*, page 86)

SCOPE MANAGEMENT

The scope of the project must be well defined and tracked to ensure a successful project. Otherwise, the schedule, cost, resources, quality, risk, procurements, etc. cannot be accurately planned, executed, monitored, or controlled.

The project manager and team will need to ensure to include only the scope necessary to complete the project are in the project (i.e., in-scope). Just as important, the project manager will need to identify and communicate to stakeholders if their requested scope will not be part of the project (i.e., out-of-scope).

Scope in Agile. Agile methodology embraces allowing the product owner or customer to change the scope throughout the project, allowing changes even late in the project.

The product backlog contains all in-scope requirements in the form of user stories. Before each iteration, the product owner or customer chooses which of the user stories (i.e., requirements) in the product backlog to work on in the upcoming iteration. After discussing each selected user story, the project team estimates the effort considering the specifications, quality, risk, etc. for each user story. The team then produces a product increment, or deliverable, based on those requirements during the iteration.

The identification of new in-scope requirements results in new or updated user stories in the product backlog. The product owner or customer will then select the user stories with the highest business value from this expanded product backlog for the next iteration.

Project versus product scope. There are two categories of scope on every project.

- Project scope. These are activities and artifacts that are necessary to produce the deliverable as specified or to meet requirements placed on the project. These artifacts (e.g., project schedule) are not part of the actual final deliverable.
    - Organizational process assets may drive project scope. Especially those required by the program management office (PMO). Will a formal or informal project schedule be created and tracked? Will all the project templates be used on the project? How the project manager answers these and other questions will result in more time, costs, and resources. Therefore, these must be in-scope for the project.
    - Enterprise environmental factors. These items are outside the control of the project team. Will this project require government approval? Meet a regulatory requirement? Does the organization require the project manager to submit weekly formal status updates, update an internal system, etc.? These and other requirements will result in more time, costs, and resources. Therefore, they must be in-scope for the project.
- Product scope. These are requirements that become a characteristic or capability of the project's deliverable. These will be part of the project's deliverables to the customer. Does the security logon meet the product requirements for password strength? Is the application's redundancy capability meeting the availability requirement?
    - Organizational process assets and enterprise environmental factors may also create product scope. Did the organization develop (i.e., organizational process asset) a security package that could be modified to meet the project's requirement? Or does the organization require the use of government-approved security package or standards (i.e., enterprise environmental factor)?

Are you confused about project verses product scope? Whether something is a project or product scope can be confusing. One way to keep them straight is to think of when you bought your cell phone.

What came with your new phone? The packaging, charging cable, earbuds, instructions, and the phone itself. All these are considered product scope. Yes, even the plastic screen protector, were delivered (i.e., "transitioned") to you, the customer.

The project scope ensures the product scope fulfills the project's objectives. But the project scope is never tangibly transitioned to the customer. Was the approved project charter required by Apple or Google included in the box when you bought your phone? Was the risk response plans addressing supplier quality risks included? No. These are examples of the project scope. Remember, project scope takes time, incurs costs, etc. so project scope must be in the project estimates and schedule. Or your project will begin and remain behind schedule and over budget.

Here is another point of possible confusion about scope. Sometimes project scope includes product scope. Other times they are mutually exclusive. Be sure to understand which of these cases is true when talking about project scope.

Scope processes. The Scope Management knowledge area processes produce outputs that have a significant impact on any project and the project deliverables.

- **How will the requirements be collected, assessed as to being in-scope or out-of-scope, and tracked?** (Plan Scope Management) The requirements management plan documents the answer to this question. Also, part of the plan scope management is the scope management plan. The focus of the scope management plan is on how the team will perform each of the Scope Management knowledge area processes. Both are part of the project management plan.
- **Here a requirement. There a requirement. Everywhere a requirement.** (Collect Requirements) This process ensures ALL requirements are gathered and documented. This documentation enables the team to trace each requirement back to the source. The project manager and team do not assess any requirement for inclusion in the project at this point. Therefore, this documentation includes requirements, even requirements that one may be able to anticipate will not be in-scope for the project.
- **What's in-scope?** (Define Scope) The project manager and team must clearly articulate the requirements that are in-scope for the

project. Just as critical, the team must also clearly articulate those requirements that will be out-of-scope. This exercise may generate considerable conversation and lobbying by stakeholders to include or exclude specific requirements. On completion of this process, only the in-scope requirements will move forward in the project as defined by the project scope statement.

- **What is being produced?** (Create WBS) The process decomposes the project deliverables into smaller components that can be planned, estimated, monitored, and controlled.
  - The creation of a hierarchical chart, or visual, of the deliverables furthers the understanding of the project's deliverables. The Work Breakdown Structure (WBS) is an excellent way to communicate the in-scope requirements to stakeholders.
  - To support the WBS, a WBS dictionary is created. This dictionary provides important additional information and context to define each WBS deliverable.

The completion of this process results in an approved scope baseline. The scope baseline includes the WBS and WBS dictionary, plus the project scope statement.

Using the scope baseline, the team will assess the progress of the project deliverables for the remainder of the project. The scope baseline will also help determine whether new requirements should or should not be part of the project.

- **Is this what the customer wanted?** (Validate Scope) The project manager and team must ensure the deliverables meet all requirements. Despite the project team's confidence, the team must validate that the interim or final deliverable meets the customer's needs. Since the customer may disagree with the team's assessment, or identify missing requirements, the project team should frequently perform Validate scope. Otherwise, potential issues will not arise until later in the project. The later the discovery of an issue occurs, typically, the higher the project impact.
- **In or out? (Control Scope)** Projects may receive requests for new requirements or modifications to existing requirements. Just implementing those changes to the scope is not acceptable. Nor is the denial of all changes. Either approach may result in an unacceptable project outcome.

To assess which changes to approve, the project manager must execute the Perform Integrated Change Control process. If the requirement is determined to be in-scope, the project manager must update the schedule, cost, etc. as part of implementing the approved requirements change. Otherwise, the project manager committed the project team to produce additional requirements without an increase in the project schedule duration, resources, or cost. This will, in many cases, have a negative impact, perhaps significantly, on the project.

It is essential to compare this approach to controlling scope in Agile. In Agile, the product owner or customer adds the new requirement change to the product backlog. The product owner or customer then prioritizes this change along with all other requirements in the product backlog.
The next sprint will then begin work on the product backlog story with the highest business value.

One should understand that Agile projects will not implement all requested requirements. Instead, controlling the project's funding or schedule manages the project scope. This results in lower priority requirements, which may have been in-scope originally, will not be done as part of the project.

Questions

1. The project manager is preparing to validate a group of deliverables with the customer. The project team just completed verify the deliverables with no known issues. The team and customer meet every two (2) weeks to validate the deliverables. What BEST describes this life cycle?
    A. Waterfall
    B. Traditional
    C. DevOps
    D. Agile

2. The project manager and team are discussing a project requirement. None remember which stakeholder requested the requirement. Which document should the team reference to determine the stakeholder?
    A. Requirements documentation
    B. Scope management plan
    C. Requirements traceability matrix
    D. Requirements management plan

3. What project output describes the project deliverables such that those deliverables may be estimated and tracked?
    A. Project schedule
    B. WBS
    C. WBS dictionary
    D. Requirements documentation

4. The project manager is meeting with the customer to review that an interim project deliverable meets the project requirements provided by the customer. What BEST describes this meeting?
    A. Control quality
    B. Control scope
    C. Validate scope
    D. Verified deliverables

5. The project manager and team want to get feedback on the proposed project deliverable to gather additional requirements. The project team developed working application pages to demonstrate a possible deliverable capability to the customer. What BEST describes this method?
   A. Prototype
   B. Observations
   C. Survey
   D. Benchmarking

6. The project manager and customer documented the criteria for reviewing the project deliverables. This criterion enables an objective assessment of the deliverables for acceptance. What process will use this criterion?
   A. Control scope
   B. Create WBS
   C. Control Quality
   D. Validate scope

7. The project team finalized the specific project documents that the sponsor requires as project deliverables. These documents include a signed project charter, approved project management plan, quality checklists, and other documents. Only the sponsor will receive these deliverables. What BEST describes these documents?
   A. Product scope
   B. Project scope
   C. Project documents
   D. Requirements

8. The project manager received a document with initial project requirements. Which document may be a source of these project requirements??
   A. Project management plan
   B. Scope management plan
   C. Requirements management plan
   D. Project charter

9. Senior managers were assessing the needs for a program of several projects to new market conditions. What BEST describes this effort?
   A. Business analysis
   B. Project Statement of Work (SOW)
   C. Project charting
   D. Collect requirements

10. The project manager and team have completed collecting all the requirements. What BEST describes the next step in the scope management plan?
    A. Develop the requirements management plan
    B. Develop the project scope statement
    C. Develop the requirements documentation
    D. Develop WBS

11. The project manager is interviewing a stakeholder about a requirement in the project charter. The stakeholder identifies another person who will impact the project and may have additional requirements. Where BEST should the project manager document this person?
    A. Requirements management plan
    B. Requirements traceability matrix
    C. Scope management plan
    D. Stakeholder register

12. The project manager has gathered a group of stakeholders together from across the organization. The purpose of this exercise is to gather project requirements. What BEST describes this data gathering technique?
    A. Interview
    B. Focus group
    C. Facilitated workshop
    D. Meeting

13. The project manager and team have identified the final project deliverables. Users will receive some of the deliverables. What BEST describes these deliverables?
    A. Product scope
    B. Project scope
    C. Deliverable
    D. Requirements

14. The project manager has determined that the project will incur considerable change to requirements during the project. To address this challenge, the project manager and team chose a life cycle that enables defining the details of each deliverable as the project progressives. What BEST describes this life-cycle?
    A. Waterfall
    B. Traditional
    C. Agile
    D. DevOps

15. The project manager and team are creating a WBS. Each level in the process is additional detail about a project deliverable. What BEST describes this approach?
    A. Decomposition
    B. Progressive elaboration
    C. Create WBS
    D. Identify requirements

16. The project manager has received approval by the sponsor for the project scope statement, WBS and WBS dictionary. What BEST describes what the sponsor approved?
    A. Schedule baseline
    B. Scope baseline
    C. Project charter
    D. Project requirements

17. The sponsor just met with the project manager to discuss a requirement. This requirement is not currently part of the approved scope baseline. Which following process BEST describes what the project management should do next?
    A. Perform integrated change control
    B. Control quality
    C. Control scope
    D. Collect requirements

18. Validate Scope is a process performed during monitoring and controlling. Which pair are outputs?
    A. Verified deliverables, accepted deliverables
    B. Verified deliverables, work performance data
    C. Accepted deliverables, work performance information
    D. Validated deliverables, work performance information

19. A new project manager has just replaced the project manager on an existing project. The new project manager wants to know how the previous project manager was managing the project's scope. What is the BEST source to answer this question?
    A. Project management plan
    B. Requirements management plan
    C. Scope management plan
    D. WBS

20. The project manager and team are interviewing a stakeholder to understand their needs and requirements. The team documents all of the stakeholder's comments. The team has two (2) more stakeholders to interview to finish this phase. Which following process BEST describes this effort?
    A. Define Scope
    B. Plan Scope Management
    C. Control Scope
    D. Collect Requirements

21. A project requirement is that the project manager submits a project budget update each month to the Project Management Office (PMO). Which BEST describes this requirement?
    A. Project scope
    B. Product scope
    C. Product requirement
    D. Organizational process assets

22. The sponsor is anxious to understand when the project will finish. Even more so on the project budget for an upcoming review with the CEO. The new project manager is eager to please the sponsor. What should the project manager focus on first?
    A. Schedule management
    B. Cost management
    C. Risk management
    D. Scope management

23. The project manager is meeting for the first time with the sponsor. The sponsor stated the project would use a preferred supplier. Based on this constraint, which of the following sources should the project manager use to help determine the project requirements?
    A. Agreements
    B. Assumptions
    C. Constraints
    D. Organizational process assets

24. The project team and manager are determining how to gather requirements on the project. Most of the team agreed to use prototyping. What BEST describes this decision-making technique?
    A. Unanimity
    B. Majority
    C. Plurality
    D. Autocratic

25. Requirements will evolve during the project. As a result, the project manager determined the best life-cycle for the project is agile. What is the BEST technique to document requirements?
    A. Requirements documentation
    B. User stories
    C. Scope document
    D. WBS

Answers

1. D. Agile
    - The Agile life cycle deploys deliverables at the end of each iteration. Next, the project team completes verifies (i.e., performs Control Quality) the iteration's deliverables and then validates (i.e., performs Validate Scope) the deliverables with the customer. Verifying and validating the scope is done for each iteration. (*PMBOK® Guide – 6th Edition*, page 131)
2. C. Requirement traceability matrix
    - The requirements traceability matrix is a critical document that tracks each requirement, both those in-scope and out-of-scope, throughout the project. When a requirement identified, the team updates the requirements traceability matrix. This update includes the identification of the stakeholder proposing the requirement along with other information. This information enables the team to trace the requirement from identification to customer acceptance of the deliverable. (*PMBOK® Guide – 6th Edition*, page 148)
3. B. WBS
    - The Work Breakdown Structure (WBS) is a hierarchical view of all the project deliverables. The WBS decomposes the project into work packages or deliverables that are produced by the project's effort. The WBS does not describe the effort. For example, a WBS deliverable might be "Project Charter". It would not be "Gather and Assess Requirements for the Project Charter" which describes the work or effort to create the project charter. This work or effort would be contained in the project schedule. (*PMBOK® Guide – 6th Edition*, page 156)
4. C. Validate scope
    - One must be clear on the purpose of Validate Scope, Control Scope, and Control Quality. The Control Quality process is performed by the project team to assess the

produced deliverable meets the project requirements as understood. The result is a verified deliverable.

- The next step, Validate Scope, is to confirm the verified deliverable meets the customer's requirements expectation. The project manager must validate the scope with the customer periodically throughout the project. By doing so, the project manager may identify missed, misunderstood requirements, or the customer may identify new requirements. The sooner in the project, these are identified, the less impact approved new or changed requirements will have on the project. It may severely impact the project outcome if new or additional requirements where identified for the first time at the end of the project.
- Identification of new requirements results in the project team performing the Control Scope process. The project manager and team must confirm the new requirement are in-scope for the project, and the change is validated and approved as part of the Perform Integrated Change Control process.
- *(PMBOK® Guide – 6th Edition*, page 163)

5. A. Prototype
- Creating a working model to demonstrate overall or a specific capability of the project deliverable is prototyping. A prototype may be very simple such as wire-frames of the screen or page layouts to specific mocked-up responses to interactive choices made during the prototype demonstration. *(PMBOK® Guide – 6th Edition*, page 147)

6. D. Validate scope
- The question states the project manager and customer documented criteria to assess project deliverables — a couple of critical points. Project deliverables indicate the focus of this effort is on the deliverables. Not the requirements. This effort also ensures an objective, not a subjective or emotional assessment, will be performed. The best answer is the Validate Scope process, where the

customer confirms the deliverables meet expectations. (*PMBOK® Guide – 6ᵗʰ Edition*, page 163)

7. B. Project scope

- Project scope deliverables focus on the work to deliver the project objectives. The sponsor or customer may require these deliverables.

- One way to identify project scope from product scope deliverables is to ask the question, will the deliverable be provided to a user? If the answer is no, then the deliverable is likely to be a project scope deliverable. For example, when a user purchases a cell phone, is the signed project charter included? No. The signed project charter is a project scope deliverable.

- (*PMBOK® Guide – 6ᵗʰ Edition*, page 131)

8. D. Project charter

- The project charter includes initial high-level requirements. The project manager and team must further define these requirements. The project charter also includes stakeholders who will provide additional requirements that may not be in the project charter.)

- Based on the question, it is essential to understand the status of the project. The project charter is the only answer that contains requirements before creating requirements.

- (*PMBOK® Guide – 6ᵗʰ Edition*, page 140)

9. A. Business analysis

- Analyzing business needs is critical to ensure programs and projects address the needs of the organization. Business analysis may start with senior management before a project begins to determine the business need and case for the program or project.

- In this situation, the outcome of the business analysis maybe a project statement of work or a draft project charter. The team may also do business analysis during the project to progressively elaborate on the business requirements.

- (*PMBOK® Guide – 6ᵗʰ Edition*, page 132)

10. B. Develop the project scope statement
- Once all the requirements are collected, the project manager and team must develop the project scope statement. This statement describes what requirements are in-scope for the project.
- Up to this point, the project team gathered all stakeholder requirements. After the project scope statement is defined, only those requirements that support the project scope statement are further developed and will be the requirements of the project deliverables.
- By definition and exclusion, the project scope statement defines those requirements that are out-of-scope for the project. Those out-of-scope requirements may generate conversations with stakeholders who challenge the exclusion of these requirements.
- (*PMBOK® Guide – 6th Edition*, page 154)

11. D. Stakeholder Register
- The stakeholder register is the source of information about all stakeholders. The stakeholder register includes name, contact, organization role information about each stakeholder. The stakeholder register also contains crucial additional information about the stakeholder, including their influence, power, etc. on the project. The stakeholder register does not contain information about specific requirements. (*PMBOK® Guide – 6th Edition*, page 141)

12. B. Focus group
- A focus group is a group of stakeholders who have a common background and project outcome expectations. A key benefit is the requirements may be better defined from the conversation that includes the input from many stakeholders. (*PMBOK® Guide – 6th Edition*, page 142)

13. A. Product scope
- Product scope is those deliverables that the user will receive from the project. The key to determining whether a deliverable is project or product based is the stakeholder who receives the deliverable. In this question, the stakeholder is users who use the project's product, service,

or result. User stakeholders include those who purchase items using an eCommerce shopping cart, complete on-line registration, purchase a cell phone, etc.

- Note that sometimes project scope includes both project and product scope. For this question, the BEST answer is product scope.
- (*PMBOK® Guide – 6th Edition*, page 131)

14. C. Agile

- The Agile life-cycle defines in detail the deliverables at the beginning of each iteration. Reassessing requirement priority at the start of iteration enables the project team to adapt to new or changing requirements and deliverables rapidly. This life-cycle requires the customer and sponsor to engage to ensure an iteration's deliverables are correctly prioritized and sufficiently defined. (*PMBOK® Guide – 6th Edition*, page 131)

15. A. Decomposition

- Decomposition is an iterative technique where a high-level objective or deliverable further defined until the lowest level may be accurately estimated and tracked. In the case of a WBS, the highest-level may be the project, second-level the phases, the third-level the major deliverables in each phase, the fourth-level sub-deliverables of each major deliverable, etc. The decomposition continues until the project's time, cost, and scope are manageable. (*PMBOK® Guide – 6th Edition*, page 158)

16. B. Scope baseline

- T The scope baseline includes the project scope statement, WBS, and WBS dictionary. The scope baseline defines the major project deliverables that are in-scope, assumptions, and constraints. Once the scope baseline is approved, any changes to the scope baseline require integrated change control approval. (*PMBOK® Guide – 6th Edition*, page 161)

17. C. Control scope

- The question states the scope baseline was approved. This statement is critical to answering the question. Therefore, the best answer is the Control Scope process. If the scope baseline were yet to be approved, the project manager would include the new requirement with the other requirements as part of Collect Requirements.

- But the scope baseline has been approved. Therefore, the project manager must perform Control Scope to ensure scope creep does not occur. Scope creep occurs when accepting new requirements without the appropriate assessment and necessary adjustments to the schedule, cost, plans, etc. Scope creek will quickly lead to the project that is out of control as the schedule, cost, plans, etc. are not sufficient to produce the new requirement.
- (*PMBOK® Guide – 6th Edition*, page 167)

18. D. Accepted deliverables, work performance information

- The only answer pair which both are Validate Scope outputs is the "accepted deliverables, work performance information" answer. The student needs to know which processes create work performance data versus information and the difference between verified and accepted (validated) deliverables. (*PMBOK® Guide – 6th Edition*, page 167)

19. C. Scope management plan

- Management plans for each knowledge area describe how those knowledge areas will be planned, executed and monitored and controlled. (*PMBOK® Guide – 6th Edition*, page 134)

20. D. Collect Requirements

- Collect Requirements gathers all needs and requirements from all stakeholders. The project manager and team are gathering requirements. The key is the team is collecting all the needs and requirements from each identified stakeholder to achieve the project objective. There is no mention of assessing the stakeholder's input or filtering requirements. (*PMBOK® Guide – 6th Edition*, page 138)

21. B. Project scope

- The requirement to submit a monthly project budget update has no direct impact on product requirements. In other words, the customer is not concerned nor can tell if the project budget was or was not submitted monthly. Therefore, this requirement is within the project scope of the project. (*PMBOK® Guide – 6th Edition*, page 131)

- Product scope includes those in-scope requirements that are part of the final project deliverable which may be a product, service or result. Examples include application background, supported languages, etc.

22. D. Scope management

- It is essential to understand the sequence of processes execution. This understanding includes both the knowledge area and the individual process levels. Are the project manager and team able to determine the project schedule without performing scope management? No. Determine the project costs? No. Determining both the project schedule and costs requires an understanding of the scope.

- Understanding the scope may be an iterative process. The team may progressively elaborate on the schedule and cost estimates from rough order of magnitude (ROM) estimate to an accurate or narrow range of values. This elaboration is true for Agile or predictive projects. The project manager and team must understand the scope before estimating the schedule or cost.

- Using good multiple-choice exam techniques is critical. One of these techniques is the elimination of answers. Is schedule management the answer? No. The question states the sponsor was also interested in the cost. Likewise, you can eliminate the cost management answer as the sponsor was interested in the schedule. Performing scope, schedule, and cost management process may lead to the discovery of additional risks. At this point, this only leaves scope management as the best choice among the answers.

- (*PMBOK® Guide – 6th Edition*, page 150)

23. A. Agreements

- A preferred supplier is a seller who has an established relationship with the buyer. The buyer in this question is the sponsor and project manager's organization. Terms and conditions are often agreed to with a preferred supplier and buyer before the project.

- The project scope must include all in-scope requirements. It is essential to understand the project scope context. Sometimes project scope may consist of both product and project scope. Other times, as in this case, just the project scope. The agreement terms and conditions include payment schedules, work hours, work location, intellectual property rights, status reporting, etc. The project manager must include all these requirements in the project scope.
- (PMBOK® Guide – 6th Edition, page 141)

24. B. Majority

- A majority is a voting technique in which half or more must vote in favor of the decision. The project manager must choose decision-making techniques wisely. Including in this case, what is the definition of a majority? More than fifty percent? Two-thirds? Eighty percent? Using the majority voting technique may leave almost half the team in favor of a different decision. If this occurs, will the team still be able to move forward in a unified approach?
- Plurality, decisions based on the greatest number in favor and unanimity, where everyone must agree on the decision, are examples of other voting techniques.
- (PMBOK® Guide – 6th Edition, page 144)

25. B. User stories

- A technique to document requirements on Agile projects is user stories. A user story template includes the role benefiting from this requirement, a description, and the business value of the requirement.
- Tools and techniques apply across life-cycles. There are no "rules" that the user story technique only applies to Agile and not predictive projects. However, remember not to imply or complicate exam questions with how it may be in your "real world." This question stated it was an Agile project. The best answer then was user stories, which are associated with Agile projects. (PMBOK® Guide – 6th Edition, page 145)A technique to document requirements

on agile projects is user stories. A user story template includes the role benefiting from this requirement, a description and the business value of the requirement.

- (*PMBOK® Guide – 6th Edition*, page 145)

.

SCHEDULE MANAGEMENT

The project schedule is one of the primary project outputs and is referenced often during the project. Is the project progressing as expected? Do additional resources need to be applied? Do events outside of the project, resource vacation schedules, weather, etc. impact the project? May resources be released back into the organization?

Typically the schedule processes are performed sequentially. For example, is a project manager able to estimate the resources needed to complete an activity before identifying that activity? No. Is a project manager able to estimate the activity duration before identifying the activity and resources? No.

The processes are also iterative. For example, the project team may identify a new activity in the schedule. If this occurs, the project team must then re-perform the processes that estimate the duration, resources, etc. before continuing to model the project schedule.

Because of the focus throughout the project, the project schedule may be viewed by stakeholders as the project plan. Remember, the schedule baseline is just one component of the project management plan.

How will the project schedule be created, maintained, and controlled? (Plan Schedule Management) The answers are in the schedule management plan. One of those critical answers is how performance will be measured. Measuring schedule performance starts with defining how to report progress, how to measure performance (Schedule Variance (SV),

Schedule Performance Index (SPI)), the tools used to create and maintain the schedule, etc.

What will produce the deliverables? (Define Activities) This process transforms the project and product scope into work tasks or activities required to produce the project's deliverables. The team must define all activities. To fully-define each activity, the team must document each activity's attributes (e.g., type of resource needed, identifier, relationship to other activities, etc.) Also, milestones mark significant project progress in creating business value.

In what order must activities be done? (Sequence Activities) Once documenting all the activities is complete, the team must determine the sequencing of those activities. Must an activity be completed before starting the next activity? May the team work on two or more activities at the same time? The result of this process is a schedule network or precedence diagram linking each activity to all the other activities.

What is needed to complete the activity? (Estimate Activity Resources) Once the sequence of activities is defined, the project manager and team must determine what resources will complete the activity. Resources may be people, materials, or tools. Does this activity require an architect? Must a software license be acquired to start this activity? Is the test environment needed to complete this activity? A resource calendar, documenting availability (e.g., team member vacation schedule), may be required for each resource.

How long will it take to complete this activity? (Estimate Activity Duration) Based on the activity attributes and required resources, the project manager and team can estimate the activity duration. To determine the duration, the project manager and team must first estimate the effort to complete the activity. Once the effort is estimated, the activity duration may be determined based on the estimated effort and amount and type of resources assigned to the activity. For example, an activity whose effort is forty hours would have a duration of five days if a senior programmer was assigned and worked eight hours a day. If the senior programmer could only work fifty percent on the activity, the duration would be ten days instead of five days. If instead the resource type was changed to a junior programmer who is less experienced and efficient, the activity duration will be longer.

Finalize the project schedule. (Develop Schedule) The project manager and team integrate the results of the previous processes to develop a model of the project schedule. The initial project schedule model may differ from the sponsor and stakeholder expectations documented in the project charter. If the schedule indicates the project will extend beyond the desired completion date, the project manager and team must model alternatives. If the schedule shows the project will complete sooner than expected, the project manager and team should still identify improvements in effectiveness and efficiency. Improvements may change an activity's resources, perform more activities in parallel, etc. The project manager and team continue to model the schedule until they are satisfied. The next step is the proposed project schedule model is reviewed and approved by the sponsor and stakeholders. Once approved, the model becomes the project's schedule baseline.

When will the project complete? Is the project on, ahead, or behind schedule? (Control Schedule) A project team member tells the project manager they have completed fifty percent of their assigned activity. Is this activity on schedule? The only information provided by the project team member, fifty percent completed, is work performance data. The project manager cannot assess the status of the activity or project schedule based on this data. To assess the project schedule status, the project manager must compare this data to the approved schedule baseline. This comparison will result in work performance information. If the schedule baseline expected fifty percent of this activity to be complete, then the activity is on schedule.

Is the project still expected to complete on time? Knowing the status of the project is important to the sponsor and stakeholders. However, just as, or even more so, is the schedule forecast. To create the forecast, the project manager must assess the schedule's past work performance data and expected future performance. The project manager must implement changes if the schedule forecast does not align with the approved schedule baseline. Adjusting the approved schedule baseline is done by executing the Perform Integrated Change Control and other processes.

Questions

1. The project's Schedule Performance Index (SPI) is 0.95 on Friday. What does the program manager report regarding the project schedule?
   A. On schedule
   B. Ahead of schedule
   C. Behind schedule
   D. Finished on schedule

2. The project manager discussed the scheduling challenges of the ABC project with another project manager. This project manager had previously completed a project that was similar to the ABC project. What BEST describes this technique?
   A. Expert judgment
   B. Analytical techniques
   C. Brainstorming
   D. Meetings

3. The project manager and team have completed the first schedule model. The project manager wants to assess the schedule model with the sponsor's milestone expectations. What document is the BEST source?
   A. Project charter
   B. Project statement of work (SOW)
   C. Schedule management plan
   D. WBS

4. The project team reported completing fifty percent of the first week's scheduled activities. The project manager calculated a Schedule Performance Index (SPI) of 0.90 for the week. What is the status of the schedule?
   A. Ahead of schedule
   B. On schedule
   C. Behind Schedule
   D. Unable to determine

5. A project schedule network begins with Activity A. The duration of Activity A is four (4) days. Once the team completes Activity A, both Activity B and C may start. The duration of Activity B is three (3) days, and Activity C is five (5) days. Complete the forward and backward passes. Start with the Early Start value of one (1).

6. The project manager wants to calculate the Schedule Performance Index (SPI) for the project. Which of the following sources provide the necessary data (choose all that apply)?
    A. Schedule baseline
    B. Cost baseline
    C. Work performance information
    D. Work performance data

7. The project manager is meeting with three project team members to estimate activities using the Triangular Distribution method. One team member believes it will take four (4) days to complete an activity. The other team members estimate it will take five (5) days and three (3) days. What is the final estimate for the activity?
    A. 12 days
    B. 5 days
    C. 4 days
    D. 3 days

8. Historically the project has performed at an SPI of 0.95. The remaining project schedule duration is one-hundred twenty (120) days. The sponsor has asked for an update on the project finish date. What should the project manager report?
    A. 120 days
    B. 134 days
    C. 114 days
    D. 127 days

9. The project manager and team are brainstorming the completion dates for all the activities to produce the deliverables. What BEST describes this process?
    A. Create WBS
    B. Estimate activity resources
    C. Define activities
    D. Sequence activities

10. The project manager and team just produced a deliverable. They are now planning in detail the next schedule iteration to create the following deliverable. The project manager and team continue this approach to provide all the deliverables. What BEST describes this approach?
    A. Rolling wave planning
    B. Progressive elaboration
    C. Decomposition
    D. Waterfall

11. The project manager and team have confirmed all the activities in the project schedule have a predecessor and successor. The only exceptions are the first and last activity. What process did the project team just complete?
    A. Define activities
    B. Define schedule
    C. Plan schedule management
    D. Sequence activities

12. The project team has completed one-thousand (1,000) hours during the period. At this point, the project has an SPI of 1.0. What is the SV?
    A. 0 hours
    B. 900 hours
    C. 1,000 hours
    D. 950 hours

13. The project manager and team are assessing potential team member's availability. The assessment includes the impact of geographical location. What document is being referenced by the project team?
    A. Human resource management plan
    B. Project calendar
    C. Resource calendar
    D. Project schedule

14. The project manager is modeling the project schedule. With each model, the shortest path changes. What BEST describes the shortest path from the first to the last activity?
    A. Critical path
    B. Total float
    C. Free float
    D. Project path

15. The project has an earned value of $1,000. The planned value on the data date is $900. What is the schedule variance (SV)? Is the project ahead of schedule?
    A. $100, behind schedule
    B. $100, ahead of schedule
    C. -$100, on schedule
    D. -$100, behind schedule

16. The project manager is preparing to update the sponsor on the project. The schedule forecast is a critical component of the update. The duration of the project per the schedule baseline is 1,000 days. Halfway through the project, the SPI = 1.0. The project manager believes that the team will perform better during the rest of the project because of executing the process improvement plan. The project manager thinks the SPI for the rest of the project will be 1.10. What is the schedule forecast to complete the project?
    A. 1,000 days
    B. 955 days
    C. 1,455 days
    D. 1,045 days

17. The project team cannot make updates to the customer's data center during the first week of January due to a change moratorium. The contract calls out this restriction. Updating the data center is critical to completing the project. What BEST describes this situation?
    A. Mandatory, internal
    B. Discretionary, external
    C. Discretionary, internal
    D. Mandatory, external

18. The project is behind schedule. The project manager has determined the best option is to add additional resources to an activity. What is this technique called?
    A. Fast-tracking
    B. Crashing
    C. Re-scheduling
    D. Monitoring schedule

19. The project manager is creating a project schedule. Activity B must start after the predecessor, Activity A, is finished. What type of precedence relationship will create this relationship?
    A. FS
    B. SS
    C. FF
    D. SF

20. The project team has determined the number and complexity of test cases to develop for the activity. The project manager estimates the effort based on a test case database that includes the complexity of test cases from previous projects. What BEST describes this estimating technique?
    A. Analogous
    B. Parametric
    C. Three-point
    D. Group

21. The project manager and team are currently discussing one of the project activities. They identified this activity would require a senior test plan developer and shared data storage that is accessible to the entire project team. Which process BEST describes this discussion?
    A. Identify activities
    B. Plan schedule management
    C. Sequence activities
    D. Estimate activity resources

22. The project manager is working on the project schedule. Two activities required the same project team member. This situation results in the project team member working eighty (80) hours one week. Working this long is not acceptable. Both activities are not on the critical path, and there is sufficient total float. What technique should the project manager use?
    A. Resource smoothing
    B. Resource leveling
    C. Critical chain method
    D. Estimate activity resource

23. The project manager wants to begin a successor activity three (3) days sooner than scheduled. What BEST describes this schedule change?
    A. Lag
    B. Schedule model
    C. Control schedule
    D. Lead

24. The project manager is performing integrated change control due to a schedule change on the approved schedule. What BEST describes the schedule?
    A. Schedule baseline
    B. Schedule model
    C. Project Schedule
    D. Schedule

25. The project manager just completed modeling the project schedule. The project schedule model has two (2) critical paths. What is wrong?
    A. One or more activity durations are incorrect
    B. One or more precedence relationships is incorrect
    C. One or more resource assignments is incorrect
    D. One or more critical paths may exist

26. The project is ahead of schedule. Which of the following is correct?
    A. SPI > 1.0 and SV < 0
    B. SPI = 1.0 and SV = 0
    C. SPI < 1.0 and SV > 0
    D. SPI > 1.0 and SV > 0

27. Key stakeholders are in the team's work area reviewing the status of the project. There is a large chart on the wall that plots two metrics. The expected number of user story points to complete in each iteration. The second line plots the number of user stories completed during each iteration. What BEST describes this chart?
    A. Burnup chart
    B. Burndown chart
    C. Information radiator
    D. Progress chart

28. The team may delay two activities on a schedule network without impacting any following activities. What BEST describes this situation?
    A. Total float
    B. Lag
    C. Lead
    D. Free float

29. Complete the forward and backward pass for the schedule network. Start with the Early Start value of one (1). What is the late start of Activity B?

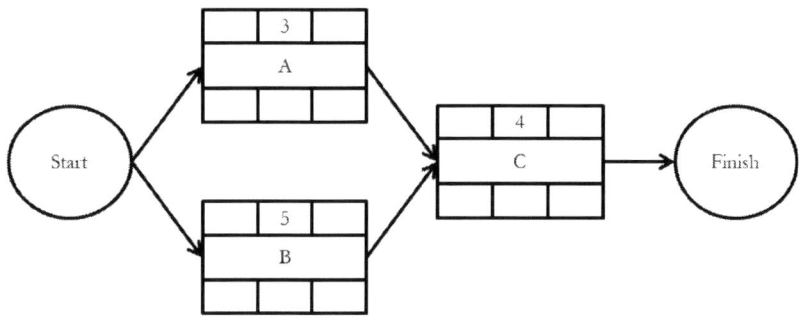

    A. 0
    B. 1
    C. 2
    D. 3

30. What is the free float of Activity B in the schedule network (question 29)?
    A. 0
    B. 2
    C. 1
    D. 3

Answers

1. C. Behind schedule
   - If the SPI is less than 1.0, the project is behind schedule. The question states, "…on Friday."
   - Friday is known as the status or data date (i.e., the date of the report). The data date is important, as SPI is a snapshot at a given moment. The project may have been or may not be at 0.95 before or after Friday. In other words, before or after the SPI was calculated.
   - (*PMBOK® Guide – 6th Edition*, page 263)

2. A. Expert judgment
   - When someone or an organization, with prior experience or expertise, provides insight, this is known as expert judgment. Someone who provides expert judgment may be known as a Subject Matter Expert (SME).
   - The expert judgment, in this case, was a project manager with previous successful experience. Note that the questions did not explicitly state successful experience. The student should assume on the exam that all activities were completed successfully per the PMBOK® Guide unless otherwise stated.
   - Other sources of expert judgment include trade associations, industry trade publications, etc.
   - (*PMBOK® Guide – 6th Edition*, page 200)

3. A. Project charter
   - Approval of the project charter authorizes the project. The project charter includes many critical sections, including constraints, assumptions, expected start and end dates, etc. One of those sections is milestones when the project will deliver the business value. (*PMBOK® Guide – 6th Edition*, page 180)

4. C. Behind schedule
   - If the Schedule Performance Index (SPI) is less than 1.0, the project is behind schedule. Earned Value (EV) is less than the Planned Value for the period (SPI = EV / PV). An SPI value of 1.0 is on schedule, while an SPI value of

greater than 1.0 is ahead of schedule. PV value from the
schedule baseline may be determined using algebra (0.90 =
9 / PV, resulting in an PV of 10). The planned value was to
complete 10 hours of the week's activities. (*PMBOK®*
Guide – Sixth Edition, page 263)

5.

Early Start	Duration	Early Finish
Activity		
Late Start	Total Float	Late Finish

Legend

- You may not get a drawn schedule network diagram in an
  exam question. So it is essential to be able to convert the
  question description into a diagram.
- Use the convention of starting on day one (1). First,
  determine the forward pass for the schedule network. The
  forward pass calculates from Start to End the Early Start
  (ES) and Early Finish (EF) for all activities. Once the
  forward pass is complete, you can perform the backward
  pass. The backward pass calculates from End to Start the
  Late Finish (LF) and Late Start for all activities. Once both
  passes are complete, then calculate the Total Float.
- Activity A – set ES to one (1). The duration of Activity A
  is four (4) days. At the end of day one (1), the team
  completed one day of work. At the end of day two (2) the
  team completed two days of work, and so on. Therefore,
  the EF of Activity A is four (4). The formula to calculate
  EF is ES + Duration – 1 = EF (1 + 4 -1 = 4).The earliest
  Activity B or C may start is day five (5).

- Activity B – set ES date to EF of Activity A plus one. The ES for Activity B is five (5). Calculate the EF the same as was done for Activity A.
- Activity C – set ES date to EF of Activity A plus one. The ES for Activity C is five (5). Calculate the EF the same as was done for Activity A and B.
- The duration of the project is nine (9) days. It will take nine days to complete the project. To verify ES and EF is calculated correctly, confirm the duration of the activities on the longest path (Start, A, C, End) equals the EF for Activity C. In this case, add the duration of Activity A and C (4 + 5 = 9). The EF of Activity C is nine (9).
- Calculation of the backward pass may now begin since the forward pass is complete. The first step is to determine the LF for the last activity or activities. In this case, Activity B and C. Since the EF for Activity C is nine (9) days and is greater than EF for Activity B, make the LF dates for Activity B and C equal to nine (9) days.
- Activity C. With the LF determine, the LS many now be calculated. The LS is five (5) days since the duration for Activity C is five (5) days. The formula is LF – Duration + 1 = LS (9 – 5 +1 = 5).
- Activity B. Calculate the LF the same as was done for Activity C.
- Activity A. You must evaluate the LS dates for both Activity B and C. Which activity, B or C, has the earliest LS date? Activity C. Therefore, the LF date for Activity A must be four (4).
- (PMBOK® Guide – 6th Edition, page 210)

6. A. Schedule baseline, D. Work performance data
   - SPI = EV / PV. The executing phase produces Earned Value (EV) or work performance data. As the team completes work on the project schedule activities, the project team members report progress or "earned value" (e.g., completed two days or 20% of a planned ten-day activity).

- Planned Value (PV) is the amount of activity value per the schedule the team would complete data date (i.e., a given date). PV amount is in the approved schedule baseline.
- For example, the team completed two (2) days of the activity (earned value), but the team planned to complete four (4) days (planned value). SPI = 2 / 4 = 0.5 The activity is behind schedule.
- (*PMBOK® Guide – 6th Edition*, page 226, 263)

7. C. 4 days
   - The Triangular Distribution formula is (tO + tM + tP) / 3. The Optimistic estimate was three (3) days, the Most Likely estimate was four (4) days and, the Pessimistic estimate was five (5) days. Inserting these values into the formula results in a four (4) days estimate for the activity. (*PMBOK® Guide – 6th Edition*, page 221)
   - The Beta Distribution formula, which weighs the Most Likely estimate higher, may also be used in some exam questions. (*PMBOK® Guide – 6th Edition*, page 245)

8. B. 134 days   D = 12?
   - The project manager must assess historical performance when developing a forecast. Were there any unique causes that influenced the previous SPI? If there was, will they or will they not affect future performance?
   - The question does not state or imply there is any reason to believe the historical SPI will be different for the rest of the project. SPI = EV / PV (0.95 = 120 / PV) results in a PV equal to 134 days. In other words, it will take 134 days to complete the remaining 120 days of earned value. The project manager should tell the sponsor the project will complete in 134 days.
   - (*PMBOK® Guide* – Sixth Edition, page 263)

9. C. Define activities
   - Define Activities is the process of determining all the activities to include in the project schedule. One approach is for the project team to review each deliverable in the WBS to determine the activities necessary to create that deliverable. (*PMBOK® Guide – 6th Edition*, page 183)

10. A. Rolling wave planning
  - Rolling wave planning is an iterative planning approach where the team defines in detail, just before beginning the work, the next deliverable or phase. With the completion of that deliverable or phase, the project manager and team plan in detail the following deliverable or phase. This "rolling wave" of planning continues until the completion of the project (*PMBOK® Guide – 6th Edition*, page 185)
  - Progressive elaboration is an iterative technique that further defines the understanding of a specific deliverable, requirement, activity, etc. For example, a requirement in the project charter should be better understood and defined in the requirements document. While any project life-cycle may use progressive elaboration at any point throughout any project, it is a common technique in Agile projects.

11. D. Sequence activities
  - The Sequence Activity process creates a precedence diagram of all schedule activities. All activities must have at least one predecessor activity and at least one successor activity.
  - There are two exceptions. The very first activity in the sequence does not have a predecessor activity. And the very last activity in the sequence does not have a successor activity.
  - (*PMBOK® Guide – 6th Edition*, page 187)

12. A. 0 hours
  - There are two ways to solve this question. First, when SPI = 1.0, the Earned Value (EV) equals the Planned Value (PV). The question states the "…project team completed one-thousand (1,000) hours…" or 1,000 hours of EV. Since the SPI = 1.0, the PV hours during this period must also be 1,000 hours. The project is on schedule. (SPI = EV / PV, 1.0 = 1,000 / 1,000). You can then use EV and PV to solve for SV (0 = 1,000 − 1,000).

- The second way is understanding the relationship between SPI and SV. An on-schedule project (SPI = 1.0) has zero Schedule Variance.
- (*PMBOK® Guide* – Sixth Edition, page 263)

13. C. Resource calendar

- The resource calendar documents the availability of individual resources. The resource calendar indicates the regular working shift and holidays observed by the resource, which may vary based on the geographical location of the resource.
- The project manager must confirm the resources needing a specific resource calendar. Resources include not only resource calendars for people but equipment. For example, lease contracts may limit or trigger additional charges if the equipment is used more than eight (8) hours a day, on weekends, moved outside a geographical area, etc.
- (*PMBOK® Guide* – 6*th* *Edition*, page 208)

14. A. Critical path

- The sequence of activities with the greatest cumulative duration is the critical path. This is the shortest path or duration to complete the project. (*PMBOK® Guide* – 6*th* *Edition*, page 210)

15. B. $100, ahead of schedule

- SV = EV – PV. Schedule Value (SV) is the difference, or magnitude, between Earned Value (EV) and Planned Value (PV). In this question, the value of the work completed (i.e., earned value) is $1,000. According to the project schedule, the team was expected to earn only $900 during this period. SV = $1,000 – $900 = $100. Since SV is positive, the project is ahead of schedule.
- The other answers were wrong due to incorrect application of the formula or assessment of the result as being ahead, on or behind schedule.
- (*PMBOK® Guide* – 6*th* *Edition*, page 226, 263)

16. B. 955 days

- This question covers many topics. Remember a vital component of any update is the forecast. It is not sufficient to report that the project is on schedule – today. The project manager must also provide the schedule forecast. Will the project be completed on schedule?

- The question states the 1,000-day project is on schedule (SPI = 1.0) at the halfway point. The Planned Value (PV) of a 1,000-day project at the halfway point is 500 days. Since the SPI = 1.0, the Earned Value (EV) must also be 500 days. (SPI = EV/PV à 1.0 = EV/500 à 1.0 * 500 = EV à 500 = EV).

- Based on this calculation, there are 500 days of PV remaining to complete the project per the schedule baseline. Since the SPI = 1.0 and the project to date is on schedule, the estimated EV must also be 500 days.

- However, the question states the project manager is forecasting an SPI of 1.10 for the remainder of the project. This SPI means the project manager is forecasting to earn value faster than the planned value of the schedule baseline. In other words, the project team will earn the value sooner than planned in the current schedule baseline for the remainder of the project. The project manager must calculate the estimate-to-complete PV for the remainder of the project. (SPI = EV/PV à 1.10 = 500/PV à 1.10 * PV = 500 à PV = 500 / 1.10 à PV = 455).

- The project manager now has both components necessary to calculate the schedule forecast. The EV to date (500 days) and the PV to complete the project (455 days). The new schedule forecast is 955 days.

- Note with a PV of 455 days to complete the second half of the project, EV for the second half of the project is reset to 455 days too. The project manager and team do not get to "keep" the 45-day improvement. Instead, this efficiency gain is returned to the organization to support other initiatives. As a result, the SPI will equal 1.0, not 1.10, at the start of the second half of the project.

- (*PMBOK® Guide – 6th Edition*, page 226, 263)

17. D. Mandatory, external
    - All dependencies impact the project schedule. This question states the dependency is based on contractual terms (mandatory) to address a customer (external) requirement. A dependency that is both mandatory and external are typically out of the control of the project team. The team must meed mandatory dependency, in this case, contract terms.
    - Internal and external dependencies are relative to the project team. The customer, while critical to the project's success, is a stakeholder that is external to the project team.
    - All the answers are valid dependency pairs. In other words, a mandatory dependency may be an external or internal dependency. A discretionary dependency may also be an external or internal dependency.
    - Discretionary dependencies are typically implemented based on the project team's preference. For example, the project team may prefer to complete all the development before starting integrated testing. Based on other factors, including the project schedule status, the project team may not be able to work as preferred resulting in changing or dropping a discretionary dependency.
    - (*PMBOK® Guide – 6th Edition*, page 191-192)

18. B. Crashing
    - Adding more resource capacity to a critical path activity to decrease the activity or project's duration is known as crashing. Crashing does not change the schedule precedence diagram.
    - There are multiple ways to add resource capacity. The project manager may ask the project team to work overtime, add additional resources to the activity, or replace a resource with a more efficient resource. Increasing resource capacity examples also include larger server capacity to execute test cases quicker, overnight vs. standard shipping, etc.
    - Often if a project is behind schedule, a project manager may reactively crash a project to recover time. However,

the project manager should always be following the process improvement plan. Process improvements that result in improved efficiency (i.e., doing more with the same resource capacity) may be considered a proactive form of crashing. Process improvement may result in lower risk, lower cost, or fewer communication channels. Therefore, the project manager must always plan, execute, monitor, and control the project's process improvement plan.

- Crashing may increase the project risk, add cost to the project (e.g., overtime pay, higher pay rate, etc.), and increase the communication channels (i.e., more resources may mean more communication channels).
- (*PMBOK® Guide – 6th Edition*, page 215)

19. A. FS

- Finish-to-Start (FS) requires the predecessor activity (Activity A) to finish before the project team may start the successor activity (Activity B). FS is typically the most common precedence relationship in the project schedule. (*PMBOK® Guide – 6th Edition*, page 190)
- The general convention is predecessor-to-successor relationship format. This convention holds for each of the precedence dependency types. For example, in a Finish-to-Start relationship, the Finish applies to the predecessor. The predecessor must finish before the successor activity may start. The Start applies to the successor activity. The successor activity cannot begin until the predecessor finishes. Finish (applies to predecessor)-to-Start (applies to successor).

20. B. Parametric

- Parametric estimating leverages past data about one or more variables. Parametric data is often in the form of a table or matrix.
- This question states historical information about test case complexity (an organizational process asset) is available. Based on the test case complexity rating, the project manager can look up the expected testing effort in the matrix (e.g. high complexity estimate is 40 hours effort,

medium complexity is 20 hours effort, low complexity is 10 hours effort).

- *(PMBOK® Guide – 6ᵗʰ Edition*, page 200)

21. D. Estimate activity resources

- The project manager and team are determining the resources needed to complete the activity. They have identified a specific role or skill set (senior test plan developer) and technical resources (shared data storage). After identifying and sequencing activities, the next project scheduling step is to identify resources. In turn, the identified resources impact the following scheduling step of estimating the activity duration. For example, the activity duration estimate will vary if experienced versus a less experienced programmer works on the activity.

- In prior *PMBOK® Guide* editions, the Estimate Activity Resource was part of the Time Management knowledge area. The Estimate Activity Resource process is now in the Resource Management knowledge area. It is included here due to its impact on schedule duration, sequence, etc.

- *(PMBOK® Guide – 6ᵗʰ Edition*, page 320)

22. B. Resource leveling

- The activities in question are not on the critical path, and there is sufficient total float. An exam assumption, unless stated otherwise, is project team members work normal working hours. Eighty (80) hours in a week are well beyond regular working hours. Therefore, the best answer is to resource level the project team by changing the sequence of the activities such that the project team member works no more than forty (40) hours a week.

- If these activities had been on the critical path, and the project manager wanted to level the resources, most likely the critical path and, in turn, the project would finish later.

- Resource smoothing is when the project manager adjusts the activities to reduce resource over allocation. Resource smoothing does not impact succeeding activities and the project completion date. Therefore, resource overallocation may still exists after resource smoothing.

- (*PMBOK® Guide – 6th Edition*, page 211)

23. D. Lead
    - Lead is starting a successor activity earlier than scheduled relative to its predecessor. For example, a successor activity with a Finish-to-Start of -3 would start three (3) days before the predecessor activity completes. (*PMBOK® Guide – 6th Edition*, page 214)

24. A. Schedule baseline
    - Once the schedule is approved, it is known as the schedule baseline. The schedule baseline is used by the project manager to determine if the project is on schedule. Any change to an approved schedule baseline requires executing Perform Integrated Change Control to determine if the change should be approved and then implemented. (*PMBOK® Guide – 6th Edition*, page 217)

25. D. One or more critical paths exist
    - A schedule model, and an approved schedule or schedule baseline, may have more than one (1) critical path. The schedule may also have more than one "near-critical" paths. Both scenarios are valid and increase the risk of the project schedule. (*PMBOK® Guide – 6th Edition*, page 210)

26. D. SPI > 1.0 and SV > 0
    - A Schedule Performance Index greater than 1.0 and a Schedule Variance greater than 0 (zero) indicates the project is ahead of schedule. (*PMBOK® Guide* – Sixth Edition, page 263)

27. B. Burndown chart
    - Agile teams use a burndown chart to show the progress of the project. There is a lot of common Agile terms in this question. The understanding of each term is essential for the exam.
    - Each Agile team defines user story points. When the team estimates requirements, they assign a relative effort value, typically in user story points, to each requirement. For example, the team estimates to complete Requirement A will take four (4) story points of effort. The team estimates Requirement B will take twice the effort, so the team assigns eight (8) story points to Requirement B. The team

plots both the estimated story points and the actual story points on a burndown chart.

- A burndown chart begins with the total number of user story points, or total estimated effort, to complete the iteration or project. The project team then "burns down" the total user story points by completing user story points during each iteration until the iteration or project finishes. The team adjusts if progress is not meeting expectations.

- Information radiator (i.e., "radiate information") is a common Agile term to describe large, highly visible charts that share information about the project. A Burndown chart is an example. Other examples include the Burnup chart, defect cycle time, etc. These charts are typically posted in the team area for everyone to see. Information radiators promote transparency.

- (PMBOK® Guide – Sixth Edition, page 226)

28. D. Free float

- When an activity can start later than its Early Start (ES) without impacting the start of any following activities, or violate a constraint, this is known as free float.

- What does it mean to violate a constraint? Let's look at an example. A schedule network has two activities. Activity A must finish before starting Activity B. And Activity B has a "must start on" date constraint. The free float is the amount that Activity A may delay starting, yet still finish in time, to meet the must start on date constraint of Activity B.

- (PMBOK® Guide – Sixth Edition, page 210)

29. C. 2

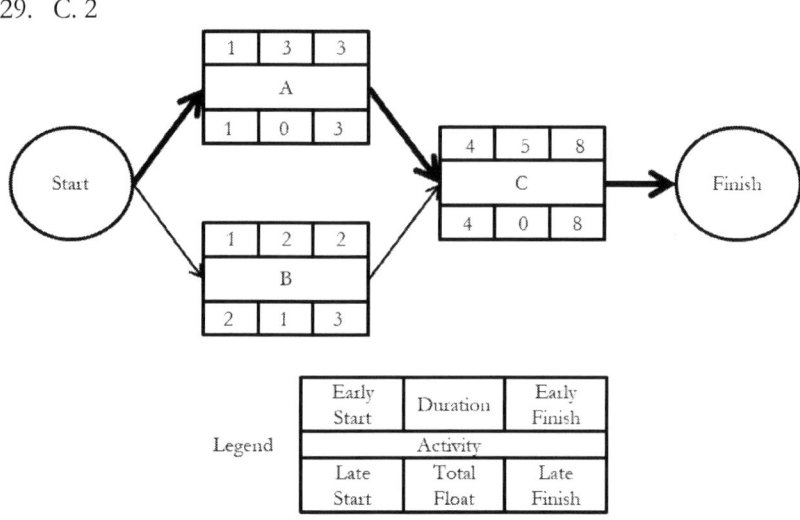

	Early Start	Duration	Early Finish
Legend		Activity	
	Late Start	Total Float	Late Finish

- The LS of Activity B is two (2).
- Use the convention of starting on day one (1). First, determine the forward pass for the schedule network. The forward pass calculates from Start to Finish the Early Start (ES) and Early Finish (EF) for all activities. After completing the forward pass, you can perform the backward pass. The backward pass calculates from Finish to Start the Late Finish (LF) and Late Start (LS) for all activities. Once both passes are completed, the Total Float may be calculated.
- A schedule network may use any period. Typically the period is one day. However, the period may be minutes, hours, weeks, etc.
- The first activity starts at the beginning of the period. In this case, at the start of day one (1). At the end of the day, the amount of work done is one (1) day. If the Activity has a duration of one (1), then the Activity is completed at the end of day one (1). If the activity must complete before starting successor activities, the earliest any successor activity may start is day two (2).
- Activity A. Make the ES one (1). Day one is the earliest Activity A may start. The EF is three (3) since the duration is three (3). Make sure you understand. The team completes One (1) day of work at the end of day one (1).

At the end of day two (2), two days of work finished. At the end of day three (3) three days of work is completed. Three days of work is the duration of Activity A. The formula to calculate EF is ES + Duration – 1 = EF (1 + 3 – 1 = 3).

- Activity B. Calculate the ES and EF the same as Activity A. Since Activity B duration is two (2), Activity B finishes on the second day.
- Activity C. When is the earliest Activity C may start? In this schedule network, both Activity A and B must complete before Activity C may start. Activity A finishes after Activity B. Therefore, ES for Activity C is the fourth (4) day. In other words, take the latest EF of all activities immediately preceding the activity and add one (1). Calculating EF for Activity C is the same as was done for Activity A and B.
- With the completion of the forward pass, the duration of the project is determined to be eight (8) days. The project will complete in eight (8) days based on this schedule network.
- The backward pass begins with the Finish of the schedule network.
- Activity C. Set the LF to the EF. Activity C cannot finish later than the EF, or the project will complete late. Beyond the eight (8) day. The LS must be day four (4). Starting Activity C any later than day four (4) would also cause the project to finish later than the eight (8) day. The formula to calculate LS is LF – Duration + 1 = LS (8 – 5 + 1 = 4).
- Activity B. The LF is three (3). Activity B must finish no later than the end of the third (3) day for Activity C to begin on the fourth (4) day. The ES of Activity C. The LS is two (2). Day two (2) is the latest Activity B may start, still complete by day three (3) and not delay starting Activity C. The formula to calculate LS is LF – Duration + 1 = LS (3 – 2 + 1 = 2).
- Activity A. The LF and LS are determined the same way as was done for Activity B.
- (PMBOK® Guide – Sixth Edition, page 210)

30. C. 1

- The free float of Activity B is one (1). Free float is the amount an activity's start may be delayed without delaying the following activity or violate a constraint. In this case, Activity B may be started on the second day and not impact the completion of Activity C. You can calculate this by subtracting LF from the EF (3 – 2) or subtracting the LS from the ES (2 – 1) of Activity B.
- In this simple schedule network, free float is the same as the total float. If Activity B starts two or more days late, or if Activity A starts one or more days later, then the entire project will finish late. One cannot assume free float equals total float for more complex schedule networks.
- (PMBOK® *Guide* – Sixth Edition, page 210)

COST MANAGEMENT

A key output of the Cost Management knowledge area is the cost baseline. This baseline is one of three baselines. Scope and schedule are the other two baselines. Baselines are critical as they defined the approved expectations of the project for what is commonly known as the triple-constraints (scope, schedule (time), and cost). The project's success will be assessed based on actual performance results relative to these baselines.

Accurate estimating of the project cost and budget is critical. Underestimating costs may result in starting a project without a sufficient budget to complete the project. Insufficient funds may result in stopping the project before achieving any or only part of the project's original business value.

Overestimating the cost may also be devastating to the organization. The result may be the project is not approved. The organization will not, when, in fact, they should have, realize the project's business value. Even if the project is approved, excessive cost estimates may limit or deny funding to other projects. These other projects will not produce their business value due to the incorrect understanding that the remaining funds were insufficient.

How will the project's cost be determined, maintained, and controlled? (Plan Cost Management) These answers are in the cost management plan. One critical answer is how performance will be measured. Answering this question starts with the tools used to track spending, agreed to performance measurements (Cost Variance (CV), defining spending reporting, etc.

Determining the cost (Estimate Costs) The project manager and team must estimate activity cost for each deliverable. Cost estimates may be determined by three-point, parametric or analogous estimating.

How much funding is required? (Determine Budget) The project's funding requirements, or budget, maybe more than just the sum of the costs of each activity. Funding also includes the cost of contingency reserves. These reserves provide funding if risk response plans are needed to address risks. This result is the cost baseline. Once the cost baseline is approved, the project manager is accountable for achieving the cost baseline.

The total project budget may include managerial reserves. Managerial reserves are funding set aside by the organization based on the project's risk. For example, some organizations may set aside five percent of the cost baseline to address unforeseen project risks. These risks include cost estimating errors. The sponsor or senior management must authorize the spending of any managerial reserve. The project's budget is the sum of the cost baseline plus the managerial reserve.

Is the project on, ahead, or behind budget? What will be the final spend amount? (Control Cost) A project team member tells the project manager they have spent fifty percent of their assigned activity cost. Is the activity on budget? The only information provided by the project team member is work performance data. The project manager cannot assess the status of the activity's cost solely on this data. To assess the project cost status, the project manager must compare this data to the approved cost baseline. This comparison will result in work performance information. In this case, if the cost baseline expected to spend fifty percent of this activity's cost, the project is on budget.

Is the project still expected to spend the project's budget? Knowing this answer is important to the sponsor and stakeholders. However, just as or even more important to the sponsor and stakeholders is the cost forecast.

The project manager must forecast the "to complete" project cost. The project manager begins by assessing past work performance data and expected future costs. The project manager must then determine if future costs will be less than, the same, or more than estimated. If less or more than the estimate, the project manager must implement changes to the approved cost baseline by executing the Perform Integrated Change Control and other processes.

Questions

1. The Budget at Completion (BAC) is $1,000,000. Due to process improvements implemented by the project team, they will be able to complete the project for $900,000. What is the Estimate to Complete (EAC)?
    A. $1,000,000 (USD)
    B. $100,000 (USD)
    C. $900,000 (USD)
    D. $1,100,000 (USD)
2. The project manager has asked the architect, senior leader, and developer to estimate the cost of each scheduled activity. The project manager has been successful in estimating costs when the most likely estimate was weighted the most. Which estimating technique weights the most likely estimate?
    A. Beta distribution
    B. Triangular distribution
    C. Parametric
    D. Analogous
3. The project manager has determined all the project costs, including contingency funding. The sponsor approved this estimate. The outcome is the project now has an approved cost baseline. What process did the team must complete?
    A. Estimate costs
    B. Control costs
    C. Determine budget
    D. Plan cost management
4. The project manager is assessing cost management performance. The project's earned value was $1,000,000, while the actual spend was $1,100,000. What's the CPI and CV? Is the budget over or under budget?
    A. CPI = 0.9, CV = -100,000, Project is over budget
    B. CPI = 0.9, CV = -100,000, Project is under budget
    C. CPI = 1.1, CV = 100,000, Project is under budget
    D. CPI = 1.1, CV = 100,000, Project is over budget

5. The project team works in three countries on two different continents. As part of the plan cost management process, the project manager must consider the currency exchange rate impact on labor costs. Currency exchange rates are?
   A. Organizational process assets
   B. Enterprise environmental factors
   C. Plan cost management output
   D. Market conditions

6. The project manager is discussing with the sponsor about the reoccurring costs after the project is finished. Should this be a concern for the project manager?
   A. No. The cost of maintaining the product, service, or results occurs after the project
   B. No. Operations needs to determine these costs
   C. Yes. The project manager must consider the impact of project decisions on the reoccurring on-going cost after the project
   D. Yes. Include these costs in the project's cost baseline

7. The customer just requested the addition of a new requirement. The project team is executing the Performing Integrated Change Control process to assess the impact. The estimate to implement the new requirement is $10,000. Actual Costs (AC) incurred to date by the project is $50,000. The team confirmed completing the remaining original requirements have an Earned Value (EV) of $30,000. What is the Estimate to Complete (ETC) if this change is approved? to Complete (ETC) if this change is approved?
   A. $90,000
   B. $40,000
   C. $50,000
   D. $30,000

8. The project team members work in two different countries with different currencies. The project's costs are defined in the cost management plan to be in USD (US dollars). The project manager must use currency exchange rates to convert all spend into USD to track and report costs. Currency exchange rates are?
    A. Organizational process assets
    B. Enterprise environmental factors
    C. Assumptions
    D. Constraints

9. The project has incurred $50,000 (USD) in cost. The project budget is $80,000 (USD). What is the estimated to complete (ETC) costs for the project?
    A. $130,000 (USD)
    B. $30,000 (USD)
    C. $80,000 (USD)
    D. Cannot determine

10. The project manager is reviewing the cost estimates with the sponsor. The sponsor asked several questions about how the estimates were determined, assumptions and constraints, and the confidence level of the estimates. Where are the answers to these questions documented?
    A. Assumption log
    B. Risk register
    C. Basis of estimates
    D. Cost management plan

11. The project has a CPI = 1.05 and has spent $1,500,000 (USD) to date. The project manager is preparing for a sponsor and key stakeholder status update. The project manager has determined the remaining cost estimates to complete the project are inaccurate. What should the project manager forecast for the project spend?
    A. Calculate and report TCPI
    B. Calculate and report EAC based on past performance
    C. Calculate and report the ETC
    D. Calculate and report EAC after re-estimating

12. The project incurred an unexpected cost. The project sponsor approved this additional spend using funds set aside by the organization. What BEST describes these funds?
    A. Budget reserve
    B. Contingent reserve
    C. Funding reserve
    D. Management reserve

13. A new project manager has completed estimating the cost for each project activity. In the project's latest status report, the project manager stated the project budget is finished. Is this true?
    A. Yes. The Estimating Costs process was completed
    B. No. The reserve cost estimates were not completed
    C. Yes. The Cost baseline was determined
    D. No. The Determine Budget process was not completed

14. The project team spent $10,000 to prototype a new technology. The new technology will not meet the project requirements. The team estimates it will take $5,000 to prototype a different technology. The team is doing a cost-benefit analysis of running the second prototype. What cost should the team use?
    A. $5,000
    B. $10,000
    C. $15,000
    D. $7,500

15. The project manager is beginning to plan the management of cost. To ensure project costs are well managed, the team should evaluate which knowledge area plans?
    A. Schedule and Risk
    B. Integration and Schedule
    C. Quality and Procurement
    D. Risk and Stakeholder

16. The project's Actual Cost (AC) is $10,000. The Cost Performance Index (CPI) is 1.0. What is the Cost Variance (CV)?
    A. $0
    B. $10,000
    C. $20,000
    D. $5,0000

17. The sponsor approved the project's cost baseline plus allocated an additional $20,000 for the project budget. Any project spend over the cost baseline will now require what?
    A. Change request
    B. Sponsor approval
    C. Project manager approval
    D. Customer approval

18. Next week there will be a critical stakeholder update. The project manager is preparing for this update by performing an Earned Value Analysis (EVA). The project manager is assessing which of the following?
    A. Scope
    B. Schedule
    C. Cost
    D. Performance

19. The project has a CPI of 0.9 after six months. The earned value is $100,000, actual cost is $110,000 with a budget at completion of $200,000. The project manager wants to determine what CPI for the remainder of the project would result in the project finishing on budget.
    A. 0.9
    B. 1.0
    C. 1.3
    D. 1.1

20. The project has a CPI (Cost Performance Index) of 0.95 and CV (Cost Variance) of $-2,000. The approved cost baseline has a $5,000 in contingency reserves. The project team has decided to use $2,000 of the contingency reserves to make up this budget shortfall. Who must authorize this budget change?
    A. Project team
    B. Project manager
    C. Customer
    D. Sponsor

21. The CPI for the project is 0.90. AC to date is $5,000, with an estimated $10,000 remaining to finish the project. The project manager has determined the CPI will remain the same for the rest of the project. What is the EAC for the project?
    A. $10,000
    B. $15,000
    C. $9,111
    D. $16,111

22. The sponsor asks the project manager for a project budget estimate. The project's charter was just approved. The project manager decides to provide a rough order of magnitude (ROM) budget. How accurate should this budget be?
    A. -5% to 10%
    B. -10% to 25%
    C. -25% to 75%
    D. 0% to 75%

23. The project manager determines the CPI (Cost Performance Index) is 0.90. Which of the following is correct?
    A. Project is over budget
    B. Project is under budget
    C. Project is on budget
    D. Unable to determine the budget status

24. A new project manager is taking over a project. The new project manager wants to understand how the previous project manager measured cost performance. What document provides this information?
    A. Basis of estimates
    B. Cost management plan
    C. Project funding requirements
    D. Cost baseline

25. The project manager is forecasting the budget. The original approved budget at completion (BAC) was $150,000. The project manager forecasts that the CPI of 1.1 will remain for the rest of the project. The actual cost to date is $100,000. What is the estimate at completion? (round to the nearest $000)
    A. $150,000. Project is on budget
    B. $164,000. Project is over budget
    C. $136,000. Project is under budget
    D. Cannot determine

26. The project manager is quantitatively determining the costs for the project. The project manager has the resource requirements for each activity and the project schedule. Which process is the project manager performing?
    A. Plan Cost Management
    B. Estimate Activity Resources
    C. Estimate Costs
    D. Determine Budget

27. The project manager is determining how to manage costs during the project. Which following process BEST describes this effort?
    A. Control cost
    B. Estimate costs
    C. Determine budget
    D. Plan cost management

28. The sponsor and project manager agree that Agile is the best life cycle for the project. The project manager must complete the project within a limited budget. What impact may this decision have on project cost management?
    A. Scope and schedule will need to be adjusted to stay within budget.
    B. Nothing. The budget is re-estimated for each iteration.
    C. Nothing. The life-cycle does not impact the need to provide a complete detailed budget at the start of the project.
    D. The project manager must emphasize the control of all costs

29. The project manager is discussing the project with a Subject Matter Expert (SME). This SME has worked on two previous projects that are similar to this project. The SME is also considered an expert in an industry association. Through that association, the SME has identified one other similar project. The PM decides to estimate the cost of the project based on these historical project estimates. What BEST describes this estimating?
    A. Expert judgment
    B. Parametric estimating
    C. Bottom-up estimating
    D. Analogous estimating

30. The project manager is familiar with the policies governing project cost management. The project manager has reached out to an accountant who is familiar with the budgeting tool and the cost reports that must be submitted. Which BEST defines these?
    A. Enterprise environmental factors
    B. Organizational process assets
    C. Cost management plan
    D. Business management plan

31. The project manager is assessing the project's cost performance during a specific work period. The actual costs incurred during this work period was $10,000. Where will the project manager find the expected earned value?
    A. Cost management plan
    B. Project management plan
    C. Cost baseline
    D. Project budget

32. The project's Earned Value (EV) = $10,000. The Cost Variance (CV) = $1,000. What is the Actual Cost (AC)?
    A. $1,000
    B. $11,000
    C. $9,000
    D. $10,000

33. The project's CPI is 1.1 with, an SPI of 0.90. Which of the following is correct?
    A. Project is over budget and ahead of schedule
    B. Project is under budget and behind schedule
    C. Project is under budget and ahead of schedule
    D. Project is over budget and behind schedule

34. The project manager and team have determined the project budget. They are now comparing the budget to the organization's financial commitment to the project. What BEST describes this process?
    A. Funding limit reconciliation
    B. Project budget reconciliation
    C. Project cost reconciliation
    D. Project budget validation

35. The project manager and team produced estimated costs for each WBS work package. The estimate included the cost of three security work packages. The sponsor, however, only wants to track security costs at an aggregate level. She asked the project manager to report only the total security costs. Which of the following will satisfy this request?
    A. Cost account
    B. Estimate account
    C. Control account
    D. Budget account

Answers

1. C. $900,000
    - The BAC reflects the original estimated cost to complete the project. When a project starts, the BAC equals EAC. The team is now able to complete the project for less than initially estimated. The EAC is $900,000. The project manager saves the original BAC is saved for future assessment relative to actual project costs. (*PMBOK® Guide* – Sixth Edition, page 264)

2. A. Beta distribution
    - The project manager has asked three (3) team members to estimate the costs. This implies a form of three-point estimating. Since the project manager will be weighting the most-likely estimate higher than the optimistic and pessimistic estimates, the PM will be using the Beta distribution estimating technique. (*PMBOK® Guide – Sixth Edition*, page 244)

3. C. Determine budget
    - Aggregation all costs for the project is one activity the project manager performs during cost management. Seeking the sponsor and possibly other key stakeholder's approval of the estimated costs is another activity. These are all activities of the Determine Budget process. The process output, if approved, is the project's authorized cost baseline. The Determined Budget process may be performed once or at multiple points throughout the project. (*PMBOK® Guide – Sixth Edition*, page 246)

4. A. CPI = 0.9; CV = -100,000; Project is over budget
    - CPI = EV / AC. When Earned Value (EV) is less than the Actual Cost (AC) (i.e., spend), the CPI is less than 1.0. In this question, the project's CPI = 0.9. The Cost Variance (CV = EV – AC) is $-100,000. The project is over budget since the project spent more (AC) than the Earned Value (EV) of the work. The project is over budget and will incur more costs to complete the activity. (*PMBOK® Guide – Sixth Edition*, page 247)

5. B. Enterprise environmental factors
    - Currency exchange rates may have a significant impact on a project's cost. It may be difficult to estimate changes to exchange rates during the project. So the project manager needs to specify how to address exchange rates in the cost management plan. Since the project team cannot influence global currency exchange rates, they are considered an enterprise environmental factor. (PMBOK® Guide – Sixth Edition, page 243)

6. C. Yes. The project manager must consider the impact of project decisions on the reoccurring on-going cost after the project is completed
    - The project manager must take into consideration when making project decisions the effect of those decisions on future on-going costs during the operations and maintenance of the project's deliverables. (*PMBOK® Guide – Sixth Edition*, page 233)

7. B. $40,000
    - Estimate to Complete (ETC) does not consider actual prior costs. These actual costs are sunk costs. The ETC, in this case, is determined by adding the EV of the remaining activities to the new requirement estimate ($30,000 + $10,000 = $40,000) (PMBOK® Guide – Sixth Edition, page 264)

8. B. Enterprise environment factors
    - The project manager and team do not determine currency exchange rates. Therefore, currency exchange rates are an example of enterprise environmental factors. (*PMBOK® Guide – Sixth Edition*, page 237)

9. B. $30,000
    - The project budget is $80,000 or Budget at Completion (BAC). Therefore, the Estimate at Completion (EAC) = BAC. The Estimate to Complete (ETC) cost is the EAC costs minus the Actual Cost (AC). In this case, ETC = EAC – AC or $30,000 = $80,000 - $50,000. (*PMBOK® Guide – Sixth Edition*, page 267)

- Be cautious about making assumptions when reading exam questions. The question provides no information about the project other than the budget and actual costs. The question does not state the project has been re-estimated nor that the Cost Performance Index (CPI) is any value other than 1.0. If either was stated then you would need to calculate EAC or use the provided EAC to calculate the ETC.

10. C. Basis of estimates
    - The basis of estimates document contains all supporting documentation about how each cost estimate was determined and analyzed. This document includes specific assumptions and constraints, a range of possible estimates, and other factors that influenced the estimates of each cost. (*PMBOK® Guide – Sixth Edition*, page 247)

11. D. Calculate and report EAC after re-estimating
    - If the project manager determines the planned spend for the remaining project activities is inaccurate, the project manager must re-estimate all remaining impacted activities. The project manager may use the bottom-up estimating technique for those activities. To determine the Estimate at Completion (EAC), the project manager would take the Actual Cost (AC) spent to date and add the re-estimates of the remaining activities (EAC = AC + re-estimate). (*PMBOK® Guide – Sixth Edition*, page 264)

12. D. Management reserve
    - A project's budget may have two types of reserves. The cost baseline may include a contingency reserve for one or more individual activities. The project manager controls the contingency reserve, which may they use at their discretion.
    - The question states the project incurred an "unexpected" cost requiring the sponsor's approval. Both these facts indicate funds for these costs were part of a management reserve.

- The project budget includes the approved cost baseline (estimated costs plus contingent reserve) and management reserve.
- (*PMBOK® Guide* – Sixth Edition, page 246).

13. D. No. The Determine Budget process was not completed

- The Estimate Costs process determines the cost of each project activity. This estimate is just one component of the project's budget.
- The cost baseline includes all the project activity costs plus all contingency reserves. The project budget is consists of the cost baseline plus any management reserves.
- (*PMBOK® Guide* – *Sixth Edition*, page 254)

14. A. $5,000

- When considering new work, one does not consider prior costs. These previous costs are known as sunk costs.
- Whether to spend additional money should not be influenced by past costs. At first, this may not be very clear. Past costs are sunk costs. There is no option, stop and don't spend more or continue or spend more, that will recover these sunk costs. However, one must consider all future costs in a cost-benefit analysis, including the risk of spending the $5,000.
- (*PMBOK® Guide* – Sixth Edition, page 263)

15. A. Schedule and Risk

- The schedule and risk management plans are critical inputs to the cost management planning. Schedule management plan determines all project activities required to produce each deliverable and requirement, the duration and resources needed for those activities, and the impact of constraints and assumptions. The risk management plan determines how risk will be identified and tracked, assessed for the probability of occurrence and impact, and how response plans will be developed and executed. The outcome from schedule and risk planning will impact the cost management planning. (*PMBOK® Guide – Sixth Edition*, page 236)

16. A. $0

- CPI = EV / AC (1.0 = EV / $10,000). You may solve algebraically for Earned Value (EV). An alternative way, in this case, is to understand that a CPI = 1.0 means EV = AC. EV therefore equals $10,000. Knowing both EV and AC enables the calculation of Cost Variance (CV). CV = EV – AC or $0 = $10,000 - $10,000.

- It is important to understand that a CPI < 1.0 means the project is over budget (EV < AC). The project spent more (AC) than the value earned (EV). A CPI > 1.0 means the project is under budget (EV > AC). The project spent less (AC) than the value earned (EV).

- (*PMBOK® Guide* – Sixth Edition, page 263)

17. A. Change request

- The project manager must determine all project activities cost estimates and any contingency reserves during cost management. These are the components of the cost baseline.

- An approved cost baseline only exists after approval by the sponsor or other key stakeholders. Once approved, any change to the cost baseline requires a change request and the execution of the Perform Integrated Change Control process. Only approved change requests will update the cost baseline.

- (*PMBOK® Guide – Sixth Edition*, page 254)

18. D. Performance

- The project manager is assessing the Performance Measurement Baseline (PMB). This baseline is an integrated assessment of the approved schedule, scope, and cost baselines. The assessment results indicate the current status of the project compared to the approved baselines.

- Key metrics must be understood to determine the project's PMB accurately. Planned Value (PV) is the value of the scope that is part of the project. For example, a seller proposed providing the deliverable's scope for $100,000.

The buyer's acceptance of this proposal implies the buyer places a $100,000 value on the deliverable's scope. This $100,000 is the PV of the deliverable's scope.

- As the seller produces increments of the deliverable, the seller is producing or Earning Value (EV). EV is never greater than PV. In this example, the seller reports completing fifty percent of the deliverable's scope. Or the EV is $50,000.

- Actual costs (AC) must also be considered and may be higher than then PV. If the AC is $60,000 for this fifty percent of EV ($50,000), the seller is -$10,000 (EV – AC) or over budget.

- Assessment of the schedule baseline must also occur in addition to the scope and cost baselines. What is the PV and EV relative to the schedule? If the seller was to produce or earn fifty percent of the scope value by this planned time, the seller is on-schedule (EV - PV).

- In summary, the project's PMB is over budget and on-schedule relative to the scope.

- (PMBOK® Guide – Sixth Edition, page 261)

19. D. 1.1

- TCPI = (BAC – EV) / (BAC – AC). With a CPI of 0.9, the project is over budget (CPI = EV/AC). The project must, therefore, for the remainder of the project, be under budget (CPI > 1.0).

- The project manager must use the to-completion-performance-index (TCPI) to determine the CPI. For remainder of this project the project must perform at a CPI = 1.11 ((200,000 – 100,000) / (200,000 – 110,000)) to finish on budget.

- The project manager must assess whether it is possible to perform at a CPI = 1.11 for the remainder of the project. If this is not possible, the project manager must re-estimate the project and request the appropriate change requests are approved to change the cost baseline.

- (*PMBOK® Guide – Sixth Edition*, page 266)

20. B. Project manager

  - The project manager has the authority to allocate or spend contingency reserves included in the approved cost baseline. The project manager should assess the project's cost performance before approving this reduction in the contingency reserve. (*PMBOK® Guide – Sixth Edition*, page 266)

21. D. $16,111

  - The sponsor and key stakeholders expect a project manager to forecast spend and Estimate at Completion (EAC) accurately. Cost Performance Index (CPI) enables estimating the project's future spend.

  - A project manager must first decide if the current CPI accurately reflects the rate of spending for the remainder of the project. In this case, the project manager determined the CPI is predictive of the future rate of spending compared to estimates. Therefore, the Estimate to Complete (ETC) of the $10,000 (USD) estimate is $11,111 (USD) ($10,000 (USD) / 0.90). EAC includes Actual Costs (AC) and the Estimate to Complete (ETC) remaining activities. EAC = AC + ETC ($16,111 = $5000 + $11,111 (USD)).

  - (*PMBOK® Guide* – Sixth Edition, page 263)

22. C. -25% to 75%

  - The student needs to know the current phase of the project in a question. The team just finished the project charter. The question does not state the project charter was approved. Therefore, the project must be in the initiating phase.

  - The project manager knows relatively little about the project during the initiating phase. The project manager may only be able to estimate within a rough order of magnitude range. The range for a rough order of magnitude estimate is -25% to 75%. For a $100,000 project, this range would be from $75,000 to $175,000.

  - (*PMBOK® Guide – Sixth Edition*, page 241)

23. A. Project is over budget
   - CPI = EV / AC. When Earned Value (EV) is less than the Actual Cost (AC), the CPI is less than 1.0. In this question, the project's CPI = 0.90. The project is over budget as more (AC) was spent than the planned or estimated Earned Value (EV) of the work.
   - For example, if the project incurred $10,000 in actual costs for an activity, but only completed 90% of the activity, the earned value is $9,000. The activity is over budget, and the project will incur more costs to complete the activity.
   - (*PMBOK® Guide – Sixth Edition*, page 263)

24. B. Cost management plan
   - The cost management plan defines how the cost performance is measured, including earned value management techniques, control accounts, etc. The cost management plan also includes the level of precision and accuracy, control thresholds, reporting formats, etc. used to plan, monitor, and control project costs. (*PMBOK® Guide – Sixth Edition*, page 235)

25. C. $136,000. The project is under budget
   - The CPI of 1.1 indicates the product to date has been under budget. The project manager expected the CPI to remain the same until the end of the project.
   - The question was, what is the estimated at completion budget (EAC = BAC / CPI). The answer is $136,364 (EAC = $150,000 / 1.1. The project manager expects the project to be under budget when completed.
   - The project manager should return excess funds to the organization so other projects and initiatives may use those funds.
   - (*PMBOK® Guide – Sixth Edition*, page 267)

26. C. Estimate Costs
   - The project manager must identify and collect all costs to complete the project. Key inputs include cost and quality

management plans, scope baseline, lessons learned register, project schedule, resource requirements, and risk register. Enterprise environmental factors and organizational process assets may also provide insight.

- Costs also include labor, licenses, equipment, materials, etc. These costs may also include the cost of financing, risk contingency reserves, and allowance for inflation.
- (*PMBOK® Guide – Sixth Edition*, page 241)

27. D. Plan cost management

- T The plan cost management determines how the team will determine and manage costs for the project. This plan includes how to perform, monitor, and control each of the cost processes in the cost knowledge area. (*PMBOK® Guide – Sixth Edition*, page 239)

28. A. Scope and schedule will need to be adjusted to stay within budget.

- The Agile life-cycle is preferred when the project team is unable to determine upfront the requirements, or it is preferred to iterate into the final project requirements.
- Choosing to leverage the Agile life cycle does not mean the budget continues to grow until the team completes the project. For some projects, there may be a fixed budget for the project that may not allow for completing all requirements. In these scenarios, the project manager must adjust the scope or schedule to produce the maximum project business value for the given budget.
- *PMBOK® Guide – Sixth Edition*, page 234)

29. D. Analogous Estimating

- Using past projects that were similar in scope, risk, schedule, etc. to estimate another project is known as analogous estimating. Using this estimating technique may address schedule challenges as it is a quick way to estimate.
- The PM must use good judgment when using analogous estimating. How similar the past and current projects are will significantly impact the accuracy of analogous estimating.

- (*PMBOK® Guide – Sixth Edition*, page 244)

30. B. Organizational process assets
    - Cost budgeting policies, procedures and guidelines, cost budgeting tools and reporting methods are all examples of organizational process assets the team may use during the Determine Budget process. (*PMBOK® Guide – Sixth Edition*, page 251)

31. C. Cost baseline
    - The cost baseline documents the cost earned values.
    - The project manager may reference the schedule baseline to find specific activities during the assessment period. The earned value cost of those activities would be compared to the actual cost to determine if the project is on, over, or under budget during the assessment period.
    - (*PMBOK® Guide – Sixth Edition*, page 259)

32. C. $9,000
    - Cost Variance (CV) = Earned Value (EV) – Actual Costs (AC). Inserting the question values results in $10,000 = $1,000 – AC. Solving for AC results in $9,000.
    - When CV is greater than zero (0) the project created more value than incurred in actual costs. In other words, the project created $10,000 in value but only incurred $9,000 in actual cost to produce that value.
    - (*PMBOK® Guide – Sixth Edition*, page 262)

33. B. Project is under budget and behind schedule
    - Recall the formulas to solve these types of questions. CPI = EV / AC. If CPI > 1.0 then EV > AC. The project team produced more earned value than the actual cost. For example, the team produced $1,000 in earned value at an actual cost of $900. The project is under budget.
    - To determine if the project is ahead or behind schedule, recall that SPI = EV / PV. In this case, the SPI is less than 1.0, so EV < PV. For example, the team completed $1,000 of schedule activities when the planned value was to complete $1,111 during this period. The project is behind schedule.
    - (*PMBOK® Guide – Sixth Edition*, page 263)

34. A. Funding limit reconciliation
   - Projects have funding constraints. This constraint should be assumed unless stated otherwise on exams.
   - You may have worked on projects where this appeared not to be the case. Remember, exam projects are large projects. And organizations don't have unlimited funding. A project exceeding the funding limit by just five percent could be millions of dollars (USD).
   - Therefore, once the project budget is determined, it needs to be reconciled with the amount of allocated project funding. If the project budget is greater, then the project manager must adjust the scope, schedule, or find other ways to reduce cost. Or a combination of those. The project manager may also ask, after exhausting other options, for additional funding from the organization.
   - The project budget may also be less than the allocated funding. Does the project team get to keep the excess to spend it as the team sees fit? No. The project manager's integrity is at stake. Excess funding is not the project manager's to spend. It must be returned to the organization to determine the best way to spend the funding, even if that means not on this project.
   - (PMBOK® *Guide* – Sixth Edition, page 253)

35. C. Control account
   - The team decomposes the WBS until the project team may accurately estimate each deliverable's work packages.
   - Sometimes this depth of decomposition is more detail than needed by the sponsor or key stakeholders. In those cases, they may ask the project manager to combine or aggregate the cost of two or more work packages. This aggregation is known as a control account. The project manager then reports the costs at the control account level and not the individual work packages.
   - PMBOK® *Guide* – Sixth Edition, page 252)

QUALTIY MANAGEMENT

What is quality? How do the project manager and team know they have met the quality requirements? Did the effectiveness and efficiency of the work being performed during the project improve? The Quality knowledge area answers these questions.

There is a cost for ensuring quality that the project manager must balance. Some people will propose that the cost of conformance is too expensive for confirming the project's quality. However, one should critically evaluate the cost of conformance against the cost of nonconformance. The cost of nonconformance may cause customer dissatisfaction to the point of canceling the project or even severely impacting the business. An example of severely impacting the business is Takata filing for bankruptcy as a result of their airbag quality issues.

How will the project's quality be determined, maintained, and controlled? (Plan Quality Management) This planning process determines how quality will be defined, measured, monitored, and controlled during the project. This plan must be a proactive plan which ensures the team is building quality into the deliverables. Not "inspected in" after being created.
The expectation is quality continuously improves as the project progresses that processes and tools and techniques become more and more effective and efficient, reducing the introduction of defects. This expectation has been demonstrated across all industries to be more cost-effective and results in higher quality deliverables.

Identifying and implementing improvements is done via the Plan-Do-Check-Act (PDCA) cycle that underlies quality improvement approaches. Improving the process efficiency and effectiveness and the product quality is critical to ensuring the project stays on schedule and within budget. The expectation of all stakeholders should be that the quality improvements will shorten the schedule, reduce the budget, and require fewer resources as the project progresses.

Is the project plans effective? Will the product design enable meeting the quality requirement? Is process improvements effective? (Manage Quality) This process implements the quality management plan into effective and efficient quality practices and tests.

The embedded practices include quality assurance, which some may misunderstand. Quality assurance is not a confirmation of the deliverable's quality. Instead, by definition, assurance confirms the confidence level that applying the defined processes, procedures, training, tools, etc. will result in the expected quality outcome. The team confirms this confidence by auditing the processes and procedures that produce the deliverable. Other practices now included in the Manage Quality process are product design, testing, process improvement, and quality reporting.

Does the deliverable meet the customer's requirements? (Control Quality) The project team performs this process to assess the deliverable attributes against the project's requirements. The result is verified deliverables. For example, the quality management plan states, "the software must load in less than one second (1) four-hundred ninety (490) times out of five-hundred (500) attempts within a sixty (60) minute period." Does it? If it does not, this will trigger an execution of the Manage Quality process. First, to determine why this requirement did not meet the requirement. And second, to restore confidence in all stakeholders that in the future, the deliverable will satisfy this requirement.

The cost of assessing the deliverable to determine if it meets the requirements is captured as part of the cost of conformance. The cost of reworking or scrapping a deliverable is the cost of nonconformance.

Questions

1. The project team is researching the acceptance criteria for each deliverable. The team will use the acceptance criteria as input to the Plan Quality Management process. What document will the team find the acceptance criteria?
   A. Requirements management plan
   B. WBS
   C. Project charter
   D. Scope statement

2. The project manager asked a team member to review an implemented change. The team member compares the expected results in the approved change to the produced deliverable. The team member confirms the implementation of the approved change was as planned by performing what process?
   A. Manage quality
   B. Perform Integrated Change Control
   C. Control quality
   D. Monitor and Control Project Work

3. The team is trying to determine the root cause of a defect. One of the team members is at the whiteboard drawing a diagram that identifies people, processes, environment, and other major categories. Team members have been shouting out possible causes under each category. What is the team creating?
   A. Cause-and-effect diagram
   B. Scatter diagram
   C. Affinity diagram
   D. Flowchart

4. The project manager and team are defining activities to include in the schedule. These activities are focused on finding ineffective processes that result in poor quality. What BEST describes the team's activities?
   A. Manage quality
   B. Plan quality management
   C. Control quality
   D. Define activities

5. The project manager and team are reviewing third-party security solutions for credit card processing. Both packages performed well on the performance tests and met all requirements. When considering the solutions, one of the solutions has more reports that track security metrics. Which of the following is an example of this difference in reports?
   A. Quality
   B. Grade
   C. Product maturity
   D. Comparable products

6. The quality manager is reviewing the quality processes of the project. The quality manager is looking for the implementation of best practices, the implementation of quality organizational process assets, and identifying opportunities for improvement. What process is the quality manager performing?
   A. Quality control
   B. Data gathering
   C. Auditing
   D. Data analysis

7. The project manager and team are modifying a tool to use on the project. The tool will track quality measurements throughout the project. If the tool indicates a deliverable measurement is outside the desired limits, the team will take corrective action. What BEST describes this tool?
   A. Control charts
   B. Cause-and-effect diagrams
   C. Scatter diagrams
   D. Histogram

8. The project manager and quality manager are defining precisely how a product attribute will be measured and verified. What BEST describes what they are creating?
   A. Quality management plan
   B. Requirements
   C. Failure cost
   D. Quality metric

9. The project deliverable is for use in another country. The team has engaged a Subject Matter Expert (SME) for their expert judgment on the country's rules, regulations, and cultural perceptions of quality. The rules, regulations, and perceptions are examples of what?
    A. Enterprise environmental factors
    B. Organizational process assets
    C. Requirement documentation
    D. Benchmarking

10. A project team member measures the performance of the product. After completing the tests, the project team member compares the data with expected results and notifies the project manager. What BEST describes what the project team member performed?
    A. Manage quality
    B. Control quality
    C. Plan-Do-Check-Act
    D. Monitor and Control Project Work

11. The project manager is presenting the project status to key stakeholders. Included in the update is the quality of the deliverables. The project manager also shares the team's process improvement recommendations from their last sprint retrospective. What process produces this information?
    A. Plan quality management
    B. Control quality
    C. Manage quality
    D. Manage stakeholder engagement

12. The project team is using Scrum, an Agile methodology. The team is discussing "what went right?" with the last iteration, and they should continue doing. The team also asks, "what could be improved? in the next iteration." What is the name of this meeting?
    A. Process improvement
    B. Review
    C. Sprint Review
    D. Retrospective

13. The project team is reviewing quality tests to verify if samples of the product conform to the customer requirements. The test results indicate the product either conforms or does not comply. The team performed which type of test?
    A. Inspection
    B. Variable
    C. Attribute
    D. Prevention

14. The project manager and team are discussing the Cost of Quality (COQ). Specifically, the team is considering the cost of defects found by the team. Which types of COQ costs are these?
    A. Failure
    B. External
    C. Internal
    D. Preventative

15. The project manager is reviewing the project spend with the business manager. The business manager is insisting on tracking training costs to learn how to assess the deliverable as part of quality. The project manager wants to put all the training costs under education. Where should the training costs go?
    A. Education budget
    B. Training budget
    C. Cost of Quality
    D. Cost of nonconformance

16. A project team member just determined the product does not meet the expected quality metric. What is the BEST next step?
    A. Perform integrated change request
    B. Create a change request
    C. Resolve the issue
    D. Notify another team member

17. The project team is identifying all stakeholders who may have an interest in the quality of the project deliverable. The customer is interested in quality. The sponsor has also mentioned quality expectations during project meetings. What project document should identify others?
    A. Requirements documentation
    B. Stakeholder register
    C. Requirement traceability matrix
    D. Risk register

18. The project manager and key team members are discussing how to implement quality during the project. This discussion ranges from choosing quality metrics, when to conduct tests, and who will perform the tests. What process is the team executing?
    A. Plan requirements management
    B. Manage quality
    C. Plan quality management
    D. Define scope

19. The team has brainstormed potential causes for a defect. The team is now organizing by grouping each brainstorming idea with similar ideas. What BEST describes this process?
    A. Cause-and-effect diagrams
    B. Flowcharts
    C. Matrix diagrams
    D. Affinity diagrams

20. Two project team members are deciding which tool should to use during the project to measure the quality of deliverable. One team member wants to be sure the team performs all the steps in the process. What tool should the team use?
    A. Checklist
    B. Check sheet
    C. Statistical sampling
    D. Questionnaire and surveys

Answers

1. D. Scope statement
   - The scope statement, part of the scope baseline, includes acceptance criteria for each deliverable. Acceptance criteria may have a significant impact on quality costs and in turn the project cost. (*PMBOK® Guide – Sixth Edition*, page 279)

2. C. Control quality
   - The team member performed the Control Quality process. One critical function of Control Quality is to verify the approved change request resulted in the expected changes to the deliverable. Otherwise, the approved change request was not successful. (*PMBOK® Guide – Sixth Edition*, page 300)

3. A. Cause-and-effect diagram
   - The question describes how a team creates a cause-and-effect diagram. The result is what looks like a "fishbone," which is one of the common names for a cause-and-effect diagram. Other common names are Ishikawa (creator of the diagram) and why-why diagrams. (*PMBOK® Guide – Sixth Edition*, page 293, 294)

4. A. Manage quality
   - The Manage Quality process converts the quality management plan into activities the team will perform to achieve the quality metrics. To ensure quality, the team must identify the causes of poor quality, which includes ineffective processes. (*PMBOK® Guide – Sixth Edition*, page 288)

5. B. Grade
   - The quality of both solutions was the same "…performed well on the performance tests and met all requirements." However, one solution has more reports. When more than one solution or product meets the requirements, the quality of those solutions is the same. However, when a solution has more features, in this case, more reports, that the solution is of a higher grade by definition. (*PMBOK® Guide – Sixth Edition*, page 274)

6. C. Auditing
   - The quality manager is performing an audit as part of Manage Quality. An audit focuses on how effective and efficient are the processes and tools and techniques to produce and verify the product meets the expected requirements. (*PMBOK® Guide – Sixth Edition*, page 292)
7. A. Control charts
   - The project team often modifies tools and techniques for the specific needs of their project. The question describes capturing data throughout the project and taking action if a measurement is outside a desired or control limit. The team modifies the upper and lower limits of control charts based on the specific needs of the project. If the project's process produces measurements that are consistently within the control limits, the process is considered to be stable and performing well. (*PMBOK® Guide – Sixth Edition*, page 304)
8. D. Quality metric
   - A quality metric describes a project or product attribute explicitly. This metric must be understood by the team to ensure appropriate assessments and tests are created and then performed as part of the Control Quality process. Quality metrics are a crucial output of the Plan Quality Management process. Examples include web page performance, help desk calls, paint color, battery run time, etc. (*PMBOK® Guide – Sixth Edition*, page 287)
9. A. Enterprise environmental factors
   - The team cannot influence enterprise environmental factors. Yet, those factors influence or impact the project. Common examples of enterprise environmental factors include laws, rules, standards, and cultural expectations and perceptions regarding quality. (*PMBOK® Guide – Sixth Edition*, page 280)
10. B. Control Quality
    - Comparing actual results (work performance data) to the expected results or quality metrics produces work performance data. This process is by definition Control

Quality. Once a project team determines the product meets all quality metrics, the product is a verified deliverable. A verified deliverable is a key milestone. The product is now ready to be validated by the customer (Validate Scope) as to whether or not the verified deliverable meets their expectations. (*PMBOK® Guide – Sixth Edition*, page 298)

11. C. Manage quality

- The Manage Quality process produces quality reports. Test and evaluation documents from the Manage Quality process are inputs to the Control Quality process. In turn, Control Quality provides quality control measurements (work performance information) as an input to Manage Quality. Manage Quality process provides quality reports (work performance reports) to other stakeholders and organizations as either awareness or to trigger action (i.e., corrective action). A sprint retrospective or retrospective is an Agile event where the team assesses and recommends improvements to be implemented in the next sprint or iteration. (*PMBOK® Guide – Sixth Edition*, page 296)

12. D. Retrospective

- Retrospective or Sprint Retrospective. Retrospectives in Agile are meetings scheduled at regular intervals for the development or delivery team to review the just completed iteration or sprint. During a retrospective, each team member identifies major items that went well, opportunities for improvement, and the team collaborates on creating a plan to implement those improvements in the next iteration or sprint. (*PMBOK® Guide – Sixth Edition*, page 274, https://www.scrum.org/resources/scrum-guide)

13. C. Attribute

- Performing a test to determine if the product conforms or not to the requirement, the test is known as attribute sampling. "Go / No Go" decisions may also be considered attribute sampling as either the decision to proceed or not is the only choice.
- Variable sampling assesses the results based on how close the product conforms to the requirement. In this case, the

requirement is compliant if the result is within a range (e.g., web page returns in between 1.0 and 1.5 seconds).

- *(PMBOK® Guide – Sixth Edition*, page 274)

14. A. Failure

- Failure costs, also known as the cost of poor quality, include all the costs associated with defects found by the team. Based on the severity of the quality issue, the team may have to rework or scrap the defective product(s). Failure costs and external costs (i.e., those found by the customer) are COQ "costs of nonconformance." *(PMBOK® Guide – Sixth Edition*, page 274)

15. C. Cost of Quality

- Training cost related to quality is part of the Cost of quality processes and assessment costs, including testing and inspections. Conformance costs plus the Cost of Nonconformance together make up the Cost of Quality. *(PMBOK® Guide – Sixth Edition*, page 282-283)

16. B. Create a change request

- The team member is performing the Control Quality process. Identified discrepancies between the expected quality metric and the actual deliverable's measurement require defect repair. The purpose of the defect repair change ticket will be to modify the deliverable to meet the expected quality metric.

- The project manager will submit the change ticket to Perform Integrated Change Control. If approved, the change is implemented by the Direct and Manage Project Work process and verified as part of the Control Quality process. (PMBOK® Guide – Sixth Edition, page 306). *(PMBOK® Guide – Sixth Edition*, page 306)

17. B. Stakeholder register

- The stakeholder register should identify all stakeholders by their role, title, interest, and impact on the project. Stakeholders who may influence or be impacted by quality decisions and outcomes should be identifiable in the stakeholder register. *(PMBOK® Guide – Sixth Edition*, page 280)

18. C. Plan Quality Management

- The Plan Quality Management process determines how quality will be managed and verified throughout the project. The team documents these decisions in the Quality Management Plan which includes the quality objectives, quality standards, roles and responsibilities, tools, procedures to address nonconformance, etc. (*PMBOK® Guide – Sixth Edition*, page 277, 286)

19. D. Affinity diagram

- Grouping ideas or "things" together based on a common theme or characteristic is known as Affinity diagramming. Once organized into groups, the team assesses each group to determine where to focus their improvement efforts. Affinity diagrams are one of the seven Data Representation tools and techniques.

- In prior editions of the PMBOK® Guide, the seven tools listed on page 293 were called the "seven basic quality tools." You may see this reference on the exam or in other materials.

- A project manager should be well versed in each of the incorrect answers. This knowledge will enable you to eliminate incorrect answers. Don't just memorize the correct answer.

- (PMBOK® Guide – Sixth Edition, page 293)

20. A. Checklist

- A checklist ensures executing a quality process that the team performs all the necessary steps.

- A checklist may be confused with check sheets. Check sheets, or tally sheets, are used to capture data while performing process steps, which may be in a checklist.

- Control charts, Pareto charts, and other graphical tools may use data from check sheets.

- (*PMBOK® Guide – Sixth Edition*, page 302)

RESOURCE MANAGEMENT

Resources "do work" by creating the project vision and plans, transforming inputs to more valuable outputs, and confirming those results produce the expected value. Therefore, perhaps the most significant impact on any project is the project team itself and other resources. While indeed poorly defined requirements, etc. will severely impact a project, no project will produce the expected value without the successful acquisition, development, and management of the project team and other resources.

Who should be on the team? What tools are needed? (Plan Resource Management) How will people be on-boarded to the team? What will be the team rewards and recognition? How will computer resources be acquired? The resource management plan addresses these and more questions.

When and how many do we need? (Estimate Activity Resources) When does the project need each type of resource? For example, the project will require more developers while creating the application and less during deployment.

What is the required capability and capacity for each resource type? Does the project need ten trucks capable of hauling twenty tons each? Thirty Java developers with five years of experience? Five apprentice plumbers?

The project manager's reputation will be built within their organization in part by demonstrating efficient use of resources. For example, does the project manager request a senior developer when a less experienced developer is sufficient. It also includes providing early notification when resources will be needed and when those resources can return to the organization.

When is the team acquired? (Acquire Resources) For many projects, the project manager may not have sufficient breadth and depth of knowledge to plan the project successfully. This need for help is especially true of large and complex projects. In most cases, the project manager has been engaging business analysts, architects, designers, and subject matter experts throughout the initiating and planning phases. Some of these people may continue with the project to completion.

However, per the *PMBOK® Guide*, the project team is not acquired until the executing phase. Waiting until the executing phase makes sense when you consider would you acquire or hire all the needed developers during the initiating or planning phases? No. All the needed testers? No. Onboarding a team member or resource early only increases the project's cost and tie up organizational resources (e.g., people, equipment) that would not be available for other projects and initiatives.

Is each team member better for being part of the project? (Develop Team) Regardless of the organizational structure (functional, matrix, or project), the project manager is responsible for ensuring each team member's experience on the project is rewarding. This responsibility may be accomplished by improving a team member's competence or creating a great work environment.

The development of team members is critical both to the organization and project as it leads to reduced staff turnover and higher performance. Would you want to work again with a project manager that did not help you improve your competencies? No. A project manager who did not provide recognition and rewards specifically addressed to your needs? No. A project manager who did not create a great work environment? No. The result is you will be less willing in the future to work again with this project manager.

How am I doing? (Manage Team) The project manager must provide specific feedback to each project team member. This feedback includes a discussion of the expectations relative to the team member's performance.

Part of providing feedback and project management, in general, is the resolution of conflicts. Therefore, a project manager must successfully resolve disputes.

There are many techniques to avoid, mitigate, or resolve conflicts. These techniques include the establishment of ground rules, effective communications, implementation of good project management practices, etc.

The choice and application of the correct conflict technique for a given situation will determine the success of the project manager. Determining the proper conflict technique includes understanding both the long-term and short-term ramifications of that choice. These conflict techniques range from withdrawal or avoidance to collaborate or problem solve. Choosing the appropriate conflict resolution technique for the particular nuances of the situation often determines who is a great project manager and the level of the project's success.

Was the resource delivered on time? Is it performing as expected? (Control Resources) This process evaluates resources other than people. For example, is the rented generator producing the expected electrical power eight hours a day? Or has it had maintenance issues and been unavailable for an hour a day during working hours? Was the generator delivered on time and to the right location? The Control Resources phase also releases the resource when it is no longer needed.

Resources that are "controlled" may be referred to as physical resources (e.g., generators, equipment, conference rooms). Examples of resources that may be considered non-physical by some include software such as subscription-based word processing, licenses, etc.

Resource Management knowledge area changes. Previous editions of the *PMBOK® Guide* focused on people rather than other resources and was called Human Resource Management.

With the sixth edition, the Resource Management knowledge area emphasizes all resources. The result is a greater focus on the physical and non-physical resources needed on the project.

This change also results in some other differences. For example, the Manage Team process focuses on people and is part of the Executing process group. Not the Monitoring and Controlling process group. One does not "monitor and control" people.

Monitoring and controlling of physical and non-physical resources is performed by the Control Resources process. This process is part of the Monitoring and Controlling process group.

Questions

1. The project manager provided a common team area for the team to co-locate with many whiteboards. The project manager often lets the team resolve local challenges and yet always supports the team by removing external obstacles. What BEST describes this team structure?
   A. Self-managed
   B. Self-organized
   C. Independent
   D. Delegated

2. The project team has completed brainstorming all the activities for the project. The team has created a list of activities, including activity attributes. What is the BEST next activity the team should perform?
   A. Plan resource management
   B. Estimate activity costs
   C. Acquire resources
   D. Estimate activity resources

3. The project manager has completed several previous projects. One skill the project manager has acquired during this period is the ability to identify, assess, and influence the sentiments of team members. The project manager demonstrates this by acknowledging their concerns and follows up on raised issues. What BEST describes this skill?
   A. Conflict management
   B. Emotional intelligence
   C. Decision making
   D. Leadership

4. The project team is struggling with who is working on which work package and schedule activities. One team member believes they are responsible for developing but not testing the work package. Another team member thinks the team member is responsible for both developing and testing the work package. What tool would BEST benefit the team?
   A. Resource breakdown structure
   B. Work breakdown structure
   C. RACI
   D. Organizational breakdown structure

5. The project manager walks by a conference room where many of the team members on a new project are engaged in a loud conversation. The conversation is about how to decide on a technical approach. The project manager pauses and listens to the passionate discussion. After a short while, the team reaches consensus and the project manager continues on their way. What BEST describes the team's development stage?
   A. Forming
   B. Storming
   C. Norming
   D. Performing

6. The project manager is concerned about a team member's performance. The project manager has provided feedback and additional training to improve the team member's performance. What process is the project manager performing?
   A. Manage team
   B. Control resources
   C. Control team
   D. Develop team

7. The project manager is in the process of selecting candidates for the project. The project manager is reviewing each candidate's competency. The project must begin in the next two weeks. What BEST describes this information?
   A. Enterprise environmental factors
   B. Organizational process assets
   C. Risk register
   D. Stakeholder register

8. The project manager has been tracking the daily usage of the computing resources for the project. The usage has been increasing rapidly as the team develops, tests, and demos the product iterations to the customer. What type of analysis is the project manager performing?
   A. Performance reviews
   B. Alternatives analysis
   C. Trend analysis
   D. Cost-benefit analysis

9. An experienced project manager is mentoring a less experienced project manager about improving the team's performance. The experienced project manager suggests the project manager is not leveraging a key technique that shows the value of team members within the project and organization. What BEST describes the technique not being leveraged?
   A. Training
   B. Team assessments
   C. Individual assessments
   D. Recognition and rewards

10. The sponsor asked the project manager for a quick estimate of a new project's resource requirements. The project manager had completed a previous project with the sponsor that is similar to this new project. What estimating tool or technique should the project manager use?
    A. Expert judgment
    B. Analogous estimating
    C. Bottom-up estimating
    D. Parametric estimating

11. The project manager and team are creating a document that describes the values, meeting guidelines, team or work agreements, etc. This document describes how the team will work together. What BEST describes this document?
    A. Team charter
    B. Project charter
    C. RAM
    D. RACI

12. A new project manager is trying to reduce team attrition while improving the team's performance. The project manager has consulted with an experienced project manager. What is the BEST process an experience manager should suggest?
    A. Acquire resources
    B. Develop team
    C. Manage team
    D. Control resources

13. The project team is in constant conflict due to scarce resources. This conflict was apparent again, just before a major deliverable was due when the project manager had to step in and make a decision. What BEST describes the project manager's response?
    A. Withdrawal/avoid
    B. Compromise/reconcile
    C. Force/direct
    D. Collaborate/problem solve

14. The project manager and key team members are determining how to estimate and manage the type and number of resources the project will need. The resources include both people and physical (e.g., equipment, material) resources. What BEST describes this process?
    A. Estimate activity resources
    B. Acquire resources
    C. Manage team
    D. Plan resource management

15. The project manager is anxious to acquire resources for the project. The project sponsor mentions every day the need to "get started" and complete the project on time. Before acquiring resources, the project must complete which phases?
    A. Initiating and executing
    B. Planning and executing
    C. Planning and monitoring and control
    D. Initiating and planning

16. The project manager is reviewing the project charter. The project charter describes the project vision, business case, and key stakeholders. However, unlike previous projects, this project charter documents more about "how" to accomplish the deliverables. Not "what" to expect of the deliverables. What is the proposed project type?
    A. Traditional
    B. Waterfall
    C. Agile
    D. Hybrid

17. The project team is creating a list of team and physical resource needs. To organize the resources, the team has decided to create a hierarchical diagram organizing resources by category and types. What BEST describes this artifact?
    A. Work breakdown structure (WBS)
    B. Organizational breakdown structure (OBS)
    C. Resource breakdown structure (RBS)
    D. Project directory

18. The project manager is executing the Acquire Resources process. The project manager must evaluate over twenty developer candidates. What is the BEST decision-making tool to help compare candidates?
    A. Voting
    B. Autocratic
    C. Multicriteria
    D. Interviews

19. A new project manager began working on an existing project. The project manager has never worked with any of the project team members before. The project manager wants to understand the team member's preferences, how they make decisions, and interact with people. What tool provides this insight?
    A. Colocation
    B. Individual assessments
    C. One-on-one meetings
    D. Interpersonal skills

20. The project manager is reviewing work performance information for a physical resource. The resource is underperforming, and the project manager will take corrective action tomorrow by requesting more resources. What process did the project manager perform?
    A. Control resources
    B. Manage team
    C. Acquire resources
    D. Estimate activity resources

Answers

1. B. Self-organized
    - Agile projects embrace servant leaders typically called Scrum masters, team leaders, or coaches. These leaders ensure the team has the environment and support they need. This support empowers the team to solve local or internal project challenges (e.g., project technical, process, etc. challenges), shields the team from external disruptions, and trusts the team will "get the job done." Self-organized teams consist of generalized specialist that can work on different tasks to assist others and keep the project progressing rather than relying on Subject Matter Experts (SMEs). (*PMBOK® Guide – Sixth Edition*, page 310)

2. D. Estimate activity resources
    - During the development of the project schedule, the team creates an activity list with activity attributes for each project activity. Both the activity list and attributes are inputs to Estimate Activity Resources.
    - The team previously developed a plan (Resource Management Plan) as to how to estimate both team and physical resources for each activity. Determining the type and number of resources is necessary before the team can Estimate Activity Cost or Acquire Resources.
    - (*PMBOK® Guide – Sixth Edition*, page 320)

3. B. Emotional intelligence
    - The ability to recognize and regulate one's own emotions is critical for leaders. Once a leader masters their own emotions, they can focus on empathizing with and influencing the team. Anticipating the team's needs, empathizing with their situation, and following up on issues, demonstrate a leader's emotional intelligence. (*PMBOK® Guide – Sixth Edition*, page 349)

4. C. RACI
    - A Responsible, Accountable, Consult, and Inform (RACI) chart is a type of assignment matrix that would identify for the team each team member's role in each work package or

activity. The assignment matrix is also known as a Responsibility Assignment Matrix (RAM).

- One key to successfully using RACIs is the project manager must ensure that only one person is accountable for each activity. Ensuring this removes confusion as to who has the authority to make decisions regarding the specific activity.
- (*PMBOK® Guide – Sixth Edition*, page 317)

5. B. Storming

- There are five stages of team development in Tuckman's ladder. While the team is new, they have advanced beyond the Forming stage as they know each other and the project's objective. However, the team has not yet reached the Norming phase as they have not adjusted their behaviors to work together collaboratively.
- The team is in the Storming phase since they are beginning to address project challenges, including determining how to reach consensus. Since the team was able to reach consensus professionally, the project manager was correct in not intervening. However, the project manager needs to be particularly sensitive during the Storming phase. If the team cannot mature beyond the Storming phase collaboratively and productively, the project will be in jeopardy.
- The other phases are Norming, Performing, and Adjourning. Throughout the project, the team may fall back to previous stages as team members come and go. Some propose, due to team member transitions often characteristic of projects in the real world, that few teams will achieve the Performing phase or able to maintain it during the entire project.
- (*PMBOK® Guide – Sixth Edition*, page 338)

6. A. Manage team

- The project manager is performing the Manage Team process by definition. (PMBOK® Guide – Sixth Edition, page 344)

- In prior editions of the PMBOK® Guide, this knowledge area called Human Resource Management. In the sixth edition, the name was changed to Project Resource Management and expanded to include planning, executing, and monitoring and controlling all resources. These resources include both people (i.e., stakeholders) and physical resources (e.g., equipment, hardware, software licenses, etc.). Unlike most other knowledge areas, some processes (e.g., Develop Team and Manage Team) apply just to the internal or organization's team resources. Keep in mind project managers do not "control" the project or organization's team resources or people. Therefore, there are no processes involving the organization's people in the monitoring and controlling phase.
- Physical resources, including seller team members, are assigned, allocated, and monitored using the Control Resources process. Keep in mind a seller's organization should be providing training, coaching, etc. for their employees. These activities may be done following the Develop Team and Manage Team processes by the seller but are outside the scope of the project. It is essential to understand that contractual agreements govern a project manager's interactions with the seller's employees. A project manager not following those contractual agreements may lead to co-employment legal challenges.

7. A. Environmental enterprise factors

- Competencies available across an organization, or an individual's competency, is outside the control of the project team. Therefore, the best answer is environmental enterprise factors. Other factors include the location of resources, market conditions that may or may not make procuring resources viable, and the organization's culture. (PMBOK® Guide – Sixth Edition, page 315)

8. C. Trend analysis

- Monitoring and controlling physical resources, in this case, tracking daily usage is an example of trend analysis

performed during the Control Resources process.
(*PMBOK® Guide – Sixth Edition*, page 356)

9. D. Recognition and rewards

- Project managers must recognize and reward desired behaviors and results. Rewarding someone or the team re-enforces their value within the project and organization. Rewards include demonstrating appreciation, a new opportunity to advance skills, monetary, time off, etc.

- Thought and planning must be applied to ensure the receiving team member or members view the recognition as a reward. This planning requires tailoring the recognition not only to the magnitude of the accomplishment but to the individual. (*PMBOK® Guide – Sixth Edition*, page 344)

10. B. Analogous estimating

- Analogous estimating is a quick method to estimate resources, time, cost, etc. when the project is similar to a previous project(s).

- However, when using analogous estimating, care must be taken. Estimating errors may be introduced if the prior project or projects are not truly similar to the project. Also, senior stakeholders, like the sponsor, may set a perceived upper estimate level based on their understanding of the similarities between the projects or without sufficiently considering differences, including market conditions, inflation, geographical location, etc. that may significantly influence the cost of resources.

- *PMBOK® Guide – Sixth Edition*, page 324)

11. A. Team charter

- How the team will work together is defined in a team charter. This document describes the expected values each team member will demonstrate during the project.

- These expectations include meeting expectations (e.g., starting and stopping on time, having an agenda, etc.), how decision-making criteria, plus other agreements to ensure a cohesive, collaborative, and well-performing team.

- (*PMBOK® Guide – Sixth Edition*, page 319)

12. B. Develop team

- A project manager is responsible for helping all team members improve their skills, knowledge, and competencies. Team members should improve in each of these attributes by the end of the project. Team members who are encouraged and provided an opportunity to grow personally are less likely to leave the project before completion and contribute to a well-performing team. (*PMBOK® Guide – Sixth Edition*, page 336)

13. C. Force/direct

- All conflict resolution techniques are valid and, for a given situation, the best choice. One may misunderstand that each method is correct as many leadership approaches today stress servant and collaborative leadership styles. However, being forceful or direct may be the best solution for a leader based on the scenario. In this scenario, the project manager had to decide due to the limited time before the due date. Force/direct was the best choice. (*PMBOK® Guide – Sixth Edition*, page 348)

- Conflict is not always negative, nor should it be avoided. Conflict may be required to identify the best ideas and approaches, resulting in a well-performing team and successful project. Whether the conflict is positive or negative, resolution techniques must be applied. Choosing the correct conflict resolution choice will ultimately determine if the conflict has a positive or negative result on the team and the project.

- Criteria to determine the best conflict resolution technique is based on the time before a resolution is needed, the criticality, and how long the solution must last. If there is sufficient time, Collaborate/problem-solve, is generally the best technique. As the outcome will last the longest since the team works together until reaching consensus. The smooth/accommodate method, while it appears to resolve the conflict successfully, may not continue long-term. As there may be someone who agreed to the resolution but never really bought-in. And therefore, they will not remain supportive over time. Withdrawal/avoid may be appropriate if the conflicting people need time to lower their emotions and reflect. Or if resolving immediately in the current setting may embarrass someone.

- One or more techniques may be applied to resolve conflict. For example, one may use the force/direct method to resolve the conflict immediately. But then the collaborate/problem-solve technique is applied as a follow-up to ensure a long-lasting resolution to the conflict.

14. D. Plan resource management

- The project manager and key team members are developing the resource management plan. They leverage many project documents, including the project schedule, requirements documentation, risk register, etc. to determine both the type and amount of needed resources. The project manager and team may repeat this process more than once during the project). (*PMBOK® Guide – Sixth Edition*, page 312)

15. D. Initiating and planning

- Prior activities before acquiring resources are to complete the Initiating phase, which includes a signed Project Charter, and to complete the Planning phase, which includes an approved project management plan. The project management plan includes approved plans for each knowledge area, time, cost and scope baselines, etc. Acquiring resources is part of the Executing phase, which follows the Planning phase. (*PMBOK® Guide – Sixth Edition*, page 328)

- When is the "team" formed? The project manager is not solely responsible for completing the deliverables in the Initiating and Planning phases. Yet the team and physical resources are not acquired until the Executing phase. How's this work? Remember, PMI assumes on the exam all projects are large projects. During the Initiating and Planning phases, the project manager works with subject matter experts (SMEs) and a limited number of other team members utilizing limited physical resources to complete these phases. It would not make sense to have full capacity available, including perhaps significant computer resources, hundreds of team members on-boarded, etc. before the project management plan is approved.

16. C. Agile

- Agile projects, by definition, have less defined project requirements until the last possible moment (i.e., just before developing the functionality to meet the requirements). Agile projects leverage progressive elaboration because the deliverable requirements are highly variable (i.e., not initially well-defined and expected to change during the project). Self-organizing teams, with little centralized control, are better suited for projects requiring an Agile framework. (*PMBOK® Guide – Sixth Edition*, page 312)

17. C. Resource breakdown structure (RBS)

- The question states, "…team and physical resource needs," which includes both people and physical resources. Potential team resource categories may be testers, developers, etc. with types as integration tester, user experience tester, backend developers, database administrators, etc.

- Potential physical resource categories may be personal computers, servers, databases, etc. with types as laptops, developer workstation, relational database, etc.

- The decomposition of each resource continues until the team can plan, monitor, and control each resource.

- (*PMBOK® Guide – Sixth Edition*, page 316)

- An artifact is a common Agile term to describe a tangible document or deliverable. In this case, an RBS document.

18. C. Multicriteria

- Multicriteria decision making leverages a matrix of criteria to assess and rank in this case each candidate. The assessment should include technical and project methodology experience, cost, availability, knowledge, and skills. But also include attitude, ability to work within a team structure, and the candidate's geographical location. (*PMBOK® Guide – Sixth Edition*, page 144, 332)

19. B. Individual assessments

- CliftonStrengths (aka StrengthsFinder) and Myers-Briggs Type Indicator® (MBTI®) are two examples of individual assessments that help the individual and others better understand how they make decisions, interact with people, and their preferences. (*PMBOK® Guide – Sixth Edition*, page 342)

20. A. Control resources

- By definition, the project manager is monitoring and controlling a physical resource and, based on their assessment, will be taking corrective action. A key point is the assessment was on a physical resource, not a team resource (i.e., stakeholder within the project organization).
- The Acquire resources process is not the correct choice. However, tomorrow if the project manager pursues corrective action by adding resources, they will be performing the Acquire Resources process.
- (*PMBOK® Guide – Sixth Edition*, page 352)

COMMUNICATION MANAGEMENT

How is the project doing? Are the project's cost, schedule, and scope on track? Does the project need additional resources? Are the team resources available for other projects? Stakeholders have these and many other questions during the project. The project manager and team must be able to efficiently and effectively communicate the project status and address all stakeholder questions and needs.

Who, what, when, where, and how much? (Plan Communications Management) Too little, too much, too frequent, too infrequent are all stakeholder communication challenges that may change during the project. Identifying individual stakeholder needs is done during Stakeholder management. The project manager and team will often find what is too much information for one stakeholder may not be enough for another. What is too frequent for one stakeholder during a specific phase may not be frequent enough during another project phase.

Communication planning determines who (which stakeholders), what (content), when (frequency), where (the source of information), and how much (level of detail) for all work performance reports. The project manager and team must also plan to ensure the usage of the appropriate technology based on the urgency, availability, confidentiality, etc. of the communication.

Is the communication plan being executed? (Manage Communications) This process provides effective and efficient flow from work performance data, to work performance information, to work performance reports, for effective communication with all stakeholders. Is it more cost-effective to communicate via a web site (pull), large email distributions (push), or meetings (interactive)? Are stakeholders receiving and understanding the communications?

Another critical process component is the disposition of communications per the organization's procedures and governmental regulations. The project manager must understand, identify, and ensure the proper disposition of all communications.

This may be referred to as document retention. The project manager must ensure that each project communication is maintained according to the organization's document retention policy. This policy identifies the type of project communication and the length of time the organization must retain that document. For specific project communications or materials, this may be as short as a few days or several years after the project's deliverable is no longer produced.

Standard document retention for communications may change due to pending legal issues. In this case, a lawsuit may require the project manager to ensure all project communications (e.g., emails, web site content, plans, etc.) retained until settlement of any legal actions.

It is common for an organization to pay a large legal settlement for improperly retaining or keeping documents. It is also true that an organization may pay a large settlement in the opposite case. In this case, a document or communication is discovered that should have been, but was not, deleted per the document retention policy.

Does the information satisfy the receiver? (Monitor Communications) The purpose of this process is to confirm that the project communications met the needs of each stakeholder. The project manager must know the difference between understanding and need. For example, a stakeholder may understand a project communication. However, the communication may not meet the needs of the stakeholder.

For example, the project may provide a total monthly project expense report to the accounting department. The accountant receiving the report understands the communication. However, the accountant needs labor expenses per organizational division (e.g., information technology, marketing, legal, etc.). The project manager must change this communication to meet this need.

Questions

1. A stakeholder complained to the project manager that the information radiator posted in the team area is not clear. What should the project manager update?
   A. Issues log
   B. Lessons learned register
   C. Communication management plan
   D. Information radiator

2. The team will be in three different regions to enable a "follow-the-sun" model. Which of the following skills will be more critical for the project manager?
   A. Political awareness
   B. Communication styles awareness
   C. Cultural awareness
   D. Time zone awareness

3. The project team needed to make a change to the production environment. The team posted announcements on web sites and invited people to the change control board meeting to discuss. After the change was approved, the team implemented the change. The team backed out the change because it impacted the accounting system. During the post-mortem, the team determined a key stakeholder was not aware of the change and would have identified the issue before implementation. Which of the following would have avoided this issue?
   A. Stakeholder communication plan
   B. Communication management plan
   C. Stakeholder register
   D. Change control board

4. Two students are studying for a project management exam. They cannot determine the process that distributes work performance reports. Which process is the correct process?
   A. Plan communication management
   B. Control communications
   C. Management communications
   D. Manage stakeholder expectations

5. The project manager realizes the organization's culture influences communication planning. What BEST describes the organization's culture?
   - A. Communication requirements analysis
   - B. Expert judgment
   - C. Enterprise environmental factors
   - D. Organizational process assets

6. The project team is working on the interactive communication model for the project. The team is debating the steps that occur during an interactive communication. Which of the following is the correct sequence?
   - A. Encode, transmit, acknowledge, decode, encode, feedback/response, decode
   - B. Encode, decode, transmit, acknowledge, encode, feedback/response, decode
   - C. Encode, decode, transmit, acknowledge, encode, feedback/response, decode
   - D. Encode, transmit, decode, acknowledge, encode, feedback/response, decode

7. The project team posts the project's progress on a web site accessible by all stakeholders. The same web site contains additional information about the project, including how to contact the project team. What method of communication is the team using?
   - A. Interactive communications
   - B. Push communication
   - C. Pull communication
   - D. Web communication

8. The project manager is reviewing a written work performance report with a communication expert. The expert emphasizes the 5Cs of written communication. Which of the following is NOT one of the 5Cs?
   - A. Comprehensive coverage of the subject
   - B. Coherent logic flow of ideas
   - C. Correct grammar and spelling
   - D. Clear purpose and expression directed toward the needs of the reader

9. Getting stakeholders to agree, working through different group dynamics, good meeting management, and keeping stakeholders engaged are examples of which skill a project manager must demonstrate?
    A. Escalation
    B. Facilitation
    C. Active listening
    D. Political awareness

10. The inclusion of stakeholders outside of the project team in project meetings is an emerging trend. Which of the following is an example of a meeting where key stakeholders may attend to get project updates?
    A. Technical design meetings
    B. Detail schedule meetings
    C. Daily standup meetings
    D. Retrospective meetings

11. The project manager is reviewing project status with the team members located in another country. As the team members provide updates, the project manager asks clarifying questions and confirms with each team member the status. What BEST describes this activity?
    A. Networking
    B. Cultural awareness
    C. Active Listening
    D. Meeting management

12. The project includes both internal and external stakeholders. The project manager is developing an appropriate communication approach. What process is the project manager performing?
    A. Manage communications
    B. Plan communications management
    C. Monitor communications
    D. Tailor communications

13. The project manager is visiting a remote facility where some of the project stakeholders work. The project manager takes time to visit each stakeholder in their office. As part of their conversation, the project manager reviews the latest project status update document. The project manager asks questions to confirm each stakeholder clearly understands the current project status. The project manager also asks if the stakeholder needs any additional information to be included in future status updates. Which of the following processes is the project manager is performing?
    A. Manage communications
    B. Plan communications management
    C. Monitor communications
    D. Manage stakeholder engagement

14. A meeting agenda and the minutes published after the meeting are examples of what type of communication?
    A. Formal communications
    B. Informal communications
    C. Official communications
    D. Unofficial communications

15. The project manager and team are planning the project's communications. The team has determined the urgency, the availability of the receiver's technology, and the project environment will influence communications. These factors influence which of the following?
    A. Communication models
    B. Enterprise environmental factors
    C. Requirements documentation
    D. Communication technology

16. The project manager and team have identified the appropriate organization's document retention policy for each document in the communication management plan. A seller has disputed whether the team fulfilled a term of the contract on the project. As a result, a legal hold is on all project documents related to the seller. What process is the team performing?
    A. Plan communication management
    B. Control communications
    C. Manage communications
    D. Control procurement

17. The project manager is reviewing team performance assessments. The project manager determines that some team members would benefit from improving their communication skills. Which of the following is NOT a communication skill?
    A. Communication competence
    B. Feedback
    C. Nonverbal
    D. Subject knowledge

18. Many stakeholders provided similar feedback regarding the lack of clarity of the project's status reports. Some stakeholders provided specific improvement recommendations and complained about the same issue with other projects. The project team made adjustments, and feedback was positive. What else should the project team update?
    A. PMIS
    B. Issue log
    C. Stakeholder register
    D. Lessons learned register

19. Key stakeholders received an email with the agenda for the project team update meeting. Once the meeting started, it became clear that not all the stakeholders had read the email. What BEST describes this situation?
    A. Push communication
    B. Interactive communication
    C. Monitor stakeholder expectations
    D. Pull communications

20. Members of the project team must determine the technical details about the product's design. It is essential that all understand the details and that everyone contributes to the solution. What is the BEST communication method?
    A. Screen sharing
    B. Video conference
    C. Face-to-face
    D. email

Answers

1.   A. Issues log
     - An information radiator graphically communicates project status on Agile projects. Information radiators "radiate information" by making the information visible to all.
     - This information radiator was posted in the team area and reflected the current project status. However, a stakeholder questioned the effectiveness of the information radiator. The next step is to log the issue in the issues log. The team will then assess and perform plan-do-act-check if a change is needed.
     - *(PMBOK® Guide – Sixth Edition*, page 390)

2.   C. Cultural awareness
     - With the team located in three locations, it is appropriate to imply each region will have different cultural norms. The project manager must be aware of the cultural differences not only to communicate effectively but to ensure each team member considers the cultural differences in all interactions. *(PMBOK® Guide – Sixth Edition*, page 376)

3.   B. Communication management plan
     - The communication management plan includes the planning, implementation, and monitoring of all project communications for effectiveness. One component of the plan is the identification of who must receive the information. In this scenario, the team missed a crucial stakeholder in the communication management plan. The project manager must ensure the plan is immediately updated. *(PMBOK® Guide – Sixth Edition*, page 377)

4.   C. Manage communications
     - One of the challenges of studying project management is the vast number of processes. Understanding major flows between those processes is critical to understanding.
     - One example is the flow between processes that create work performance data (Direct and Manage Project Work), work performance information (various Monitoring and Controlling processes), and work performance reports

(Monitor and Control Project Work). The distribution of work performance reports to appropriate stakeholders occurs by executing the Manage Communications process.

- *(PMBOK® Guide – Sixth Edition*, page 382)

5. C. Enterprise environmental factors

- The culture of the organization is outside the control or influence of the project and project team. An enterprise environmental factor. Other examples include communication channels, tools, the geographic distribution of team, etc. *(PMBOK® Guide – Sixth Edition*, page 368)

6. D. Encode, transmit, decode, acknowledge, encode, feedback/response, decode

- Encode, transmit, and decode is the basic communication model. However, interactive communication between two or more people is more complicated. The sender must encode (i.e., convert thoughts and ideas into the English, Spanish, etc. language) and transmit (i.e., speak English) those words to the receiver. The receiver must decode (i.e., convert English into thoughts and ideas) and acknowledge the receipt of the communication.

- It is essential to understand that acknowledging does not mean agreeing. Not realizing this difference may lead to miscommunications and misunderstandings among people from different cultures, as the definition of acknowledging may vary across cultures.. Acknowledging means "I got the message", it does not mean "I understand or agree."

- The communication model continues with the original receiver encoding a feedback message, transmitting that message, and the sender decoding the message.

- *(PMBOK® Guide – Sixth Edition*, page 372)

7. C. Pull communication

- The context of pull or push depends on the receiver's perspective. The receivers must "pull" information from the web site by accessing the web site and locating the desired information. Pull communication may be an excellent choice to share information with a large group of stakeholders. But may not be the right choice if the urgency or "ease of use" are factors to consider. Yes, going to a web site may be considered by some stakeholders to be relatively difficult to access compared to push communications that arrive on their phone as text messages. It is the receivers' perspective as to what communication technology is "easy to use" and should be given preference over the sender's "ease of use." (*PMBOK® Guide – Sixth Edition*, page 374)

8. A. Comprehensive coverage of the subject
    - The 5Cs of written communication include the other three answers plus Concise expression and elimination of excess words, and Controlling flow of words and ideas.(*PMBOK® Guide – Sixth Edition*, page 362, 363)

9. B. Facilitation
    - Each of the facilitation skills in the question is required for a project manager to execute the Manage Communications process effectively. This process ensures the communication has been appropriately created, understood by the receiver, and enables the receiver to provide feedback. (*PMBOK® Guide – Sixth Edition*, page 381)

10. C. Daily standup meetings
    - Agile daily standup meetings occur each day in the team's work area. The meeting is timeboxed (limited) to fifteen minutes and only project team members may speak. Each team member shares what they accomplished since the last daily standup, what they will accomplish before the next standup and if there are any impediments to their work. Other stakeholders do not talk but may attend to get a project progress update. Stakeholders may stay after the meeting to discuss obstacles or other topics with specific team members. The remaining team members return to project work. (*PMBOK® Guide – Sixth Edition*, page 364)

11. C. Active listening
    - The project manager is demonstrating the characteristics of active listening. These skills include acknowledging, asking clarifying questions and rephrasing and repeating messages to confirm understanding. While the project manager may

be demonstrating cultural awareness, these same active listening skills apply regardless of team member's culture. (*PMBOK® Guide – Sixth Edition*, page 386)

12. B. Plan communications management
    - Determining the best approach for each stakeholder or stakeholder group, what organizational assets exist to ensure effective and efficient communications, and the project needs are occur during the Plan Communications Management process. (*PMBOK® Guide – Sixth Edition*, page 366)

13. C. Monitor communications
    - The question context is in the broader context of engaging stakeholders, so the project manager is performing the Manage Stakeholder Engagement process. But the project manager is specifically asking if the project status report meets stakeholder needs. Seeking the answer to this question is the purpose of the Monitor Communications process.
    - As is often the case, the project manager switches between multiple processes during the same scenario or discussion. Manage Stakeholder Engagement process includes many activities to ensure the project meets all stakeholder needs. In this case, ensuring specifically the information needs are met (Monitor Communications).
    - (*PMBOK® Guide – Sixth Edition*, page 388)

14. A. Formal communications
    - Reports, formal (e.g., scheduled) meetings, meeting agendas and minutes, presentations, etc. are all examples of formal communications. These communications may be internal, external, or both. The project manager and team are accountable for the security, storage, retrieval, etc. of these communications based on the organization's documents retention policies. (*PMBOK® Guide – Sixth Edition*, page 361)

15. D. Communication technology
    - The question lists several influences when choosing communication technology. For instance, if it is an urgent

communication, a phone call instead of email is more appropriate. The project team must also be aware of the confidentiality of the information. Other influences include will the team be able to communicate face-to-face (F2F), is the team located in different time zones? (*PMBOK® Guide – Sixth Edition*, page 370)

16. C. Manage communications

- An organization's document retention policy determines the ultimate disposition of each type of document in the organization. A document may be any communication (e.g., voice mail, text message, written status report, emails, social media posting, etc.). A legal hold is an action taken by the organization to ensure all documents which may be subject to a court order are available and may override the standard retention period for a communication. If a project team cannot produce a communication, the organization may be held in contempt of court. The Manage Communication process ensures the proper storage, distribution, retrieval, and disposition of all communications. (*PMBOK® Guide – Sixth Edition*, page 379)

17. D. Subject Knowledge

- Although the breadth and depth of one's knowledge on a subject may add creditability to the communication, it is not a communication skill. Presentation is the fourth communication skill. The presentation skill is not limited to PowerPoint presentations. Instead, presentation skill is the delivery of any communication clearly and concisely, to the appropriate stakeholders, and meets the needs of the target audience. (*PMBOK® Guide – Sixth Edition*, page 384)

18. D. Lessons learned register

- The project team made improvements to the project status reports that were well received. This feedback should trigger the action to capture this knowledge in the lesson learned register. Also, stakeholders "…complained about the same issue with other projects" states the issue is throughout the organizations.

- Each project manager and team are responsible for improving the effectiveness and efficiency of their project, the organization, and future projects. A primary way to capture and share this knowledge is through the lessons learned register.
- (PMBOK® Guide – Sixth Edition, page 393)

19. A. Push communication

- Although sent to each desired stakeholder, one challenge with push communications is the inability to determine if the receiver read and understood the message. This question describes a scenario where some stakeholders did not read the communication. The project manager and team should perform the Monitor Communication process and determine if changes to the communications management plan are needed to improve the effectiveness and efficiency of meeting agenda communications. (PMBOK® Guide – Sixth Edition, page 374)

20. Face-to-face

- The most effective communication method is face-to-face (F2F). The effectiveness is due to the richness of F2F communication, which is interactive and includes both verbal and nonverbal. Technology challenges (e.g., poor cell phone connection), verbal only (e.g., phone calls), provide no means to ask questions (e.g., video), etc. impact other communication methods. (PMBOK® Guide – Sixth Edition, page 374)

RISK MANAGEMENT

All project discussions and actions are about risk. Every conversation changes the confidence level of the project achieving its objectives. Did the deliverable meet the customer's expectations? If yes, then the risk may not change or may be reduced as it is more likely the project will produce acceptable deliverables. If no, then the risk of the project not being able to produce acceptable deliverables just increased.

Do risks always result in a negative outcome (e.g., over budget, behind schedule, etc.)? No. There may be incentives for a project to complete by a specific date, achieve a particular market share, etc. These positive risks, receiving the incentive, will motivate the project manager and team to implement plans ensuring the project achieves the incentive.

How will risks be addressed? (Plan Risk Management) Internal (e.g., project's schedule, budget, etc.) and external (e.g., global economic conditions, organizational changes, etc.) forces result in a constant flux of the project's risk. Therefore, it is critical to have an effective plan to manage risk throughout the project. How will risks be identified? When will the risk be assessed and reassessed? The Plan Risk Management process answers these and more questions.

Here a risk, there a risk, everywhere a risk. (Identify Risks). The project manager and team must proactively search for all potential risks to the project objectives. Risk identification starts with assessing the triple-constraints (scope, schedule, and cost). For example, if the project team identifies an event that may cause a scheduled task to complete late, the team must also consider the impact on the other constraints (scope and cost).

The project manager and team must use good brainstorming and other techniques to ensure the identification of all risks. At this point, the team should capture every potential threat. A missed risk not identified until later in the project may have a significant effect on the scope, schedule, and cost of the project. This impact may result in an unsuccessful project, perhaps even canceling the project, after considerable labor and expenses have occurred. Poor risk management will result in a negative perception of the project manager's ability to successfully lead projects.

What are the critical few risks? (Perform Qualitative Risk Analysis) A project team may identify many risks. The project manager and team quantitatively assess the risk's probability of occurrence and impact. The team then ranks each risk based on this assessment.

Is it possible to assess risks quantitively? (Perform Quantitative Risk Analysis) Yes. But first, the team must evaluate the quality of the data. Sufficient numerical data about the risk must be available to perform quantitative assessments.

The required data quality may not be available for any risks. Other times it may be only available for a few specific risks. Therefore, the project manager and team may be able to quantitatively assess and rank only a few, if any, of the project's risks. Quantitative assessments may also require expert judgment and tools to be available to evaluate the results.

How may the project team influence a risk's probability of occurrence and impact? (Plan Risk Responses) For each identified risk, that the team cannot eliminate, the project team creates a risk response plan. Risk response plans vary based on the chosen risk strategy.

The project team may identify a different technology, process, etc. that eliminates the underlying root cause of the risk. This results in the project manager being one-hundred percent confident the risk event will not occur (negative risk) or will occur (positive risk). Avoiding negative risks and exploiting positive risks occurs as an outcome of the project team discussing and brainstorming a risk response.

The project team may be willing to accept the risk. In this case, the project team will not create a risk response plan. In other words, if the risk event occurs, the team will "deal with it" at that time. The team may choose the accept strategy when there is a low probability of occurrence or impact.

Accepting the risk may also occur for risk events outside the control of the project team. For example, the project team has identified that if a competitor enters the market, it will influence the project's risk. But will a competitor enter the market? What features will the competitor's product have? This information is typically not available to the project team until the competitor makes a formal public announcement. This lack of data makes it challenging to create response plans in advance. The project team may have to accept this risk even though the impact may be significant.

The team creates risk response plans for the remaining risks that were neither eliminated or accepted. While the risk response plan is unable to eliminate the probability of occurrence or impact, the plan may have a significant influence on both. The result is less overall project risk.

Since all project discussions have an underlying risk component, the project manager is always reassessing the project's risk. This on-going reassessment may result in a previously eliminated or accepted risk now requires a risk response plan. Likewise, a response plan for other risks may no longer be necessary. This flux in the project's risk assessment is highest early in the project. The risk of a well-managed project should reduce as the team completes project milestones.

We have a plan. (Implement Risk Responses) Projects may spend considerable effort to create risk response plans. The risk owner is responsible for ensuring the risk response plan as approved is implemented. This responsibility includes the implementation of the contingency plan if the initial response is ineffective.

Have the project's risks changed? (Control Risk) The project manager must always be looking for ways to influence a risk's probability of occurrence and impact. For negative risks, this means reducing the probability of occurrence or impact. For positive risks, increase one or both. Did a stakeholder request a new requirement? Was the project budget reduced? Did the schedule tasks complete as expected today? As you can see, every discussion has an underlying risk component. Therefore, the project manager, risk owner, and team must continuously reassess the project's risks and adjust as necessary the response plans.

Questions

1. The construction project must meet the approved budget to be profitable. The project manager was concerned that significant repair expenses might occur on the equipment. To address this risk, the project manager purchased a maintenance contract for all the equipment. What BEST describes this risk strategy?
   A. Avoid
   B. Mitigate
   C. Transfer
   D. Share

2. The team determined all identified risks' impact and their probability of occurrence. The team has also created risk response plans. The project team decided to assess how quickly they would need to implement each risk response plan if the risk event occurs. What BEST describes this assessment attribute?
   A. Urgency
   B. Proximity
   C. Strategic impact
   D. Detectability

3. The sponsor and project team are discussing risks. The team wants to tailor a probability and impact matrix for the project. Before starting that work, the team must understand what about the sponsor?
   A. Organizational authority
   B. Influence over other stakeholders
   C. Commitment to the project
   D. Risk appetite

4. The project charter specifies the need for the project to implement the Agile methodology. The requirement is needed as the stakeholders anticipate evolving requirements. What type of risk BEST describes this concern?
   A. Variable risk
   B. Ambiguity risk
   C. Known risk
   D. Unknown risk

5. The project team, sponsor, and project manager are brainstorming to determine what risks may occur during the project. The team has interviewed other stakeholders, subject matter experts, and project team members who were part of previous similar projects. What process is the team performing?
   A. Plan risk management
   B. Monitor risks
   C. Identify risks
   D. Perform qualitative risk analysis

6. The project team and project manager are looking for people who may be able to identify possible project risks. Where should they look?
   A. Requirements documentation
   B. Assumptions log
   C. Stakeholder register
   D. Issues log

7. The project charter listed a requirement for quantitative assessment of significant risks. Four risks have been identified as substantial risks, either individually or because of their aggregate impact on the project's overall risk assessment. What is required to perform a quantitative risk?
   A. High quality data
   B. Risk assessment expertise
   C. Specialized risk tools
   D. Ability to interpret the results

8. The team identified many risks. The new project manager is not sure what process to execute next and consults a more experienced project manager. Which of the following is the recommendation?
   A. Monitor risks
   B. Perform Qualitative risk analysis
   C. Perform Quantitative risk analysis
   D. Plan risk responses

9. A key stakeholder is discussing the project with the sponsor and project manager. The stakeholder mentions their concern about a project risk several times. Neither the sponsor nor the project manager shares the same level of concern. What BEST describes the stakeholder's assessment of the risk?
    A. Detectability
    B. Proximity
    C. Strategic impact
    D. Propinquity

10. An expert is performing a risk analysis of the project's cost estimates. The output represents a range of possible project completion cost values by performing several thousand iterations. What best describes this analysis?
    A. Sensitivity analysis
    B. Simulation
    C. Decision tree analysis
    D. Influence diagrams

11. An audit assessing the efficiency and effectiveness of the risk response plans just finished. The audit determined the plans did not reduce risks as much as anticipated increasing the project's costs. As a result, the PMO increased the overall project risk. Which process audits response plans?
    A. Plan risk responses
    B. Implement risk responses
    C. Monitor risks
    D. Identify risks

12. The project team is discussing the root cause of a risk event. The team should use which data analysis tool to identify the root causes?
    A. Assumption and constraint analysis
    B. SWOT
    C. Document analysis
    D. Fishbone

13. The project team is selecting strategies and developing actions to influence the probability of occurrence or the impact of project risks. What process is the team performing?
    A. Plan risk management
    B. Monitor risk
    C. Plan risk responses
    D. Perform qualitative risk analysis

14. The project team is using a control chart to track the test performance of the product. The team has developed a risk response plan if a special cause event occurs. What type of risk is product performance?
    A. Variable risk
    B. Ambiguity risk
    C. Known risk
    D. Unknown risk

15. The project team is organizing the risks on the project. The team identified an organizational process asset that they modified to complete this effort. The risks are now in a hierarchical chart. What BEST describes this asset?
    A. RBS
    B. WBS
    C. Decision matrix
    D. Risk chart

16. The requirements management plan, cost management plan, resource management plan, and the baselines all provide excellent sources to identify risks. This project will utilize multiple sellers, each providing a part of the project's deliverables. Which one of the following sources may also identify risk for this project?
    A. Stakeholder register
    B. Agreements
    C. Assumptions log
    D. Issues log

17. A risk owner implemented the risk response plan before a scheduled network outage. By following the plan, the risk owner could ensure the development environment was available to the developers. The risk owner is executing what process?
    A. Implement risk responses
    B. Plan risk management
    C. Monitor risks
    D. Perform integrated change control

18. The Identify Risk process was just completed for the first time by the project team. The team will track the identified risks by a unique number, assigned a risk owner to each, and will update with new risks during the project. What is this key output?
    A. Assumption log
    B. Issues log
    C. Risk register
    D. Lessons learned register

19. The team assigned numeric values to each identified risk. These values were assigned based on the perceived risk's probability of occurrence, impact, and other factors. What BEST describes this assessment?
    A. Quantitative analysis
    B. Qualitative analysis
    C. Risk data quality analysis
    D. Risk parameter analysis

20. A risk subject matter expert is working with a project team to communicate to key stakeholders the project's risk assessments. The team identified three assessment criteria for each risk (impact, probability, and strategic impact). What tool would BEST communicate the project's risk assessment?
    A. Risk register
    B. Probability and impact matrix
    C. Bubble chart
    D. Risk matrix

21. During a project meeting, the team identified a new risk that would increase the project's cost. After a brief discussion, the team determined a change to the project schedule would eliminate the risk. Which risk strategy did the team implement?
    A. Avoid
    B. Transfer
    C. Mitigate
    D. Exploit

22. A risk event just occurred on the project. The risk owner is a new project team member. Where would the risk owner find the risk response plan?
    A. Organizational process assets
    B. Project documents
    C. Risk report
    D. Risk register

23. The project manager is talking to a risk expert about potential risks to the project. The expert suggests the project manager contact the PMO for a list of risk categories. What BEST describes this list?
    A. Prompt list
    B. Risk category list
    C. Risk list
    D. Impact list

24. The project team identified four sources of project risks. The team further decomposed these sources into a risk breakdown structure (RBS). What tool or technique BEST describes this effort?
    A. Risk breakdown
    B. Risk category list
    C. Risk categorization
    D. Risk alignment

25. A new project manager needs to communicate the probability of occurrence, impact, and the ability to detect for each risk. The project manager is unsure of how to effectively communicate this information. An expert might suggest which of the following?
    A. Histogram
    B. Bar chart
    C. Area Chart
    D. Bubble Chart

Answers

1. C. Transfer
   - Insurance is a common example of implementing the transfer risk strategy. One type of insurance is maintenance contracts that transfer the unknown impact of repair costs to another party for a known fee (i.e., insurance premium). (*PMBOK® Guide – Sixth Edition*, page 442)

2. A. Urgency
   - Urgency defines how quickly must a response plan be implemented to be effective after the risk event occurs. For example, loss of electrical power to preventive care and critical care medical clinics may be similar in both the probability of occurrence and impact. However, the urgency to restore power to the critical care clinic may be considerably higher than the preventative care clinic. (*PMBOK® Guide – Sixth Edition*, page 424)

3. D. Risk appetite
   - The team must understand the sponsor, other key stakeholders, and the organization's "appetite" for risk. This understanding is critical and will vary based on the type, probability, and impact of the risk.
   - Risk appetite is the amount of risk that an organization is prepared to accept in pursuit of the project's objectives. Often the higher the reward or opportunity, the greater the appetite for risk. The converse is also true — the higher the penalty or loss, the lower the appetite for risk.
   - A team must determine the risk appetite before taking actions to influence the risk's probability or impact. Let's use a car example. There is a much lower risk appetite for a critical risk event (e.g., the engine stops in traffic, brakes fail, etc.) that poses a safety risk than a risk event that requires a scheduled service (e.g., emission failure).
   - (*PMBOK® Guide – Sixth Edition*, page 407)

4. B. Ambiguity risk
   - Ambiguity risks are non-event risks, where it is not possible to accurately determine the probability of occurrence and impact due to a lack of knowledge.
   - For example, Agile project methodologies delay requirements, design, and development decisions to the last possible moment. This approach enables the team to discuss, incrementally build, and demo small increments of the product to the customer. Based on customer feedback, the team adjusts the next product increment and demos again. The team and customer repeat this methodology until the final product reflects the requirements of the customer.
   - Does this Agile approach reduce risk? Yes, but there is no discrete event. By how much? One cannot assess the impact of this approach versus another, yet it is clear this approach reduces the risk of delivering unsatisfactory deliverables. (*PMBOK® Guide – Sixth Edition*, page 398)

5. C. Identify risks
   - The team is using tools and techniques to gather possible individual and overall project risks. This process will be repeated throughout the project, not just during the Planning phase.
   - However, the team must identify risks as early as possible. This early identification allows the maximum amount of time before the risk event may occur to influence the probability of occurrence or impact.
   - (*PMBOK® Guide – Sixth Edition*, page 414)

6. C. Stakeholder register
   - The stakeholder register documents all stakeholders who may be impacted by or influence the project. This project document includes organizational position, requirements of interest, etc. for each stakeholder. The project charter is another document that identifies risks but is not a choice in this question. (*PMBOK® Guide – Sixth Edition*, page 409)

7. A. High quality data
   - This question is challenging. Each answer may be correct based on what is needed to perform quantitative analysis.
   - The right exam technique approach to these types of questions is to ask, "Which answer is required to be true for the others to true?" For example, if the project has access to experts, would the data still need to be of high-quality? Yes. If specialized tools were available, would the data need to be of high-quality? Yes. By using this exam technique, you can eliminate three of the answers as they all depend on the availability of high-quality data.
   - (*PMBOK® Guide – Sixth Edition*, page 429)
8. B. Perform Qualitative risk analysis
   - Exam questions expect you to know where in the processes the project is based on the question. "The team identified many risks." indicates the team has completed the Plan Risk Management and Identify Risks processes.
   - The best next step is to qualitatively assess both the probability of occurrence and impact for each identified risk. Based on this analysis, the team may elect to accept the risk (i.e., not develop a risk response plan) or escalate the effort to change the probability of occurrence or impact of the risk.
   - Please keep in mind there are positive and negative risks. For positive risks, the team wants to develop and execute risk response plans to increase the possibility of occurrence and impact. For negative risks, the team seeks to develop and execute risk response plans to decrease the likelihood of occurrence or impact.
   - (*PMBOK® Guide – Sixth Edition*, page 419)
9. D. Propinquity
   - Propinquity describes a perceived risk event by the stakeholder(s). Based on the question, the stakeholder perceives the risk as high. The project manager and team must address the risk and the risk response planning in a manner acceptable to the stakeholder(s) to address their perception.

- Solutions include changing the perception of the stakeholder. This approach would be an Agile example of "maximizing the work not done." Convincing the stakeholder, it is a misconception on their part, eliminates the need for risk response planning (i.e., maximizing work not done).
- (*PMBOK® Guide – Sixth Edition*, page 424)

10. B. Simulation
   - A simulation model is used to evaluate numerous outcomes of individual project risks. Monte Carlo analysis, or simulation, provides a range of costs and assigns a probability to each potential outcome. (*PMBOK® Guide – Sixth Edition*, page 433)

11. C. Monitor risks
   - The project team must always be alert for new risks, changes to existing risk profiles (probability of occurrence or impact, risk strategy, etc.), and the efficiencies and effectiveness of risk processes. Therefore, the team continually executes the Monitor Risks process throughout the project.
   - Each discussion and event during a project changes the project's risk. A task just completed on time increases the probability of meeting the schedule baseline. A seller's invoice for more than the planned cost decreases the probability of meeting the cost baseline. In this case, the project manager and team may create a risk response plan to avoid impacting the project's budget.
   - (*PMBOK® Guide – Sixth Edition*, page 453)

12. D. Fishbone
   - The team may use a fishbone diagram to conduct root cause analysis. The fishbone diagram is also known as Ishikawa or cause-and-effect diagram. (*PMBOK® Guide – Sixth Edition*, page 415)

13. C. Plan risk response
   - The team must first select a strategy for each identified risk. If the team determines to "accept" the risk, the team does not plan any further. For other risk strategies, the team

puts together a risk response plan to minimize negative outcomes from threats or to maximize positive results for opportunities. (*PMBOK® Guide – Sixth Edition*, page 439)

14. A. Variable risk

- Variable risks are non-event risks that occur when conditions occur outside the expected range or may occur throughout the project. In this case, a new test resulted in performance that fell outside the control limits of the control chart.

- Variable risks may be classified as non-event risk because the expectation was there would be no impact on performance, and there is no identified future event that triggered the poor performance. The trigger event may have been an inadequate test environment, design, hardware failure, etc.

- The team prepared for this variable risk by developing a risk response plan to identify and resolve the cause of poor performance if it occurred.

- (*PMBOK® Guide – Sixth Edition*, page 398)

15. A. RBS

- Risk Breakdown Structure (RBS) enables teams to organize risk by categories. This question includes many topics and techniques.

- First, the RBS acronym is used more than once (Resource Breakdown Structure and Risk Breakdown Structure). The context of the topic should identify which RBS applies.

- The question also states that the RBS is an organizational process asset that is made available to be leveraged by project teams. Teams may modify organizational process assets to their specific project needs.

- (*PMBOK® Guide – Sixth Edition*, page 406)

16. B. Agreements

- This question models many exam questions. All the answers are correct because they are good sources to identify risks on all projects.

- The best approach to correctly answer these types of questions is to eliminate the answers that are not the BEST answer. This question states the project "…will utilize multiple sellers…" and therefore, agreements is the only answer that applies just to projects with sellers. Reviewing agreements are critical to identifying risks.
- (*PMBOK® Guide – Sixth Edition*, page 413)

17. A. Implement risk responses

   - The project manager assigns a risk owner to each risk response plan. The risk owner is responsible for ensuring the implementation of the risk response plan to address the targeted risk. In this case, to ensure during network outages do not impact the development team.
   - Remember, the project manager, while remaining accountable for the project overall, is not responsible for all project activities. The risk owner is one example where someone other than the project manager was responsible. Other examples include schedule tasks, WBS deliverables, requirements owners, etc.
   - (*PMBOK® Guide – Sixth Edition*, page 413)

18. C. Risk register

   - An output of the Identify Risks process is the risk register. The risk register is a single source for all risks. All other project risk management processes leverage the risk register.
   - Each risk is identified and described with sufficient detail, identifies the risk owner responsible for the risk and risk responses. The risk register may contain additional information.
   - The team should first look for an organizational process asset to see if the organization has a risk register template before creating one.
   - (*PMBOK® Guide – Sixth Edition*, page 417)

19. B. Qualitative analysis

   - Perform Qualitative Risk Analysis process is completed based on the stakeholders' perception of the risk. The team may assign numeric values to the risk's probability of occurrence, impact, and other factors.

- The team may determine these values from a probability and impact matrix. These numeric values enable calculating the earned monetary value and risk severity.
- However, stakeholder perception is the basis of qualitative analysis. This perception naturally includes bias and is done without the numerical data rigor or analysis required for quantitative analysis. The result is a subjective, relative qualitative assessment of risks. Which is valuable and is all the team can perform if sufficient numeric data is not available.
- (PMBOK® Guide – Sixth Edition, page 420)

20. C. Bubble chart
- Some tools and techniques communicate only two-dimensions (e.g., impact and probability of occurrence, or probability of occurrence and strategic impact, etc.).
- A bubble chart enables a third assessment criterion. In this case, strategic impact. The size of each bubble varies based on strategic impact.
- (PMBOK® Guide – Sixth Edition, page 425)

21. A. Avoid
- The risk is a threat as it would result in increasing the project's costs. This threat is a negative risk the team must address by one of the appropriate negative risk strategies.
- The team could eliminate the risk by reducing the probability of occurrence or impact to zero. Therefore, the project's impact was "avoided."
- Project teams discover that through the collaborative planning of risk responses, the team can avoid many negative risks on the project. Two strategies, escalate and accept, may be applied to both negative and positive risks. These same strategies used for individual risks may also apply at the project level.
- (PMBOK® Guide – Sixth Edition, page 443)

22. D. Risk register
    - The risk register contains all the information about each identified risk. This information includes the risk strategy, risk response plan, contingency plans, and the identification of secondary risks. While the project manager remains accountable, the risk owner is responsible for ensuring the successful implementation of the risk response plan. (*PMBOK® Guide – Sixth Edition*, page 448)

23. A. Prompt list
    - The prompt list contains a predetermined list of risk categories. The project team may use a prompt list while brainstorming potential individual risks to the project.
    - The prompt list may also help assess overall project risk. These overall risks may be political, economic, social, technical, legal, or environmental (PESTLE), Other frameworks include TECOP (technical, environmental, commercial, operational, political) and VUCA (volatility, uncertainty, complexity, ambiguity).
    - (*PMBOK® Guide – Sixth Edition*, page 416)

24. C. Risk categorization
    - Identifying the source of risk is one way to categorize risks. For example, a single category may include all the transportation or distribution risks. Manufacturing, legal, supply source, etc. are other examples of possible risk categories.
    - Categorizing risks may identify areas of higher risk. Categorizing may also help determine that a single risk response plan may address more than one risk.
    - (*PMBOK® Guide – Sixth Edition*, page 425)

25. D. Bubble chart
    - It can be challenging to communicate the relationship between three critical variables. In this case, risk probability of occurrence, impact, and the ability to detect the risk. One effective solution is the bubble chart. (*PMBOK® Guide – Sixth Edition*, page 426)

PROCUREMENT MANAGEMENT

Projects done today without any contractual services are rare. It may be more likely the entire project is done with contracted services, including contracting project management services.

For this section, we will assume the project manager is an employee of the organization sponsoring the project, and the rest of the project team, up to and including the entire team, is contractors.

Successful project managers leverage the expert judgment of Subject Manager Experts (SMEs). Nowhere is this more critical than with procurement. Even project managers with years of procurement experience rely on purchasing managers, contract administrators, and attorneys plus others during procurement planning, executing, and closing.

Since procurement will result in legal agreements or contracts, the details (i.e., terms and conditions) of each procurement are critical to the success of the project. The project manager is accountable for ensuring all procurement contracts align with and facilitate creating the project deliverables. Therefore, the project manager, who is the SME for the project, must work closely with the purchasing manager, contract administrator, and attorney to ensure the contractual terms and conditions will result in a successful project.

The project manager must confirm the contract will deliver the expected deliverable before formally agreeing to the agreement. This emphasis on upfront understanding and planning is critical since contracts may reduce project flexibility. This potential reduction in flexibility is due to the nature of some legal contracts. These types of contracts may specify in detail the what, when, who, where, and how much will be delivered.

For example, if a fixed-price contract does not include an essential requirement, the seller will typically require additional funding to provide this requirement. Immediately the project's cost is now over budget, and the schedule may be behind. Also, at this point, it may be too challenging to bid the new requirement and switch sellers competitively. The result may have a significant impact as the buyer, the project manager, or their organization, is now in a weak negotiating position.

Cost-reimbursable contracts, including time and material contracts, still require considerable upfront planning to complete a project successfully. Sometimes that does not occur as the seller of the services is less concerned with what they must deliver. The cost and schedule risks are mostly or all on the buyer in cost-reimbursable contracts. The seller will deliver whatever, whenever the buyer specifies. All the while, the seller is assured any cost, and perhaps profit will be paid by the buyer.

Project managers must ensure their management that the project supports the separation of contractual service employees (i.e., seller employees) from the organization's employees (i.e., buyer employees). Without this separation, the buying organization is at risk of co-employment litigation. Co-employment occurs when the buyer's organization acts in a manner that it appears the buyer employs the seller's employees. The result may be the buyer becoming liable for providing compensation and benefits to the seller's employees. As if those seller employees were employees of the buyer.

Understanding how to avoid the legal liability of co-employment is a precarious journey. Yet the project manager is responsible that their organization is not liable for co-employment. All project managers should continuously educate themselves on the latest rulings and seek SME input regarding the latest co-employment practices.

The project needs help! (Plan Procurement Management) There are many reasons a project manager and organization may wish to enter into procurement contracts with one or more sellers. These efforts to source work is a result of the make-buy decisions completed in this planning process. Common reasons include unavailable expertise within the organization; the organization does not wish to invest in the needed services (e.g., build a data center versus cloud services), etc.

Another reason is risk management. An organization may wish to self-insure or transfer the cost of a potential loss to an insurance company for a fixed, known fee (i.e., buy insurance). Transferring risk is a common risk planning response strategy. The team and key stakeholders must evaluate as to whether the organization wants to make or buy a project deliverable.

After determining the make-buy decision for each project need, then the project manager and organization must find sellers who can provide the deliverable or service. The first step to finding capable sellers is the development of the selection criteria. This selection criteria will be used to evaluate sellers and is one of the critical outputs of this process.

Choosing a seller. (Conduct Procurement) As a reminder, all project managers must adhere to the PMI® ethics and professional conduct. Project managers must be ethical in all interactions, and this certainly applies in the case of the Conduct Procurement process.

Selecting potential sellers is relatively easy if the organization has preferred or pre-arranged sellers. For instance, an organization may have an existing agreement for seller A to provide computer server capacity. In this case, the project manager will work with the procurement manager and seller A to confirm the agreement meets the project needs or modify the existing agreement if it does not.

Selecting the best seller among more than one capable seller is challenging. The project manager will need to ensure the selection criteria accurately evaluates each seller's capability against the project needs.

Equitably sharing information amongst sellers is critical to ensure fairness. Any preference or information given to one seller over another during this process may result in legal action taken by one or more sellers. Even if the seller chooses not to pursue legal action, the business partner relationship between the buyer organization and seller may be damaged. Therefore, the project manager must ensure the entire process is fair and equitable to all sellers and should seek subject matter expert input throughout the process.

Are the terms and conditions being met by the project team? Seller? (Control Procurement) Most interactions between a project manager and the seller must be formal. The reason for the formality is both the buyer (i.e., project manager and team or organization) and the seller (i.e., contracted service provider) have to meet specific contract terms and conditions. That is correct. The buyer must fulfill, not just the seller, each term and condition.

If either the buyer or seller defaults on even a single term and condition, regardless of the perceived magnitude, then the contract may be in default and trigger legal actions. If the project manager is unaware or decides not to hold a seller accountable for a term and condition, the organization may lose legal rights and compensation that would have been otherwise available to the organization.

The seller delivered as contracted. Now what? (Close Project or Phase) The process of closing contracts is part of the Integration process group in the PMBOK® Guide – Sixth Edition. Not the procurement knowledge area. In prior editions of the PMBOK® Guide, the team performed these activities in the Close Procurement process.

The project manager must ensure the proper closing of each procurement. Based on the contract terms and conditions, this process may end with a final payment to the seller.

Executing this process may occur throughout the project. The reason is understandable when considering a seller who completes their contract early in the project. That seller would not want to wait for the final payment until project completion, which for some projects could be many months into the future.

Questions

1. The procurement manager is insistent the team ensures all potential sellers have equal access to all information about the Request for Quote (RFQ). What technique or tool should the team use?
    A. Expert judgment
    B. Bidder conferences
    C. Advertising
    D. Industry publications

2. The project manager received the latest seller's status report. The report includes both completed schedule activities and the most recent summary of invoices. What BEST describes this information?
    A. Contract status
    B. Work performance data
    C. Work performance information
    D. Project status

3. The project manager acquired people for the project through a contract that specified the required experiences and skills. The contract does not explicitly state the deliverables in detail. What BEST describes this type of contract?
    A. FP
    B. CPIF
    C. T&M
    D. CPFF

4. The project team has determined to procure two critical requirements for the project. The team wishes to make this need known to qualified buyers, begin the preparation of bid documents, and create a procurement SOW. Whose role should BEST lead this effort?
    A. Project manager
    B. Procurement manager
    C. Procurement SME
    D. Sponsor

5. The project team and procurement SME are reviewing different contract types. The team wants to choose the type of contract best suited for the project needs and then tailor that contract to exactly the project needs. What BEST describes these types of contracts?
   A. Organizational process assets
   B. Enterprise environmental factors
   C. Procurement SOW
   D. Procurement documentation

6. The project team entered into a contract with a seller. The contract will pay the seller $200,000 to produce a simple web site. The contract contains clearly defined requirements. What BEST describes this contract type?
   A. FPIP
   B. FPEPA
   C. FP
   D. CR

7. A project team member within a large organization has been working closely with a seller. The seller has provided a contract for specified services. The team member has reviewed the contract and agrees with the terms and price. Who should sign the contract for the buyer?
   A. Project team member
   B. Project manager
   C. Project sponsor
   D. Procurement manager

8. The project manager and procurement manager have sent procurement statements of work (SOW) to three sellers. The managers are currently conducting bidder conferences. What process are they performing?
   A. Plan procurement management
   B. Conduct procurements
   C. Control procurements
   D. Estimate activity resources

9. The seller has completed their contractual work. The project itself continues for another six months. What is the BEST next step?
    A. Continue and finish the project
    B. Perform close procurements
    C. Perform control procurements
    D. Perform conduct procurements

10. The project manager and seller's project manager have identified a need to change the contract's deliverable. What is the next step?
    A. Perform integrated change control
    B. Control procurements
    C. Create a change request
    D. Approve change request

11. Each team member needs a software package license. There are ten team members. The organization pays a set price per copy, and the project manager purchases the licenses on-line through a procurement system. What BEST describes this contract?
    A. FP
    B. PO
    C. CR
    D. SLA

12. The project manager and key business subject matter experts are not sure how to choose from two technical solutions for the project. They have decided to source the project work to a seller and would like each seller to recommend a solution. What type of bid should they, along with the procurement manager, send to prospective sellers?
    A. RFI
    B. RFQ
    C. RFP
    D. CP

13. The buyer and seller disagree about whether or not a deliverable meets all the requirements. What best describes this situation?
    A. Appeals
    B. Claims
    C. Dispute
    D. Issue

14. The project manager and team are reviewing the schedule activities. For each activity, they are assessing the organization's skills and capability to complete that activity. They have determined two activities require special skills the organization does not possess. What BEST describes this process?
    A. Plan procurement management
    B. Conduct procurements
    C. Estimate activity resources
    D. Control procurements

15. Market place conditions, seller's reputation, and legal advice regarding procurement are examples of what?
    A. Organizational process assets
    B. Enterprise environmental factors
    C. Requirements documentation
    D. Procurement documentation

16. The buyer and seller agree to split any costs that exceed the specified cost amount. Likewise, they will split any savings on the project that results from completing the project below the specified cost amount. What is this contract type?
    A. FP
    B. CPFF
    C. CPIF
    D. T&M

17. The buyer is assessing sellers with Agile experience using a multi-decision criteria matrix. The Agile methodology enables the potential sellers' development team to progressively elaborate requirements with the customer. Which of the following source selection criteria should be weighted more than others in the matrix?
    A. Qualifications only
    B. Fixed budget
    C. Quality and cost
    D. Highest technical score

18. The project team is preparing a procurement document that describes the needed services. Rather than provide tangible deliverables, the seller will provide specific services. What BEST describes this document?
    A. Terms of Reference
    B. Statement of Work
    C. Request for quote
    D. Request for information

19. The procurement manager is facilitating a meeting with the project team. The purpose of the meeting is to finalize the selection of sellers. During the meeting, each proposal is reviewed, discussed, and assessed. Which following process BEST describes this meeting?
    A. Plan procurement management
    B. Control procurements
    C. Conduct procurements
    D. Proposal evaluation

20. The project manager emails the procurement manager seeking information about sellers that can be on-boarded quickly and can perform the work. The procurement manager responds immediately with a list of potential sellers. What BEST describes this information?
    A. Prequalified sellers
    B. Seller performance evaluations
    C. Lessons learned
    D. Industry leaders

Answers

1. B. Bidder conferences
   - Gathering all potential sellers together during a bidder conference is one way to ensure all sellers get the same information. The team may conduct more than one bidder conference.
   - However, competing sellers may be reluctant to meet together. Regardless the project team must ensure that all sellers have equal access to the same project information as another seller throughout the Conduct Procurement process.
   - Advertising and industry publications focus on finding potential sellers. While each provides some basic initial information to sellers, neither ensures information is shared equitably with sellers throughout the entire selection process.
   - (*PMBOK® Guide – Sixth Edition*, page 487)
2. B. Work performance data
   - Can you determine the status of the project with work performance information? No. While commonly called status reports often, the report only includes work performance data.
   - That is the case in this question. The buyer or project manager received data from the seller about completed schedule activities and spend to date. This work performance data must be compared to the schedule and cost baselines while performing Control Procurements to produce work performance information. Once analyzed, the project manager can tell if the schedule and costs are on target or not.
   - (*PMBOK® Guide – Sixth Edition*, page 496)
3. C. T&M
   - The project team may enter into time and material (T&M) contracts when the project needs to add people with specific skills or experiences. T&M contracts may also

enable the team to meet workload demand during certain phases. For example, when many implementers are needed to deploy the project deliverable in a short time frame. (*PMBOK® Guide – Sixth Edition*, page 472)

4. C. Procurement SME

- The project manager must be fully engaged in all procurements to ensure the accuracy of the project's requirements in procurement documents.
- However, the project manager is often not an expert in legal contracts, aware of the organization's current preferred sellers, etc. A procurement SME (Subject Matter Expert) has the expert judgment required to lead and guide the team through the organization's procurement process.
- The procurement SME may report organizationally to the procurement manager who may have the authority to sign contracts but is not involved directly with the procurement processes for each project.
- (*PMBOK® Guide – Sixth Edition*, page 468)

5. A. Organizational process assets

- A key phrase in the question is "…tailor that contract to exactly the project needs…" The project team modifies organizational process assets to the specific needs of the project.
- There are two major types of contracts: Fixed Price and Cost-Reimbursable. The procurement SME often begins working with the team by using a template of the chosen contract type and then modifies the template's terms and conditions, deliverables, cost, schedule, etc. to the specific needs of the project.
- (*PMBOK® Guide – Sixth Edition*, page 471)

6. C. FP

- This contract is a Fixed-Price (FP) contract. The seller will receive $200,000 to deliver specific requirements.
- If the seller's cost is higher than planned, the seller will still only receive $200,000. If the buyer wishes to make changes

to the requirements, the seller may request additional money to complete those changes.

- *(PMBOK® Guide – Sixth Edition*, page 471)

7. D. Procurement manager

- The key words "… within a large organization…" in the question influences this answer. The best answer for large organizations is the procurement manager, although the title may vary (e.g., purchasing manager). The other roles are unlikely to have the authority to sign contracts on behalf of the large organization.
- Please keep in mind the PMBOK® Guide has traditionally focused on large projects. However, for smaller organizations, procurement may be decentralized, and the project manager may have the authority to sign contracts. The key is to clearly understand who within the buyers' organization has this authority.
- *(PMBOK® Guide – Sixth Edition*, page 460)

8. B. Conduct procurements

- Adhering to the PMI code of ethics is essential for the project manager, procurement manager, and all project members. Being ethical is expected for all activities.
- While conducting procurement activities any question of unfairness, unethical, etc. behavior by any member of the buyer's organization may expose the organization to legal actions by one or more the sellers. This risk may be highest during Conduct Procurements.
- *(PMBOK® Guide – Sixth Edition*, page 460)

9. C. Perform control procurements

- Unless the terms and conditions state otherwise when sellers complete their contractual work, they expect specific actions to be taken by the buyer. These actions include confirming the final deliverables are accepted, making the final payment, etc.
- The Control Procurement process is performed multiple times throughout the contractual period to monitor

progress. Control Procurement is performed one final time with a seller after the completion of each contract.

- In prior PMBOK® Guide editions, performing these activities a final time to close contracts occurred during the Closing phase as part of the procurements processes (Close Procurements).
- (*PMBOK® Guide – Sixth Edition*, page 492)

10. C. Create a change request

- The sequence of events begins with identifying the need for change. The next step is to create a change request to document the change. This change request is submitted to the Perform Integrated Change Control process to assess the proposed change across all knowledge areas for impact.
- If the change is approved, then all the steps identified in the change request must be performed, which includes updating the appropriate documents (e.g., agreements, requirements, quality metrics, etc.). The sequence of performing any change on a project should be well understood.
- (*PMBOK® Guide – Sixth Edition*, page 496)

11. B. PO

- A Purchase Order (PO) is a type of fixed-price contract. PO contracts have a predetermined price per quantity for a specific item.
- In this question, a predetermined price for a software license. A PO may also specify other terms and conditions such as payment schedule (e.g., on-order, within 30 days). PO contracts typically do not require authorized signatures. But instead, the contract is agreed to when the seller provides, in this case, the licenses.
- (PMBOK® Guide – Sixth Edition, page 471)

12. C. RFP

- A Request for Proposal (RFP) is a bid document that seeks the seller's input as to the best solution to complete the project. The seller may provide technical, project management, etc. recommendations.

- A buyer sends an RFP to sellers when the approach or solution is not easily determined or if the buyer's organization is not aware of leading industry approaches.
- When selecting a seller using an RFP, the buyer must assess the proposed solution itself along with all the other typical assessment criteria (e.g., cost, seller capability, terms, and conditions, etc.).
- (*PMBOK® Guide – Sixth Edition*, page 477)

13. B. Claims

- Contested changes or terms and conditions of a contract are known as claims. Because contracts are legally binding to both parties, disagreements involving contracts are more formal.
- All parties must closely monitor adherence to the contract terms and conditions. If either the buyer or seller believes the other did not meet a contract term, they must raise a claim or that party may lose its legal rights under the contract.
- It is best if both the buyer and seller reach an agreeable resolution to each claim. If they are unable to reach an agreeable solution, a claim proceeds to become a dispute and, finally, an appeal through the legal system.
- (*PMBOK® Guide – Sixth Edition*, page 498)

14. A. Plan procurement management

- During Plan Procurement Management, the team and key stakeholders determine which project deliverables, and in turn, which activities or requirements, they will procure through a seller.
- A seller is an organization outside of the project team. While often a seller is external to the project's organization, a seller may be within the project buyer's organization.
- Please keep in mind if a seller and buyer are in the same organization, legal entity, the buyer and seller cannot enter into a legal contract. For example, a Google project cannot enter into a legal agreement with another Google team to provide services. By definition, a legal contract must be

between two separate legal entities. Contracts must also include an offer, acceptance of the offer, consideration (i.e., compensation), and legal (i.e., the contact must be for legal activities, not illegal activities).

- However, the two teams in this example may wish to complete many of the procurement process steps to ensure understanding, agreement of internal charges, and maintain good relationships.
- (*PMBOK® Guide – Sixth Edition*, page 466)

15. B. Enterprise environment factors

- Each of these and other factors influence the make-buy decision on each project. And are outside the control of the project, making them enterprise environmental factors.
- Are the needed skills available in the market place? Are those skills too expensive? Reviewing lessons learned, what is the organization's experience with the seller? Did the seller provide similar deliverables in the past, or is this new work for the seller, which may invalid past experiences?
- (*PMBOK® Guide – Sixth Edition*, page 470)

16. C. CPIF

- This contract is a Cost Plus Incentive Fee (CPIF) contract. The buyer receives payment for all costs that are allowable under the contract plus an incentive fee defined in the contract. The seller achieving specified contract performance objectives determines the incentive fee.
- For example, the contract may specify an 80/20 (buyer/seller) sharing of cost if the cost exceeds a certain contractual amount. In this case, the buyer will only pay 80% of the actual costs after costs exceed the specified contract amount. On the other hand, the seller will pay the buyer 20% of any cost savings, an incentive fee, if the seller completes the work under the specified contract amount.
- (*PMBOK® Guide – Sixth Edition*, page 472)

17. B. Fixed budget

- All projects have the triple-constraints of time, cost, and scope. Traditional or waterfall methodology projects focus on determining the scope requirements very early in the project planning phase. Once identified, the scope requirements are fixed and may be changed only through formal change procedures.

- Agile projects instead promote changing requirements, and the priority of those requirements, up to the last possible moment. A fixed budget on an Agile project instills the discipline that the project will only implement the highest business valued requirements. This control requires the fixed budget is less than what it takes to complete every imaginable customer requirement, regardless of the requirement's business value. The result is the project consumes the budget and therefore ends, before producing deliverables with every possible requirement.

- (PMBOK® Guide – Sixth Edition, page 474)

18. A. Terms of reference

- Not all contracts provide tangible deliverables (e.g., construction of a building, new web application). Contracts may provide services (e.g., deployment, security, cleaning services).

- For service contracts, a Terms of Reference (TOR) may be created instead of a Statement of Work (SOW). A TOR scope is limited to activities or areas of knowledge and describes the tasks the seller is to perform, what is provided by the buyer for the seller (e.g., desks, phones), etc.

- (PMBOK® Guide – Sixth Edition, page 478)

19. C. Conduct procurements

- The team is performing Conduct Procurements. Key outputs of this process are selected sellers and signed agreements (i.e., contracts). These outputs trigger the need to update the project management plan and many project documents. Requirements documentation, communication plan, stakeholder plan, cost, schedule and scope baselines, resource calendars, risk register, etc. must be updated to include the chosen sellers and the terms and conditions, deliverables, etc. of the agreements. (*PMBOK® Guide – Sixth Edition*, page 482)

20. A. Prequalified sellers

- Large organizations may have a list of previously well-performing sellers with basic agreements already in place. This capability facilitates the Conduct Procurements process because the seller's performance is known.

- Plus, basic or master agreement terms and conditions may already be negotiated and agreed to between the parties. These terms and conditions may include predetermined costs for services. These agreements are known as master agreements. Master agreements reduce the contract negotiation process scope to just reaching an agreement on the deliverables specific to a project. Updates to the prequalified seller list occur during the Control Procurements process.

- (*PMBOK® Guide – Sixth Edition*, page 501)

STAKEHOLDER MANAGEMENT

Who is a project stakeholder? Anyone or any organization that could impact the project or who perceives to be impacted by the project. Is the project manager a stakeholder? Yes. Is the project team? Yes. The project impacts or influences both these stakeholders.

Who proposes project requirements? Stakeholders. Every project requirement and deliverable are a result of input from a stakeholder. Therefore, it is essential to identify all stakeholders as early as possible. The longer it takes to identify all stakeholders, the longer it may take to identify all the requirements. Any delay in identifying a requirement may lead to significant schedule delay and cost increases as the project progresses.

Who's a stakeholder? (Identify Stakeholders) The project manager performs the Identify Stakeholder process as part of the Initiating phase, confirming the importance of early identification of stakeholders. The other significant activity during the Initiating phase is the creation and approval of the project charter. Before seeking project charter approval, the project manager must ensure all key stakeholders have been identified and had an opportunity to provide input to the project charter. Often these stakeholders are senior leaders within the organization. Missing input from a stakeholder will delay the project charter approval. Or perhaps even worse, missed major requirements, risks, invalidation of the business case, etc. will be identified shortly after approval.

A key stakeholder management document is the stakeholder register. The stakeholder register contains information such as name, contact information, organizational position, etc. It also includes assessment information about the stakeholder's influence and impact, how supportive the stakeholder is of the project, etc. Since the stakeholder register contains personalized information, maintaining the confidentiality of this information must be considered.

Stakeholders may change during the life of the project. The project manager must immediately execute the Identify Stakeholder process when this occurs, or after identifying a new stakeholder. Changing or newly identified stakeholders, especially when they are senior managers or the project sponsor, may result in significant changes to the project. These changes may include budget and priority changes up to and including canceling the project.

How will the stakeholder engagement be managed? (Plan Stakeholder Engagement) It is critical the project manager clearly understands the project's expected business outcomes. This understanding is essential to planning, managing, and monitoring stakeholders' influence and impact on those outcomes. Is a key stakeholder resistive to the project? Then a plan must be developed and implemented to move the stakeholder's engagement to supportive. Is there a champion for the project? Then a plan must be implemented to maintain this stakeholder's engagement.

Meet and greet. (Manage Stakeholder Engagement) The project manager and perhaps other project team members must execute the stakeholder management plan. Otherwise, a stakeholder who was supportive of the project may become less so and become disgruntled. Touching base, often meeting in person with key stakeholders, is critical. Meeting face-to-face is an opportunity for a stakeholder to provide feedback on the project, raise issues, identify new requirements, etc. The earlier the awareness of this input, the more likely the success of the project.

Is the stakeholder now supportive of the project? Is the stakeholder less supportive? (Monitor Stakeholder Engagement) Is each stakeholder's engagement at the level required for the project's success? If no, then the engagement efforts are not working. Planning for new engagement efforts must begin, implemented, and reassessed.

Questions

1. Several project managers are discussing which knowledge area plan has the greatest impact on the project. Which of the following plans has the most impact on a project?
   A. Risk management plan
   B. Project management plan
   C. Stakeholder management plan
   D. Requirements management plan
2. The project manager did a stakeholder analysis after meeting with a stakeholder who just got promoted. In the new role, the stakeholder is now responsible for the project funding and a champion for the project. What stakeholder analysis classification BEST describes this stakeholder?
   A. Interest
   B. Contribution
   C. Knowledge
   D. Ownership
3. The project manager is frustrated with a stakeholder's participation. The project manager rated the stakeholder as resistant, yet for the project to succeed, the stakeholder must be supportive. The project manager and team have updated the stakeholder engagement plan to address this issue again. What tool or technique are they using to assess and track this issue?
   A. Conflict management
   B. Negotiation
   C. Expert judgment
   D. Engagement assessment matrix
4. The project manager just completed a power/influence grid on critical stakeholders. The project manager's analysis also identified one of the stakeholders has a significant influence on their peers. What BEST describes this influence?
   A. Impact
   B. Upward
   C. Sideward
   D. Downward

5. The project manager just reviewed the stakeholder engagement assessment matrix. The project manager has been meeting with a stakeholder to get the stakeholder more supportive of the project. But the stakeholder remains neutral. The meetings do not seem effective. What process is the project manager performing?
    A. Manage stakeholder engagement
    B. Plan stakeholder engagement
    C. Identify stakeholders
    D. Monitor stakeholder engagement

6. The sponsoring organization recently re-organized. The sponsor remains in the same role, but another key stakeholder has been replaced on the project. The gate review in two weeks will be seeking stakeholder approval to close the current phase and authorization to start the next phase. What process is triggered by these events?
    A. Plan stakeholder engagement
    B. Identify stakeholders
    C. Monitor stakeholder engagement
    D. Manage stakeholder engagement

7. The project's deliverables are critical to the success of the sponsoring organization. The organization's senior-most leader rarely attends project update meetings. But one time the project manager escalated an issue to the senior manager who quickly resolved it. What stakeholder mapping BEST describes this stakeholder?
    A. Impact/Influence
    B. Power/Interest
    C. Power/Influence
    D. Salience model

8. The project manager meets with a key stakeholder each Friday for coffee. They talk about a range of topics, including project progress. The project manager often describes or shows the latest product increment seeking the stakeholder's input. The stakeholder shares any organizational priority changes that may or will influence the project. Which following process BEST describes this discussion?
   A. Manage stakeholder engagement
   B. Plan stakeholder engagement
   C. Identify stakeholders
   D. Monitor stakeholder engagement

9. The deployment support organization has just changed vendors. The new vendor will provide this deployment service just before the project's deliverable is released. What should the project manager do?
   A. Manage stakeholder engagement
   B. Plan stakeholder engagement
   C. Identify stakeholders
   D. Monitor stakeholder engagement

10. The customer had many suggestions about the product increment during the sprint review. At one point during the review, the customer suggested the team engage a user experience subject matter expert. Afterward, during the sprint retrospective, the team decided they must perform what process?
    A. Identify stakeholders
    B. Plan stakeholder engagement
    C. Manage stakeholder engagement
    D. Monitor stakeholder engagement

11. A project manager just finished meeting with the second stakeholder identified in the project charter. Both stakeholders mentioned other people who will be influenced by the project. Where should the project manager log this information?
    A. Issue log
    B. Change log
    C. Project charter
    D. Stakeholder register

12. The project manager wants to assess key stakeholders based on their authority, how quickly the project team needs to respond to the stakeholder's needs, and how appropriate it is for their engagement on the project topic or knowledge area. What is the BEST assessment tool or technique?
    A. Impact/Influence
    B. Stakeholder cube
    C. Power/Influence
    D. Salience model

13. The project manager and team are meeting to determine how to assess stakeholders and ensure the stakeholders remain engaged throughout the project. What process is the team performing?
    A. Plan stakeholder engagement
    B. Identify stakeholders
    C. Monitor stakeholder engagement
    D. Manage stakeholder engagement

14. The project manager is struggling with a key stakeholder. The stakeholder is in a power struggle with the sponsor. The project manager must resolve this conflict for the success of the project, but none of the conflict management techniques have worked. What may the project manager try next?
    A. Expert judgment
    B. Meetings
    C. Negotiation
    D. Escalation

15. The project manager was presenting the project vision to stakeholders about the project vision. Each stakeholder committed their support to the project. What skill did the project manager demonstrate?
    A. Cultural awareness
    B. Leadership
    C. Networking
    D. Political awareness

Answers

1. C. Stakeholder management plan
   - The *PMBOK® Guide* does not specify one knowledge area that has a more significant impact than another on a project. The importance of many knowledge areas and those plans vary from project to project. For example, the importance of procurement management differs considerably from a project with no procurement needs compared to a project where all team members, deliverables, and services are out-sourced.
   - To answer this question, which knowledge area identifies and manages "resources" that impact or influence the project or are impacted or influenced by the project? Stakeholder management. Those "resources" are individual people or groups of people (i.e., organizations). Who determines which requirements are in scope? Stakeholders. Who defines the appropriate quality metrics? Stakeholders. Who approves funding? Stakeholders. Who…? Stakeholders. One must not understate the importance of identifying and managing stakeholder expectations on any project.
   - (*PMBOK® Guide – Sixth Edition*, page 504)

2. B. Contribution
   - The classification of a stakeholder who assigns funds, people, or other resources is Contribution. This role classification includes stakeholders who support the project objectives through words and actions across the organization. These stakeholders also protect the project team from frivolous interruptions and organizational politics. (*PMBOK® Guide – Sixth Edition*, page 512)

3. D. Engagement assessment matrix
   - The project team determines the necessary engagement level of each stakeholder. Then each stakeholder's current engagement level is assessed by the team as unaware, resistant, neutral, supportive, or leading. If the desired engagement level is not the stakeholder's current level of

engagement, the team creates a plan to align the stakeholder's engagement to the desired state for the success of the project. (PMBOK® Guide – Sixth Edition, page 522)

4. C. Sideward

- When stakeholders influence their peers, it is known as sideward influence. The other directions of influence are upward, downward, and outward. Each of these influences is about the project or product deliverables. For example, the procurement manager has an outward influence on sellers, while the project manager's influence is downward toward the project team. As the sponsor promotes the project objectives to senior leadership, that influence is known as upward. (*PMBOK® Guide – Sixth Edition*, page 513)

5. D. Monitor stakeholder engagement

- The Monitoring Stakeholder Engagement process assesses the efficiency and effectiveness of stakeholder engagement. What if the tools and techniques have not produced the expected results? For example, comparing the stakeholder's current engagement level (resistant) to their planned engagement level (supportive) results in work performance information. The efforts did not produce the expected results. Corrective actions such as asking a peer of the stakeholder to engage, applying different conflict techniques, etc. must be taken and then re-assessed. (*PMBOK® Guide – Sixth Edition*, page 530)

6. A. Plan stakeholder engagement

- The stakeholder engagement plan is updated throughout the project as stakeholders' roles change. Other triggers, like project phase start or completion (i.e., gate reviews), may result in a stakeholder's engagement changing from neutral to leading. Keep in mind Identify Stakeholders occurs before Plan Stakeholder Engagement. This sequence is unique compared to other knowledge areas. First, you must identify there is a new stakeholder, and then you plan how to maintain or change that stakeholder's engagement for the success of the project. (*PMBOK® Guide – Sixth Edition*, page 518)

7. C. Power/Influence
   - A stakeholder's role is a basis for their power or authority within the organization. In this case, the stakeholder is the "senior-most leader" in the organization. The question also states the quick resolution of an escalated issue. This implies the senior manager has a lot of influence or ability to make changes within the project or organization that impact outcomes. In a Power/Influence grid, this manager would be high in both power and influence. (*PMBOK® Guide – Sixth Edition*, page 512)

8. A. Manage stakeholder engagement
   - The project manager is communicating and working with a key stakeholder to ensure the project is meeting the stakeholder's needs and expectations. The outcome is increased stakeholder support for the project. The project manager is using feedback, negotiation, observation, conversation, and other tools and techniques to achieve or maintain this key stakeholder's engagement. (*PMBOK® Guide – Sixth Edition*, page 522)

9. C. Identify Stakeholders
   - Sellers are also known as contractors and vendors. This new deployment vendor will impact and influence the deployment of the project's deliverable. This change is an example were agreements with sellers are potential sources of new stakeholders. The project manager should perform the Identify Stakeholders process and ensure the new stakeholders are aware of the project's objectives. (*PMBOK® Guide – Sixth Edition*, page 510)

10. A. Identify stakeholders
    - The question indicates this is a Scrum Agile project. The sprint review is where the project team shares the latest product iteration (i.e., version) with the customer. The purpose of a sprint review is to get feedback from the customer. In this scenario, the customer identified another stakeholder for the team. During the sprint retrospective,

the team determines what improvements to make in the next sprint. The team recognizes the need to perform the Identify Stakeholder process to understand the influence or impact the user experience SME has on the project. (*PMBOK® Guide – Sixth Edition*, page 507)

11. D. Stakeholder register
    - The single source of information about each stakeholder is the stakeholder register. As such, the project manager references the stakeholder register throughout the project.
    - In addition to contact information, organizational role, etc. the register contains an assessment of the stakeholder's influence, impact, and support of the project. As a result, the project manager should maintain confidentiality about this information.
    - (*PMBOK® Guide – Sixth Edition*, page 514)

12. D. Salience model
    - The Salience model assesses stakeholders based on three components.
    - Power. The ability to influence outcomes.
    - Urgency. How quickly the team must respond to a stakeholder's needs or questions.
    - Legitimacy. Does the stakeholder represent the knowledge area or have expertise in the subject (e.g., typically a quality manager addressing quality issues has more legitimacy than a chief financial officer).
    - (*PMBOK® Guide – Sixth Edition*, page 513)

13. A. Plan stakeholder engagement
    - "The project manager and team are meeting to determine how…" indicates the team is planning. The team is not assessing or meeting with the stakeholders, which would imply they are performing other processes.
    - Be cautious about reading too much into an exam question. It is essential and expected on the exam that you will need to determine precisely wherein the process is the question before answering. One helpful way to assist in this

determination is to understand the purpose and key benefits of each process.

- (*PMBOK® Guide – Sixth Edition*, page 516)

14. A. Expert judgment
   - One may think of expert judgment to be limited to those with technical, process or procedural expertise. But expert judgment is very broad and includes soft skills too. In this case, an individual with deep knowledge of the organization's politics and culture is the best next approach. This person ideally would be a peer to both the key stakeholder and sponsor, understand the history, and well versed in conflict management. (*PMBOK® Guide – Sixth Edition*, page 526)

15. B. Leadership
   - A project manager must show strong leadership to convince the stakeholders of the project's vision and business value. (*PMBOK® Guide – Sixth Edition*, page 534)

OVERVIEW

This section contains additional questions and answers that cover all the previous chapters.

This study guide provides a primary page reference for each question. Often the terms, as in the rest of this book, are referenced many times within the PMBOK® Guide – Sixth Edition. Therefore, the student is encouraged to search the PMBOK® Guide – Sixth Edition for further understanding and context.

This search for further understanding also includes the following topics.

- It is easy to get lost by studying one process or knowledge area at a time in isolation. Don't forget all the processes are integrated and may be performed more than once during the project. Therefore, it is essential to understand the underlying flows. What process creates or produces the product, service, or result? Creates and publishes project communications? When does the project deliverables transition to operations? When does the project start? In each of these cases, there is only one answer. PMBOK® Guide – Sixth Edition, page 25, shows all the processes and knowledge areas.

- As with the processes and knowledge areas, once must know the flow data, information, and reports (i.e., outputs to inputs) across the processes. Which process group produces data? Which process group transforms that data into information? Which process group provides reports based on that information to drive decisions? PMBOK® Guide – Sixth Edition, page 27, shows this critical flow from work performance data to information to reports.

- What influences on a project reside outside of the project? These are classified as either enterprise environmental factors (EEFs) or organizational process assets (OPAs). Because of their influence, one or both are often inputs to many processes. EEFs and OPAs are two examples where you may learn them once and then use that knowledge often on the exam.. See the PMBOK® Guide – Sixth Edition, page 37, to start your understanding.

- The organization structure type has a significant influence on the project. Who has the authority to assign team members to project work? Will key team members be part-time or full-time? Do you work in a matrix organization? See the PMBOK® Guide – Sixth Edition, page 47, for an overview of the influence of the organization's structure on a project.

- Is a project manager a leader or manager? These are not synonymous terms. See the PMBOK® Guide – Sixth Edition, page 64, to understand the difference between leaders and managers.

- There's a lot of project documents! You should know which process produces, updates, and consumes each document. It would be necessary for you to understand the purpose of each document and the data or information contained in the document. For a single reference of all the documents, see the PMBOK® Guide – Sixth Edition, page 89.

- Is there math? Yes. You will be expected on the exam to calculate answers based on formulas. For example, you will need to be able to calculate how well the project is doing relative to the approved schedule and cost baselines. You will also need to interpret the results. Is the project ahead, on or behind schedule?

Another example is the To Complete Performance Index (TCPI). The calculation is a little complex. Therefore, while you should prepare for, you may not have to calculate it on an exam. However, you will need to understand that TCPI determines the cost performance that must be achieved for the remainder of the project to meet the cost baseline. Will the team be able to perform at that level? That is for you as the project manager and team to decide. For a single reference of all the formulas, see the PMBOK® Guide – Sixth Edition, page 267.

- What's the relationship between process groups? Where are most resources and time spent? Part 2 of the PMBOK® Guide – Sixth Edition, including page 541, provides a good summary of the entire standard.

- What changed from the previous editions? For example, a web site of exam prep questions asked: "what are the inputs to the Acquire Project Team process?" Yet I cannot find the Acquire Project Team process in the PMBOK® Guide – Sixth Edition. Why is that? Because in the sixth edition, Acquire Project Team became Acquire Resources. Appendix X1, the PMBOK® Guide – Sixth Edition, page 639, documents all the changes from the fifth edition.

- The PMBOK® Guide – Sixth Edition is influenced more by Agile than prior editions. The PMBOK® Guide – Sixth Edition, Appendix X3, page 665, covers predictive, iterative, incremental, and Agile project life-cycles. One should be knowledgeable about these different life-cycles.

- There is a lot of information to understand. The PMBOK® Guide – Sixth Edition, Appendix X4, page 673, may aid your understanding. This appendix provides a summary of key concepts for each knowledge area. You should test yourself on the information as it should be considered a basic understanding.

Keep in mind, don't let your organization's adherence to the PMBOK® Guide – Sixth Edition, or lack of, influence you on the exam. The exam is on the full standard. Being influenced by tailoring or lack of adherence in your organization will lead to incorrectly answering questions.

- The PMBOK® Guide – Sixth Edition, Appendix X5, page 679, provides some considerations if the team should tailor a knowledge area. It is not expected that everything must be applied to every project. That would result in inefficient projects. On the other hand, one must be cautious as improper tailoring will also lead to ineffective and inefficient projects.

- The PMBOK® Guide – Sixth Edition, Appendix X6, page 685, provides a list of process tools and techniques. There is a lot of them! This appendix provides insight to help you prepare a study approach. Some tools and techniques, expert judgment, etc. are used by many processes. Therefore, you can often learn these once and then that knowledge across all the processes. Other tools and techniques, histograms, etc. may only be used by one or two processes.

Questions

1. The project manager and project team will determine project costs by estimating in detail the cost of each activity component and aggregate or roll up the cost. Which of the following BEST describes this estimating approach?
   A. Parametric
   B. Analogous
   C. Bottom-up
   D. Top-down

2. Cost of Quality has two major components. Which component captures the cost of planning, inspection, and testing?
   A. Cost of non-conformance
   B. Cost of conformance
   C. Quality cost
   D. Testing cost

3. The Resource Management Plan process describes how to perform which of the following? (Mark ALL that apply)
   A. Staff acquisition
   B. Training
   C. Releasing staff
   D. Role

4. What technique must a project manager use to address challenges during the project due to the scarcity of resources, priorities, and time? Choose the BEST answer.
   A. Conflict management
   B. Planning
   C. Reserve analysis
   D. Communications

5. Analyzing root causes, reviewing the project charter, and conducting SWOT meetings are all done during which process? Choose the BEST answer.
   A. Qualitative Risk Management
   B. Quantitative Risk Management
   C. Identify Risks
   D. Plan Risk Management

6. The project team has determined that they want a contract where the seller is responsible for delivering all scope for a predetermined set price. What BEST describes this type of contract?
   A. Cost Plus Percentage of Cost
   B. Cost-Reimbursable
   C. Time and Material
   D. Fixed Price

7. Which one is NOT one of the triple-constraints?
   A. Cost
   B. Time
   C. Life-Cycle
   D. Scope

8. You are meeting with Alexa to ask for her help with another stakeholder. This stakeholder is a peer in the organization with Alexa. Alexa promises to meet with the stakeholder to persuade them to support the project. Alexa has provided funding for the project. What BEST describes Alexa's role?
   A. Project team member
   B. Customer
   C. Sponsor
   D. Business partner

9. A stakeholder asks the PM if a specific deliverable is in the WBS. The deliverable is NOT in the WBS. Therefore, the deliverable is:
   A. In-scope
   B. Out-of-Scope
   C. Maybe in-scope
   D. Maybe out-of-scope

10. Which of the following BEST describes costs that are in cost baseline, are approved, used to cover potential cost overruns, and controlled by the project manager?
    A. Contingency Reserve
    B. Management Reserve
    C. Padding
    D. Buffer

11. The project team develops a process map that shows the value from the source to the customer. What BEST describes a tool to facilitate this effort?.
    A. Flow chart
    B. Scatter diagram
    C. Fishbone
    D. Control chart

12. What is the BEST document a project manager may use to ensure everyone knows their role and responsibility?
    A. TCPI
    B. RACI
    C. Organization chart
    D. Resource chart
13. The project manager has decided to wait to see if the team can resolve a conflict. What type of conflict resolution approach is this?
    A. Smooth/Accommodate
    B. Withdrawal/Avoid
    C. Compromise/Reconcile
    D. Collaborate/Problem Solve
14. Effective communication is made up of which components? Choose the BEST answer.
    A. Nonverbal, body language
    B. Nonverbal, verbal
    C. Verbal, body language
    D. Verbal, paralingual
15. The project manager and project team identified a significant risk to user security. The team is unable to eliminate this risk. What BEST describes the options the team may pursue?
    A. Avoid
    B. Transfer
    C. Accept
    D. Mitigate
16. The project team has selected the seller. The project team is pleased with how flexible the seller is in regards to project scope changes. What BEST describes this type of contract?
    A. Cost Plus Award Fee
    B. Cost Plus Fixed Fee
    C. Time and Material
    D. Fixed Price
17. Select the BEST answer that defines a project.
    A. Temporary. Has defined begin and end dates and creates a unique product, service, or result
    B. On-going. Has defined begin and end dates and creates a unique product
    C. Temporary. Has defined begin and end dates and creates the same product
    D. On-going. Does not have defined begin and end dates and creates the same product

18. A stakeholder is an account payable clerk. They want to track shipping costs for each shipper so they can create only one invoice for each shipper at the end of the month. Write a user story in the proper format.

19. The project manager is using three-point estimating to determine the activity duration. The Pessimistic estimate is four (4) days, the Most Likely estimate is three (3) days, and the Optimistic estimate is two (2)days. What is the estimated Beta Distribution?
    A. 3.3
    B. 2.0
    C. 3.0
    D. 2.5

20. The total project budget or funding requirements consist of:
    A. Cost Baseline
    B. Cost Baseline + Management Reserve
    C. Cost Baseline + Contingency Reserve
    D. Management Reserve

21. Who is responsible for ensuring the development and training of team members while on the project team? Choose the BEST answer.
    A. Project manager
    B. Sponsor
    C. Team member
    D. Training manager

22. Whenever possible, which conflict resolution approach is BEST as it typically results in the best solution and addresses the root cause of the conflict?
    A. Smooth/Accommodate
    B. Withdrawal/Avoid
    C. Compromise/Reconcile
    D. Collaborate/Problem Solve

23. Interactive, push, and pull communications are all types of (choose the BEST answer)?
    A. Communication technologies
    B. Project communications
    C. Manage communications
    D. Communication methods

24. The project manager is concerned about the maintenance of the phone system expiring before being replaced. As a result, the PM purchases an extension of maintenance support. Buying extended maintenance is an example of which of the?
    A. Transfer
    B. Mitigation
    C. Acceptance
    D. Avoidance

25. The project team has entered into a contract with a seller to provide specific technical skills for an hourly rate. Embedded in the hourly rate is the buyer's profit. What BEST describes this type of contract?
    A. Cost Plus Percentage of Cost
    B. Cost-Reimbursement
    C. Time and Material
    D. Fixed Price

26. A project manager has struggled to get resources to focus on project activities. Instead, resources continue to be reassigned to work on process-related work. The project manager does not have the authority to reassign the resources to the project. What type of organizational structure is this?
    A. Strong Matrix
    B. Projectized
    C. Coordinator
    D. Functional

27. You have assumed the project manager role for an existing project. The project's objective is to replace a software system that has considerable technical debt. Which life-cycle would be the BEST to use on this project?
    A. Predictive or Waterfall
    B. Agile or Iterative
    C. DevOps
    D. Matrix

28. The Earned Value (EV) is three (3) days. The Planned Value (PV) is four (4) days. What is the schedule variance (SV)? Please write the formula AND calculate the answer.
    A. 4
    B. -1
    C. 1
    D. 3

29. Life cycle costing includes which costs?
    A. Deployment costs
    B. Design through testing costs
    C. Startup through testing costs
    D. Startup through operations and maintenance cost
30. Who is responsible for ensuring ALL project rewards and recognition are appropriate for individual team members and the team as a whole during the project? Choose the BEST answer.
    A. Sponsor
    B. Team lead
    C. Project Manager
    D. Functional Manager
31. The project team consists of the project manager, an architect, and two (2) developers. How many communication channels exist within this team? (Show formula AND answer)
    A. 3
    B. 4
    C. 2
    D. 6
32. Which process captures all the project's risks in the risk register?
    A. Plan Risk Management
    B. Plan Quality Management
    C. Identify Risks
    D. Identify Stakeholders
33. The PM is performing a process to assess how well the risk response plans mitigated known risks that have occurred on the project. What process describes what the PM is doing?
    A. Develop Risk Response Plans
    B. Identify Risks
    C. Risk Audit
    D. Quantitate Risk Management
34. The PM, project team, and procurement manager are determining the appropriate document to send to sellers. They want to get each seller's input as to how the seller would provide a solution for the specified requirements. What best describes the correct procurement document?
    A. Request for Information (RFI)
    B. Invitation for Bid (IFB)
    C. Request for Quote (RFQ)
    D. Request for Proposal (RFQ)

35. A project manager is working with a sponsor to evaluate projects for selection. Project A has an IRR of 30%; Project B has an IRR of 29%; Project C has an IRR of 25%; Project D has an IRR of 29%. Which project should the PM recommend if all other factors are considered equal?
    A. Project A
    B. Project B
    C. Project C
    D. Project D
36. Most project effort and cost occur in which phase?
    A. Planning
    B. Executing
    C. Initiating
    D. Closing
37. The project has a Schedule Performance Index of 0.97. Is the schedule?
    A. Ahead of schedule
    B. On Schedule
    C. Behind Schedule
    D. Cannot determine
38. A project activity's Actual Cost (AC) = $10,000); Planned Value (PV) = $10,000; Earned Value (EV) = $9,000. What is the Cost Variance and Cost Performance Index?
    A. -$1,000
    B. $8,000
    C. 0.9
    D. 1.1
39. Choose the BEST plan that defines specific actions to continuously improve the efficiency of project processes and the development of the project deliverable(s).
    A. Project Management Plan
    B. Quality Management Plan
    C. Process Improvement Plan
    D. Cost Management Plan
40. What describes a team that is spread across an office campus, geographical area, or works remotely. Choose the BEST answer.
    A. Stakeholders
    B. Virtual Team
    C. Infrastructure team
    D. Development team

41. The project manager has created work performance reports. The project manager is in the process of distributing the reports. The project manager is performing which process?
    A. Plan Communication Management
    B. Manage Communication
    C. Control Communication
    D. Manage Stakeholder Expectation

42. A risk that can be identified, analyzed, and proactively monitored that may have a contingency reserve is known as which of the following?
    A. Known Risk
    B. Unknown Risk
    C. Identified Risks
    D. Specific Risks

43. The PM and project team have identified an application outage as a risk to the project. The project team identified two potential causes of application outages. The server and the database. The application server is guaranteed to have a 90% uptime, and the database is also guaranteed to have a 90% uptime. What is the probability the application will be available?
    A. 95%
    B. 90%
    C. 72%
    D. 81%

44. The PM has not led previous projects where a seller was responsible for part of the scope. Therefore, the PM has engaged a Procurement Manager who will lead the negotiations on this project with the seller. Since a Procurement Manager is involved, the PM is no longer responsible for understanding the contract. Is this true?
    A. Yes. The project manager is not responsible for understanding the contract
    B. No. The project manager is still responsible for understanding the contract

45. The PM is identifying stakeholders during the Initiating phase of the project. What is the critical output created during this effort?
    A. Stakeholder Management Plan
    B. Project Management Plan
    C. Stakeholder Register
    D. Communication Management Plan

46. The sponsor asked you to lead the project as the team leader. The sponsor provided you with a draft of the project charter. Is the project started?
    A. Yes, with the sponsor selecting you as the project manager
    B. Yes, with the creation of the project charter
    C. No, not without assigning the team
    D. No, not until the signing of the project charter
47. Complete the forward and backward pass for the schedule network. Start with the Early Start value of one (1). What is the duration of this project?
    A. 14 days
    B. 13 days
    C. 12 days
    D. 11 days

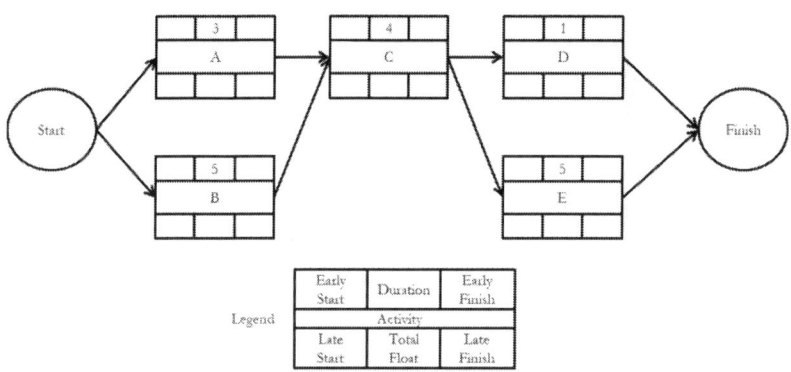

48. Using the schedule network, calculate the total float for Activity D.
    A. 0 days
    B. 1 day
    C. 2 days
    D. 3 days

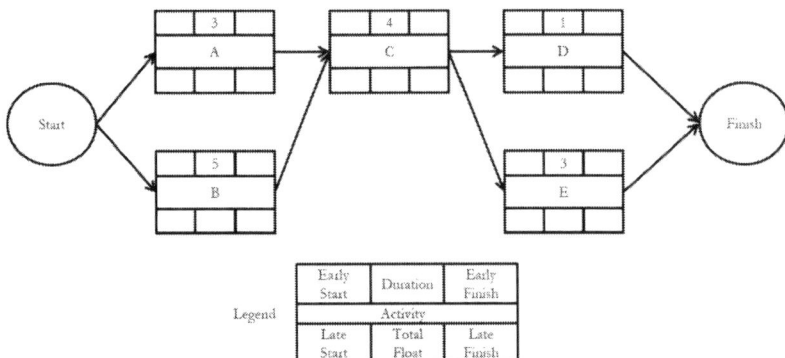

49. Using the schedule network, what is the Critical Path?
    A. Start, A, C, D, End
    B. Start, B, C, E, End
    C. Start A, C, E, End
    D. Start B, C, D, End

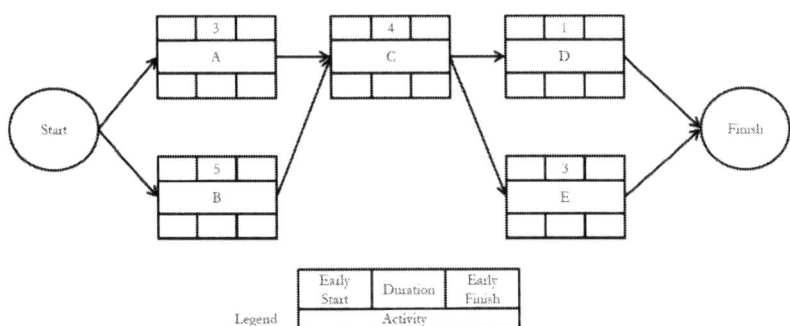

50. Using the schedule network, what is the duration of this project?
    A. 14 days
    B. 13 days
    C. 12 days
    D. 11 days

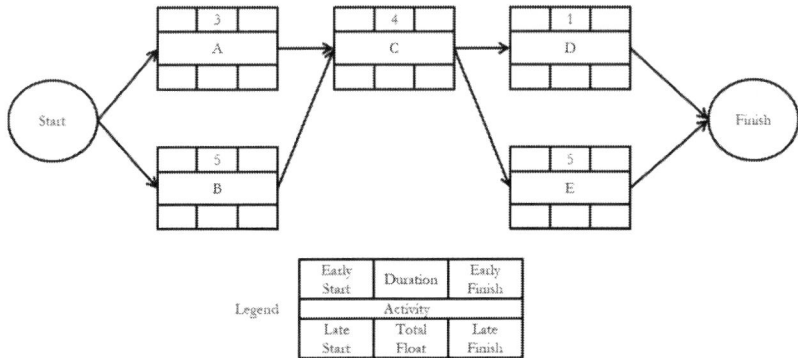

Legend

Early Start	Duration	Early Finish
	Activity	
Late Start	Total Float	Late Finish

51. A project activity's Actual Cost (AC) = $10,000; Planned Value (PV) = $10,000; Earned Value (EV) = $8,000. What is the Cost Performance Index (CPI), and is the project over or under budget?
    A. CPI = 0.8 and the project is under budget
    B. CPI = 0.8 and the project is over budget
    C. CPI = 1.25 and the project is under budget
    D. CPI = 1.25 and the project is over budget

52. Which stakeholder is ultimately accountable for the quality of the project?
    A. Project Manager
    B. Quality Manager
    C. Sponsor
    D. Quality Team Member

53. Mark ALL the potential challenges of a virtual team?
    A. Travel expenses
    B. Cultural
    C. Team-building
    D. Access to expertise

54. The project manager is reviewing specific organizational policies on how, where, and how long to retain seller contracts? What Organizational Process Assets BEST defines this policy?
    A. Plan Communication Management
    B. Document Retention Policy
    C. Project Communications
    D. Stakeholder Register

55. Which item should be on every meeting agenda? Choose the BEST answer.
    A. Project risk
    B. Project cost
    C. Project schedule
    D. Project scope

56. The PM and project team just completed just completed a document to be given to each potential. This document has described all the scope that the project team wants to have a seller provide and will be used by the seller to prepare their response. What BEST describes this document?
    A. WBS
    B. Procurement Management Plan
    C. Statement of Work (SOW)
    D. Contract

57. The project manager is executing Control Procurements. What is the BEST activity for the PM to perform?
    A. Approve change request
    B. Assess seller proposals
    C. Review deliverables and issue payment
    D. Assess seller contract terms & conditions performance

58. A stakeholder asks the project manager to add a requirement. The project manager confirmed the requirement is NOT in the Project Scope Statement. What process if the project manager performing?
    A. Control Scope
    B. Validate Scope
    C. Plan Scope Management
    D. Define Scope

59. The project team reported on the percent of work completed on each of their execution phase activities. This information is an example of which of the following?
    A. Work Performance Data
    B. Work Performance Information
    C. Work Performance Reports
    D. Status Reports

60. The PM has determined during Control Schedule that the project is behind schedule. The PM has evaluated several options and has decided to add additional developers. Choose the BEST description of this approach.
    A. Resource leveling
    B. Crashing
    C. Resource Adjustment
    D. Resource Addition

61. The project manager and team have re-estimated the remaining project spend to be $1,000,000. Actual Costs (AC) to date is $500,000. What is the Estimated-At-Completion (EAC)?
    A. $1,000,000
    B. $500,000
    C. $750,000
    D. $1,500,000

62. The project manager, along with the quality manager, is conducting an audit of the planned processes developed to ensure the achievement of the quality metrics. What process is performing this audit?
    A. Plan Quality Management
    B. Control Quality
    C. Manage Quality
    D. Identify Risks

63. What are two (2) significant outputs from the Acquire Resources process?
    A. Physical resource assignments
    B. Training plan
    C. Resource calendars
    D. Project Calendars

64. The project team includes the project manager, an architect, and two (2) developers. The project manager requests an additional developer who joins the team. How many MORE communications channels now exist?
    A. 4
    B. 10
    C. 6
    D. 8

65. As a project manager, you know there are several sources to help you and the team identify risks. Which one of the following BEST identifies an often overlooked area because it states uncertainty as a fact?
    A. Requirements
    B. Market Conditions
    C. Assumptions
    D. Cost

66. The PM and project team has received all the sellers' proposal responses. The team is now assessing those responses to determine which seller to choose. What BEST describes this process?
    A. Plan Procurement Management
    B. Conduct Procurements
    C. Perform Quantitative Risk Analysis
    D. Define Schedule

67. Four (4) sellers were involved in the project that is now finished. Choose the BEST answer.
    A. Perform Close Project or Phase once
    B. Perform Close Procurement once
    C. Perform Close Project or Phase for each seller and Close Project or Phase once for the project
    D. Perform Close Procurement and Close Project or Phase for each seller

68. What component is NOT part of the scope baseline?
    A. WBS
    B. Project Charter
    C. WBS Dictionary
    D. Project Scope Statement

69. The project team is reviewing an updated Risk Register template from a recently closed project. The team plans to modify this template for their needs. What BEST describes this template?
    A. Enterprise Environmental Factors
    B. Organizational Process Assets
    C. Expert Judgment
    D. Documentation

70. What BEST describes an approved realistic schedule?
    A. Time Management Plan
    B. Project Schedule
    C. Project Network Diagram
    D. Schedule baseline

71. The project manager wants to forecast the cost performance index (CPI) required to complete the remaining project work per the current forecasted budget. What formula or technique should the PM use?
    A. CPI
    B. CV
    C. EAC
    D. TCPI

72. A team member wants to gather data from the entire population. However, the customer's requirement called for collecting data from only a sample of the population. The project team decides to sample the population. The BEST reason for this decision?
    A. Takes too long
    B. Testing the population is a type of gold plating
    C. Testing the population results in more data than necessary
    D. Testing the population results in too many defects

73. What is the sequence of team-building stages?
    A. Forming, Norming, Storming, Performing, and Adjourning
    B. Storming, Norming, Forming, Performing, and Adjourning
    C. Forming, Storming, Performing, Norming, and Adjourning
    D. Forming, Storming, Norming, Performing, and Adjourning

74. The project manager is determining which communication technologies to use for project communications. Choose ALL the factors that the project manager must consider?
    A. Urgency
    B. Skype
    C. Ease of use
    D. Sensitivity and confidentiality

75. Which of the following documents tracks risks?
    A. Risk Management Plan
    B. Risk Register
    C. Issues Log
    D. Change Log

76. What must be required to be a legally binding contract?
    A. An offer, acceptance, consideration, legal capacity, and legal purpose
    B. An offer and acceptance
    C. An offer, acceptance, and consideration
    D. An offer, acceptance, consideration, and legal purpose

77. Which process approves changes?
    A. Perform Integrated Change Control
    B. Direct and Manage Project Work
    C. Validate Scope
    D. Monitor and Control Project Work

78. Which management plan defines ALL the project work?
    A. Stakeholder Management Plan
    B. Time Management Plan
    C. Project Management Plan
    D. Scope Management Plan

79. What is the project status if CPI is 0.95 and SPI is 1.0?
    A. Under budget and on schedule
    B. Over budget and behind schedule
    C. Over budget and ahead of schedule
    D. Over budget and on schedule

80. Which process has as one of its outputs "accepted deliverables"?
    A. Perform Quality Assurance
    B. Plan Quality Management
    C. Validate Scope
    D. Control Quality

81. During what stage is the "project team working well and working through issues efficiently and effectively"?
    A. Norming
    B. Forming
    C. Performing
    D. Adjourning

82. Who is primarily responsible for understanding communications? Choose the BEST answer.
    A. Sender
    B. Receiver

83. The team assesses threats, opportunities, strengths, and weaknesses using which tool or technique?
    A. SWOT
    B. Risk Register
    C. Risk Response Plan
    D. Risk Management Plan

84. The seller has not delivered a critical requirement. This significant default makes completing the project impossible. What BEST legally describes this event?
    A. Default
    B. Material Breach
    C. Termination
    D. Force Majeure

85. The project manager will be meeting with the customer to review the deliverables. What is the BEST approach to preparing for this meeting?
    A. Review WBS
    B. Review the Scope Statement
    C. Review Control Scope
    D. Review the Scope Baseline

86. The functional manager has informed the project manager that she does NOT have any engineers free till July. Which of the following describes this statement?
    A. Assumption
    B. Constraint
    C. Requirement
    D. Presupposition

87. To which of the following does the project scope statement provide unambiguous clarity? Choose the BEST answer.
    A. What is in-scope for the project
    B. What is out-of-scope for the project
    C. What is in-scope and out-of-scope for the project
    D. What is the scope management plan for the project

88. In a strong matrix organization structure, the project manager's authority is:
    A. Moderate to high
    B. High to almost total
    C. Low
    D. Little to none

89. The project manager has identified a stakeholder in a Power/Interest grid who has significant (high) power and a very high interest in the project. How BEST should the project manager manage and control this stakeholder?
    A. Manage closely
    B. Keep satisfied
    C. Monitor
    D. Keep informed

90. The project manager and project team are in the process of creating the project WBS. A tool or technique used to break the project down to a level of detail that can be estimated is BEST called?
    A. Project work
    B. Variance analysis
    C. Brainstorming
    D. Decomposing
91. The project has total costs of $10,000. Revenue from the project is $2,000 per year. What is the payback period?
    A. 10 years
    B. 2 years
    C. 5 years
    D. Need more information to determine
92. The sponsor suggests the project manager should add more developers. The project manager is aware of the Law of Diminishing Returns. The Law of Diminishing Returns states:
    A. The more resources, the more project work can be completed
    B. Never refuse an offer of more resources
    C. The output continues to diminish until the additional cost exceeds the benefit
    D. Any additional resources above the planned resources will result in less total work done
93. A project manager just reported the project had spent $1M (million) so far. The $1M is an example of (choose the BEST answer).
    A. Sunk costs
    B. Fixed costs
    C. Variable costs
    D. Direct costs
94. What tool or technique is a hierarchical view of all the project deliverables?
    A. WBS Dictionary
    B. Requirements Traceability Matrix
    C. Organization chart
    D. WBS
95. What is the approved version of the Project scope statement, WBS, and WBS Dictionary called?
    A. Scope baseline
    B. Schedule baseline
    C. Project baseline
    D. Project Management Plan

96. When should the Validate Scope process be executed?
    A. At the end of the phase or interim deliverable
    B. Middle of the project
    C. During planning
    D. End of the project
97. Which execution process produces the work and provides the overall management of all project work?
    A. Develop Project Management Plan
    B. Direct and Manage Project Work
    C. Control Scope
    D. Monitor and Control Project work
98. The project manager is beginning their first project. The project manager has worked on several projects before as a team member. They understand that *PMBOK® Guide – Sixth Edition* states it is permissible to tailor processes to the project needs. They begin immediately eliminating parts of the project charter template.
    A. Tailoring processes are important for the project to be a success
    B. Tailoring will allow the project to more effective and efficient
    C. Based on the skills acquired from the project manager's experience as a team member, they are ready to tailor
    D. The project manager should seek mentoring to acquire more skills before tailoring.
99. The sponsor shared that they expected the customer to change requirements throughout the project with the project manager. Which life cycle is BEST for this project?
    A. Predictive
    B. Interactive
    C. Agile
    D. Incremental
100. The quality manager is assessing the deliverable. The assessment will determine the degree of conformity to requirements. What BEST describes this assessment.
    A. Statistical sampling
    B. Variable sampling
    C. Attribute sampling
    D. Quality sampling

Answers

1. C. Bottom-up
   - Start with determining the individual activity costs in detail. Then use those costs to calculate the total or higher-level project costs. Calculating costs this way is known as bottom-up estimating.
   - The team may also use bottom-up estimating to estimate activity duration, Estimate At Completion (EAC), etc. in addition to costs.
   - (PMBOK® Guide – Sixth Edition, page 244)
2. B. Cost of conformance
   - The team must analyze the cost of conformance versus nonconformance to determine how much testing, training, inspection, etc. should be done.
   - One should not assume the project requires perfect quality. Often perfect or completely defect-free quality is too expensive due to the cost of conformance activities.
   - What is too expensive is determined by the customer's willingness to pay for conformance. As a process nears perfect compliance, the costs to achieve even higher levels of quality typically rise exponentially.
   - (PMBOK® Guide – Sixth Edition, page 283
3. All. A. Staff acquisition, B. Training, C. Releasing staff, and D. Role
   - The resource management plan is a critical document that describes how all resources will be acquired, their role on the project, if training is needed, and when the resources will be released. Managing and controlling resources is critical to ensuring the project delivers business value on time and within the estimated costs.
   - A project manager does not delay project activities due to delays in onboarding resources or incur additional costs by not releasing resources promptly. Resources include both people and equipment, software, licenses, etc.
   - (PMBOK® Guide – Sixth Edition, page 318)
4. A. Conflict management
   - The ability to successfully resolve conflicts is a critical project manager skill. Conflict often occurs on projects. Competing with other projects for essential people,

resources, budgets, team ground rules, roles, etc. are all sources of potential conflict.

- Successful project managers are very good at determining the importance, intensity, time constraints, and other factors that influence choosing the correct action to address each conflict in the context of the moment.
- (*PMBOK® Guide – Sixth Edition*, page 348)

5. C. Identify Risks

- The risk register is a key project document and an output of the Identify Risk process. The team draws from many sources to identify risks. These sources may include root cause analysis, reviewing documentation such as the project charter, assessing strengths, weaknesses, opportunities, and threats (SWOT), etc.. The project team is always looking to identify new risks. (*PMBOK® Guide – Sixth Edition*, page 415)

6. D. Fixed-price

- The seller is the party who will provide the deliverables(s), product, service, or result, per the terms and conditions of the contract. The buyer is the one who receives the deliverable. For fixed-price contracts, the seller is responsible for delivering the contract terms and conditions, including deliverables, for a fixed-price.
- The buyer must ensure all requirements are clearly defined upfront in the fixed-priced contract. Any discrepancy or additional requirements may result in the seller changing the price or other terms and conditions of the fixed-price contract.
- (*PMBOK® Guide – Sixth Edition*, page 471)

7. C. Life-cycle

- Cost, time (schedule), and scope are the triple constraints. If one of these constraints changes, at least one or both of the other two constraints also change.
- For example, "speed costs money" is a common phrase. If a project manager wants to crash a project schedule, adding more resources will increase the cost. In this example, reducing the time constraint results in needing to increase the cost constraint.
- It is vital to remember that cost, time, and scope constraints exist on every project within the PMBOK® Guide – Sixth Edition and the exam. These limit the project. There is "no extra" time or cost nor an undefined

scope. If there was, this would indicate poor project management practices.

- See the Performance measurement baseline. (*PMBOK® Guide – Sixth Edition*, page 88)

8. C. Sponsor
   - All people or groups who may influence, or may be influenced by the project are stakeholders. Alexa is a specific type of stakeholder. The project sponsor.
   - The project's sponsor provides resources, including funding. The sponsor may be the highest organizational person on the project. The project sponsor is accountable for the project's organizational success.
   - (*PMBOK® Guide – Sixth Edition*, page 723)

9. B. Out-of-scope
   - The Work Breakdown Structure (WBS) is a hierarchical view of all the project's work, including project reporting updates, interim deliverables, testing, documents, etc. By definition, then if a project deliverable, or work, is not in the WBS, it is out-of-scope for the project.
   - The WBS dictionary provides additional detail, or clarification, on WBS items. The WBS, WBS dictionary, and other components are part of the scope baseline.
   - (*PMBOK® Guide – Sixth Edition*, page 157)

10. A. Contingency reserves
    - May be either additional funding included in the cost baseline or extra time included in the schedule baseline. After estimating both project cost and schedule, the team may add a contingency reserve to the baselines for known-unknown risks.
    - Using the contingency reserve is at the discretion of the project manager. Not the project team or management.
    - (*PMBOK® Guide – Sixth Edition*, page 245)

11. A. Flowchart
    - A flow chart shows the process or steps, including decision points, that lead to increased customer value. This technique may be called value stream mapping. A SIPOC (Suppliers, Inputs, Process, Outputs, Customers) is one type of flow chart used to assess a value stream. (*PMBOK® Guide – Sixth Edition*, page 284)

12. B. RACI
- A Responsible, Accountable, Consult, and Inform (RACI) matrix is useful to define and communicate individual roles and responsibilities. In turn, all stakeholders can understand everyone's role and responsibilities.
- It may not be straightforward to understand the difference between accountable and responsible. An accountable person must justify decisions while a responsible person has control over completing work.
- For example, an electrician is responsible for completing the building wiring according to code. The construction project manager is accountable for the electrical, plus all other work, per the project performance baseline. The project manager is the one who will have to justify to the customer any decisions that led to any differences between the expected project performance baseline and actual results. Therefore, in this example, the project manager is accountable and must answer to the customer. While the electrician is responsible for the electrical work.
- (PMBOK® Guide – Sixth Edition, page 317)

13. B. Withdrawal/Avoid
- Each of the answers is a valid approach to conflict management. The project manager must choose the best approach for the unique characteristics of each situation. The project manager's ability to manage conflict will either improve or degrade the team's performance.
- The question describes the withdrawal or avoid conflict management technique. It is important to note that withdrawal from conflict is most likely not a long term solution. Often the original issue that caused the conflict remains and will cause conflict again. Therefore, the project manager may need to follow up with a different conflict management technique later to completely address the original issue that caused the conflict.
- (PMBOK® Guide – Sixth Edition, page 348)

14. B. Nonverbal, verbal
- Effective communications contain many components. Often those components are classified as either verbal or nonverbal.
- On the exam, it is often best to choose the broader of the provided terms. For example, nonverbal includes body language but also actions. Verbal includes paralingual

(pitch, tone, tempo, etc.) but also the words that were chosen by the speaker
- (*PMBOK® Guide – Sixth Edition*, page 361)

15. D. Mitigate
- The team may not be able to avoid some risks. This inability may be due to limited time, influence, availability of experts, costs, etc.
- Often the next best strategy is to mitigate the risk. What can the team do to reduce the probability of occurrence or the impact of a negative risk? Or both?
- The question indicates the team is addressing a negative risk. If on the exam, a risk strategy for positive risks was an answer, it may be appropriate to eliminate that answer from possible answers. Keep in mind the accept risk strategy applies to both negative and positive risks.
- (*PMBOK® Guide – Sixth Edition*, page 443)

16. C. Time and Materials
- Time and material (T&M or TM) contracts consist of two basic parts. Time, where the seller is typically paid a fixed fee or price for each hour worked. This fixed fee component includes profit. The second component is material where the buyer reimburses the seller for expenses (e.g., travel, licenses, etc.).
- The seller's profit is included in the fixed fee for hours worked. The seller's profit is not contingent on working efficiently or even producing deliverables.
- Since profit is assured, sellers are typically very receptive to scope changes. Even if the work completed is discarded, the seller receives payment for all hours worked and expenses incurred. The burden is on the buyer to manage scope creep and cost increases to ensure project deliverables produce business value efficiently without budget overruns.
- Not to exceed and other variations of T&M contracts may be used to incent the seller to work efficiently. These types of T&M contracts are preferred, especially for Agile projects.
- (*PMBOK® Guide – Sixth Edition*, pages 78, 471)

17. A. Temporary; has defined start and end dates; and creates a unique product, service or result
- The answer is the basic definition of a project. However, one must apply some judgment to this definition.

- Temporary does not mean quickly completed. Likewise, differences between similar products, services, or results may be enough for them to be considered unique. For example, consider building two power plants. Each power plant will take years to build even though both leverage a similar design. Building each power plant would be separate projects as each is a temporary endeavor and unique based on local approval and environmental requirements, different stakeholders, etc.
- (*PMBOK® Guide – Sixth Edition*, page 542)

18. "As an accounts payable clerk, I want shipping costs tracked by each shipper, so that there is a single payment to the shipper at the end of the payment period."
    - The answer is in a standard user story format, "As an [role], I want [describe requirement] so that [business value]. User stories are used in Agile to capture requirements. The product owner prioritizes those requirements in the product backlog.
    - When the development team is ready to begin to work on the requirement, further elaboration of the story will occur. In this case, with the accounts payable clerk and the development team to further define the requirement. The development team will then implement the solution during a sprint.
    - (*PMBOK® Guide – Sixth Edition*, page 155)

19. D. 2.5 *C 3·0*
    - The beta distribution formula is (Optimistic Estimate + 4*Most Likely Estimate +Pessimistic Estimate)/6.
    - $(1 + 4*2 + 6)/6 = 2.5$
    - (*PMBOK® Guide – Sixth Edition*, page 245)

20. B. Cost Baseline + Management Reserve
    - Total product funding includes the cost baseline plus the management reserve. The management reserve is determined and controlled by the sponsor and other management leaders – not the project manager.
    - The purpose of the management reserve is to fund unforeseen risks to the project. These are unknown-unknowns risks. Spend management reserve requires change control.
    - The cost baseline includes the contingency reserve and work package cost estimates.

- (*PMBOK® Guide – Sixth Edition*, page 255)

21. A. Project manager
    - Project managers are responsible for ensuring training is available for each team member. When done correctly, development and training will lead to a team whose measurable effectiveness and efficiency grows throughout the project. The team will be producing more with less effort.
    - Personal growth opportunities for team members will also lead to a current team member's willingness to work on future projects led by the project manager.
    - (*PMBOK® Guide – Sixth Edition*, page 342)

22. D. Collaborate/Problem Solve
    - Conflicts frequently occur on a project. The key to choosing the best answer is in the question. "Whenever possible." If there are sufficient time and resources, applying the collaborate/problem-solve technique engages all members to solve the root cause of the conflict. This technique will lead to long term resolution.
    - All conflict resolution techniques are valid. One must choose the appropriate technique for each given situation. Sometimes this may mean selecting more than one technique to resolve the conflict entirely. For example, one may use the avoid technique to address an immediate issue. Then later following up, if necessary, with a different technique to ensure long term resolution.
    - (*PMBOK® Guide – Sixth Edition*, page 349

23. D. Communication methods
    - The project manager must choose the appropriate communication method. The project may push critical information to stakeholders. Less time-critical or large amounts of information may be posted to a site for stakeholders to pull as desired. All projects, indeed Agile projects, embrace frequent real-time interactive communications between the customer and the development team.
    - For the exam, know that instant messaging, texting, and some forms of social media may be considered interactive communication tools. It is important to remember, however, that acknowledging receipt of a message is an important component of communication. And the sender may not receive confirmation the receiver read the instant

message in real-time. Nor confirmation the receive understood the instant message in real-time.

- This understanding can make for a difficult exam question. When in doubt, default to the textbook answer. In this case, the PMBOK® Guide – Sixth Edition lists instant messaging, texting, and some forms of social media as interactive communications. Don't overthink or let your experience bias your answer as to whether or not the receiver may have read the instant messages in real-time or not.

- Face to Face (F2F) interactive communication is always the best choice if possible. F2F includes video conferencing.

- (*PMBOK® Guide – Sixth Edition*, page 443)

24. A. Transfer

- Insurance is a common method to transfer risk from one party to another. For a set fee, the insurance premium, the buyer purchases an insurance contract from the seller. The seller then accepts responsibility if an event occurs to reimburse the buyer the agreed-to amount. You transfer risk when you purchase accident and liability car, home or renter's insurance. Extended warranty or maintenance agreements are also forms of insurance that for fee transfer the risk of mechanical breakdown to the insurer (seller).

- The transfer risk strategy may include actions the buyer must take to impact the probability of occurrence or impact. For example, how far you drive to work influences the probability of occurrence or impact regarding auto accidents. Reducing the distance driven (mitigate), or by taking public transportation (avoid), typically reduces the transfer costs (insurance premium). Don't overthink these types of questions on an exam. The best answer, given the information provided to this question, is the transfer risk strategy.

- (*PMBOK® Guide – Sixth Edition*, page 443)

25. C. Time and Material

- The information in the question defines a Time and Material (T&M, TM) contract. T&M contracts are a blending of two contract types. Fixed Price (FP) and Cost Reimbursable (CR). The FP component is the hourly rate, which is a fixed amount. The CR component is the buyer must reimburse the seller for all expenses (materials) purchased to fulfill the contract.

- (*PMBOK® Guide – Sixth Edition*, page 472)
26. D. Functional
    - Organization structure plays a significant role in project accountability and responsibilities. The key point of the question is, "The project manager does not have the authority to re-assign the resources…" In a functional organization, the functional manager determines who within the functional area works on what assignments. These assignments include which functional team members work on a project. (*PMBOK® Guide – Sixth Edition*, page 47)
27. A. Predictive or Waterfall
    - Technical debt occurs on projects when past decisions impact the ability to efficiently and effectively make future decisions and changes. For example, consider a prior decision to support all previous cell phone operating system versions. Updating those earlier versions to new security and market features would have a tremendous impact on deployment velocity. If technical debt is too high, it may be very costly in both time and resources to make changes. Hence why companies often announce that a prior version or versions are no longer supported.
    - Often when replacing existing systems with high technical debt, the new system must implement many of the current expected market features. For example, today, financial sites often require two-step user authentication. This authentication requires the user to enter their credentials (user name and password) and then enter a code texted to their registered phone to log on. Any new financial site today must, on the first day, provide this same level of security.
    - Meeting this expectation may best be done using a predictive or waterfall approach. Because of the market expectations, a project team will most likely not be able to provide two-step authentication across many sprints incrementally using Agile. It would not be acceptable first to deploy basic password authentication. Then deploy on-line password resetting in the next sprint. And finally, deploy two-step authentication in a future sprint. Agile projects with long release cycles may be better suited for a waterfall approach.
    - (*PMBOK® Guide – Sixth Edition*, pages 19, 74)

28. B. -1
   - Calculate the Schedule Variance (SV) by subtracting Earned Value (EV) from Planned Value (PV). If the team only completed three days of work when the team planned on completing four days, is the team ahead or behind schedule? Behind. The team completed less work than planned during the period. SV = EV − PV (-1 = 3 − 4).
   - SV is for a given period. Note that the question did not state the period. The period could have been hours, days, weeks, months, or the entire project duration. It does not matter. However, the period must be the same for both EV and PV values. On an exam, unless otherwise stated, you may assume the period is the same for EV and PV values.
   - (PMBOK® Guide – Sixth Edition, page 262)

29. D. Startup through operations and maintenance costs
   - Life cycle costs include all costs over the entire life of the product, service, or result. These costs include not only the costs incurred during the project but costs after the project.
   - These post-project life cycle costs include ongoing maintenance, support, license, product retirement, and other costs. The post-project life cycle costs may exceed the total original project costs. In some cases, many times over the original project cost. Therefore, life cycle costs may be a critical decision criterion.
   - (PMBOK® Guide – Sixth Edition, page 293)

30. C. Project Manager
   - An essential tool and technique used during the Develop Team process is recognition and rewards. The project manager is responsible for ensuring a recognition plan is in place for all project team members.
   - What is considered a valued reward differs for each team member. For example, some team members may want formal recognition in front of a large audience. Other team members would find this embarrassing. Successful project managers ensure the team member being recognized values the reward.
   - (PMBOK® Guide – Sixth Edition, page 341)

31. D. 6
   - The formula for calculating communication channels is N(N-1)/2. There are four team members (project manager, architecture, and two developers). 4(4-1)/2 = 6.

- Project managers need to understand the larger the project team or number of stakeholders, the more challenging the communication planning. It is not a linear relationship. The communication channels formula mathematically validates this concept. Adding one more team member, in this case, increases the communication channels from six to ten. $5(5-1)/2 = 10$.
- This non-linear relationship is one reason the recommendation for Agile teams is between three and nine members. See the Scrum Guide (https://www.scrumguides.org).
- (*PMBOK® Guide – Sixth Edition*, page 370)

32. C. Identify Risks
    - This question is an excellent example of using the elimination technique on multiple-choice exams. The key phrase in the question is, "Which process captures…"
    - Plan Risk Management. Creates a plan for the project to identify, assess, manage, and control risks. The output is a plan. While a plan to capture, evaluate, and address risks the output of this process, no risks are captured during this process. Therefore, eliminate this answer.
    - Plan Quality Management. The process creates a plan for quality activities on the project. Not directly related to risk management. Therefore, eliminate this answer.
    - Identify Stakeholders. This process identifies and captures information about all stakeholders. A key output is the stakeholder register. Stakeholders, anyone who influences or is impacted by the project, are a primary source to identify risks. However, if a stakeholder mentions a risk during the Identify Stakeholders process, the project team switches to the Identify Risks process to capture that risk. After recording the risk, the project team, in this case, returns to performing the Identify Stakeholder process. It is essential to understand the project manager and team do not perform any process in isolation. Instead, they may switch from one process to another. Or return to previously completed or partially completed processes. Identify Stakeholders does not capture risks, therefore eliminate this answer.
    - Identify Risks. A key Identify Risks process output is the risk register. Only risks documented in the risk register are "identified." The team then assesses, applies a risk strategy,

develops a risk response plan, assigns a risk owner, etc. to those risks.

- Eliminating known incorrect answers is a valuable multiple-choice exam technique. If you are unsure of the question's answer, try eliminating one or more provided answers. Then choose the remaining answer, or choose from the remaining answers, to improve your chance of selecting the correct answer.
- (*PMBOK® Guide – Sixth Edition*, page 409)

33. C. Risk Audit
   - The project manager is assessing the effectiveness and efficiency of the risk response plans. An audit is an inspection to determine if a plan or process produces the expected outcome.

   - In other words, an audit determines if the plan or process was effective and efficient in producing the expected result. In this case, did the risk response plans effectively and efficiently implement the risk strategy and address the risk as planned?

   - (*PMBOK® Guide – Sixth Edition*, page 456)

34. C. Request for Quote (RFQ)
   - This question is the definition of RFQ. The buyer is asking the seller to propose how to implement the requested product, service, or result. The seller will also provide a quote to implement the seller's proposal.

   - In this case, while the requirements are defined, the requirements are not defined to the point where no options are available for the seller to propose alternatives. The seller is free to choose the best solution with the most attractive cost to secure the business.

   - (*PMBOK® Guide – Sixth Edition*, page 477)

35. B. Project A
   - Choose the project or decision with the greatest IRR.
   - Calculating IRR may be considered too difficult for inclusion in most exams. However, knowing which project or decision should be chosen based on IRR is expected of project managers. This type of question may be on the exam.

- Do not overthink these types of exam questions. In "the real world," multiple decision criteria are often considered. For example. Will this project be done to meet regulatory requirements? If so, the organization needs to do the project, perhaps without regard to an IRR assessment. Is the payback period critical? If so, IRR may not have a strong influence on the decision.
- The question does not imply nor states the need for any other decision criteria. Therefore, you should not "expand" the question by considering other decision analysis techniques when answering this question.
- (PMBOK® Guide – Sixth Edition, pages 34, 473)

36. B. Executing
    - Most time and costs occur while performing the processes in the Executing Process Group.
    - Did you choose the planning phase? Considering the number of processes in the planning process group, this is a common misunderstanding. Another possible misconception is the team spends a majority of their time planning to minimize time and cost during execution.
    - (PMBOK® Guide – Sixth Edition, pages 25, 555)

37. C. Behind Schedule
    - Schedule Performance Index (SPI) of less than 1.0 indicates the project is behind schedule. The project earned less Earned Value (EV) during the period based on Planned Value (PV).
    - For example, the project manager asked a team member after five days of working on an activity if they completed the activity. The activity was to take five days (PV) to complete. The team member said they needed one more day to complete the activity. In other words, the team member only earned four days of value (EV). The SPI = 0.8 ($4/5 = 0.8$). The team member is behind schedule.
    - SPI determines schedule efficiency and may be used to predict future project performance. If the project manager expects past events, that led to an SPI of 0.97 to continue, the project manager can forecast when the project schedule will complete. For example, if one-hundred (100) workdays

remain and the SPI = 0.97, it will take one-hundred and three (103) days to complete (100 / 0.97 = 103). SPI = EV / PV.

- You should expect to be able to calculate SPI and other performance measurements on exams.
- (PMBOK® Guide – Sixth Edition, page 267)

38. A -$1,000

- CV = EV – AC. -$1,000 USD = $9,000 USD - $10,000.

- It is essential to understand to use Actual Cost (AC) to calculate Cost Variance (CV) instead of Planned Value (PV). The reason is why would a project manager use a planned cost value when actual costs are known. They would not.

- Earned Value (EV) costs equals Planned Value (PV) costs at the beginning of the project. A project manager would not start a project that has a negative cost variance. Remember, unless stated, exam questions assume a well-run project. Would you start a project without enough funding to complete? No.

- EV cost remains the same throughout the project unless the project manager determines that re-estimating must occur.

- For example, the team estimated a project activity cost to be $1,000. This $1,000 is the PV and EV at the start of the project. However, the activity cost $1,500 (Actual Cost) to complete. The cost variance is -$500 ($1,000 USD - $1,500). The project is over budget.

- (PMBOK® Guide – Sixth Edition, pages 263, 267

39. B. Quality Management Plan

- Continuous improvement planning is part of the quality management plan. The project manager is accountable for improving the effectiveness and efficiency of the team's process execution and production of deliverables throughout the entire project. Doing so may reduce spending, if over budget, to perhaps enough to return the project to within the cost baseline or to return excess funding to the organization. Likewise, improvements may return the schedule, if behind, to the schedule baseline or return resources back to the organization sooner to work on other initiatives.

- In prior editions of the *PMBOK Guide* defined, process improvements in the Process Improvement Plan. The sixth edition no longer specifies this plan. This change is a good reminder that it is essential to validate exam preparation materials to ensure the content is current.
- (*PMBOK® Guide – Sixth Edition*, page 286)

40. B. Virtual Team
- Also known as distributed or remote teams. These terms apply to any team that does not sit close together in the same work area.
- Cultural differences, time zone differences, and efficiently and effectively communicating amongst team members are some of the challenges of virtual teams. Research has proven that project teams, even located on different floors within the same building, demonstrate characteristics of a virtual team.
- The benefits of virtual teams include access to subject matter experts anywhere in the world. Plus, virtual teams may enable the "follow the sun" technique as team members in different time zones end and begin their workday. This technique allows for a sustainable method to work around the clock on project deliverables.
- Colocation is when the team works physically next to each other. This arrangement facilitates collaboration and communication. Real-time face-to-face (F2F) communication is best if at all possible. F2F communication is a principle of Agile.
- Today's globally sourced projects may not be able to collocate the entire team. In these cases, the project manager must leverage different communication technologies, like video conferencing, to minimize the challenges of virtual teams.
- (*PMBOK® Guide – Sixth Edition*, page 311)

41. B. Manage Communications
- Work performance reports are a crucial input to the Manage Communications process. A key output of Manage

Communications is project communications. Project communication is a general term for all project communications.

- The student should prepare for exam questions that require knowledge of process inputs and outputs. This question incorporates some key concepts. Know the difference between work performance data, information, and reports. Know process flows, including basic ones like "What process publishes communications to stakeholders?" "What inputs are required by this process?" "What process produces these reports?"
- (*PMBOK® Guide – Sixth Edition*, page 382)

42. A. Known risk

- This question defines known risks. A contingency reserve for cost or time is determined when implementing risk strategies for known risks. Cost and schedule baselines include the contingency reserve, which the project manager controls.
- There other risks that may not be known to the project team (e.g., a competitor entering the project's targeted market, etc.). These are unknown risks. The result is the project team is unable to determine an effective risk strategy and risk response plan. Management may create a management reserve, which is in addition to the cost or schedule baseline, to address unknown risks. The sponsor or other organizational leaders control the management reserve.
- (*PMBOK® Guide – Sixth Edition*, page 399)

43. D. 81%

- Correctly assessing a risk's probability of occurrence is critical. In this example, there are two components, the server, and the database. Each component has a ninety percent availability. Both must be available for the web site to work.
- Incorrectly assessing the risk would conclude that since each component is ninety percent available, then the web site would also be accessible ninety percent of the time. That is incorrect. One cannot assume both the server and database unavailability occurs precisely at the same time every time. One may be unavailable, while the other remains available.

- To determine the probability that one or both are unavailable, you must use the concept of rolling throughput. To calculate rolling throughput, multiply together the probability of occurrence of each component. In this case 90% (0.9 * 0.9 = .81 or 81%). So the probability of both the server and database, the web site, will be available is 81%.
- The impact is the other component of assessing risk. Assessing both the probability of occurrence and impact occurs during Perform Qualitative Risk Analysis. Based on the availability of data, calculating rolling throughout may also be done during the Perform Quantitative Risk Analysis.
- (*PMBOK® Guide – Sixth Edition*, page 423)

44. B. No. The project manager is still responsible for understanding the contract
    - The procurement manager typically negotiates several contracts with various sellers across multiple projects. Therefore, it is not expected the procurement manager knows the specific requirements of each project.
    - Therefore, the project manager must ensure the expected scope of both the product and project, to be delivered by the seller, are included in the contract. Product scope is those requirements that are either part of or directly support, the product, service, or result. For example, a cell phone camera specifications, the phone's packaging material, etc. would be considered product requirements. Required status reporting frequency and format, requiring seller employees to be on-site, expenses covered, etc. would all be considered project requirements.
    - (*PMBOK® Guide – Sixth Edition*, page 461)

45. C. Stakeholder register
    - Each stakeholder, or stakeholder group, must be identified in the stakeholder register. Documenting stakeholders in the stakeholder register begins during the Identify Stakeholders process. While the project manager and team must identify all stakeholders early, stakeholders may change or new ones found throughout the project.
    - The impact of new stakeholders during a project may be significant, including the new sponsor considerably less support of the project than the original sponsor. Perhaps to the point of canceling the project.

- The stakeholder register also documents stakeholder support, which may vary, during the project. The project manager should be implementing activities throughout the project to achieve or maintain stakeholder support of the project. The result of the efforts will also result in updating the stakeholder register.
- Many processes update the stakeholder register. The influence of each process on the stakeholder registration should be understood.
- *(PMBOK® Guide – Sixth Edition*, page 507)

46. D. No, not until the signing of the project charter
    - The signing of the project charter authorizes the project manager to apply the organization's people, funding, and other resources to the project. This authorization is the start of the project.
    - It is essential to understand all significant activities and milestones within the PMBOK® Guide. It is easy to "get lost."
    - For example, the Develop Project Charter process is part of the Initiating phase along with Identify Stakeholders. Since both these processes are like all the other processes, it may appear the project has started. Besides, the project manager may begin working during the Initiating phase, along with some team members. However, the project has not yet started.
    - The people, funding, etc. engaged before the signing of the project charter are typically minimal compared to the project itself. These minimal resources focus only on preparing and assessing the project charter and may or may not continue on the project if the charter is approved.
    - *(PMBOK® Guide – Sixth Edition*, page 76)

47.

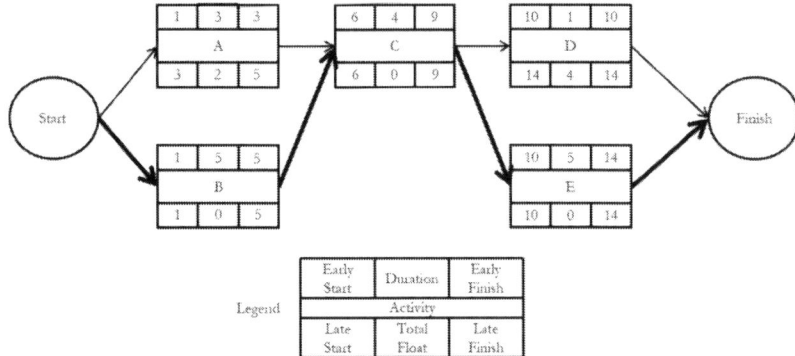

- This schedule network is assumed to be in units of days. That is not necessary. You may have a schedule network that is in hours, weeks, months or any other period that is appropriate for the project. Regardless of the period, the performing of the forward or backward pass is the same.
- A forward pass is from the Start to the Finish of the schedule network. Starting with one (1) as the starting day, you "pass" or calculate from Start to Finish.
- It may be easier for you to think of each day starting in the morning when you arrive at work. The beginning of each day is the Early Start (ES) date or time. When you leave later that day, that is the Early Finish (EF) date or time. So you arrive in the morning, work all day, and then leave to go home. The result is you worked one (1) day or duration.
- Activity A has a duration of three (3) days. It takes three days, starting the morning of day one (1) and working until the end of day three (3) to complete Activity A. The ES is one (1), and the EF is three (3). If you prefer a formula to calculate it is ES + Duration − 1 = EF. It is essential to understand you don't just add ES and duration. That would incorrectly calculate EF as four (4) days.
- Activity B has a duration of five (5) days. Since Activity B starts at the same time as Activity A, the ES for Activity B is one (1). Calculate EF for Activity B the same as was done for Activity A. (ES + Duration -1 = EF, 1 + 5 − 1 = 5)
- Activity C has a duration of four (4) days. When can Activity C start? Not until the completion of predecessor

activity or activities with the largest EF. In this case, that is Activity B (EF = 5 days). Since Activity B EF is five (5), the ES for Activity C is six (6). You then calculate EF for Activity C the same as before.

- Activities D and E. When can these activities start? After Activity C EF. This constraint results in the ES for both Activity D and Activity E to be ten (10) days. You then calculate EF for Activities D and E the same as before.

- How many days will it take to complete the project? Fourteen (14). Fourteen days is the earliest Activity E will finish.

- The backward pass begins with the Finish of the project and works back to the Start. How late can the project finish? The activity with the largest Early Finish (EF) determines when the project ends. This project will finish fourteen (14) days after starting. The EF of Activity E. If the project was to finish any later, then EF is not accurate. Set the Late Finish (LF) to the largest EF of the last activity or activities. In this case, set LF to fourteen (14) days for both Activity D and E.

- Activity E has a duration of five (5) days. What is the Late Start (LS) day? Take the LF – Duration + 1 = LS. (14 – 5 + 1 = 10). Activity E must start no later than the tenth (10) day, or it will not complete by the fourteenth (14) day.

- Activity D has a duration of one (1) day. The LF of Activity D must be no later in this case as Activity E. Therefore set Activity D LF to fourteen (14) days. How late can Activity D start? Remember, the team can work until the end of the fourteen (14) day of the project. The LF of Activity D. The team could start at the beginning of the fourteenth (14) day and finish by the end of the day since Activity D duration is one (1) day. Therefore, the Late Start for Activity D fourteen (14). The team may start on the tenth (10) ES day or wait until the fourteen (14) LS date and still finish Activity D on time. (LF – Duration + 1 = LS. (14 - 1 + 1 = 14)

- Activity C must finish by the ninth (9) day. Otherwise, Activity E will not start in time for the project to finish by the fourteenth (14) day. This constraint makes the LS for Activity E day six (6). (LF – Duration + 1 = LS. (9 – 4 + 1 = 6)

- Activity A and B. Since Activity C has an LS of day six (6). Therefore, both Activity A and B must have an LF of five (5). Using LF – Duration + 1 = LS formula, you can calculate the LS for Activity A and B.
- The critical path is Start-B-C-E-Finish. The critical path is the longest path with the shortest duration. This definition can be confusing but must be understood. What is the longest path? The critical path, which in this case is Start-B-C-E-Finish. What is the shortest duration to complete the project? The critical path, which in this case is fourteen (14) days long. The project will finish in fourteen (14) days.
- *(PMBOK® Guide – Sixth Edition*, page 210)

48. C. 2 days

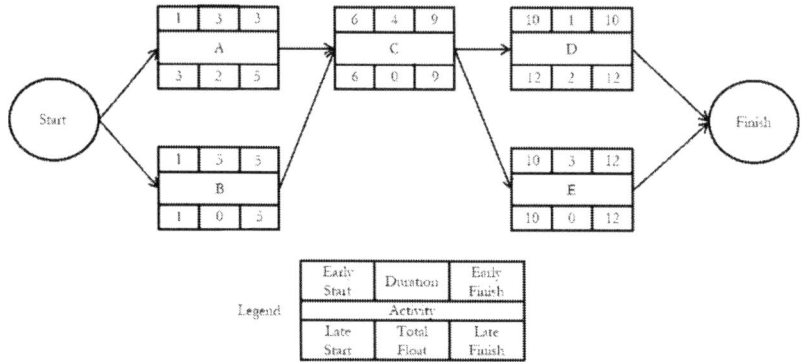

- The amount an activity may be delayed or extended from its early start date without impacting the project finish date or violating a constraint is known as total float.
- A project's total float may be positive, zero, or negative. However, activities on the critical path often have zero (0) total float. The critical path in this question has zero total float.
- Activity A could start two (2) days later than the early start day without impacting the project finish date. Activity D could also start two (2) days after the early start date.
- Use either LS – ES or LF – EF to calculate total float. The total float for Activity D is three (3.) (LS – ES 12 – 10 = 2 or LF-EF 12 – 10 = 2).
- *(PMBOK® Guide – Sixth Edition*, page 210)

49. B. Start, B, C, E, End

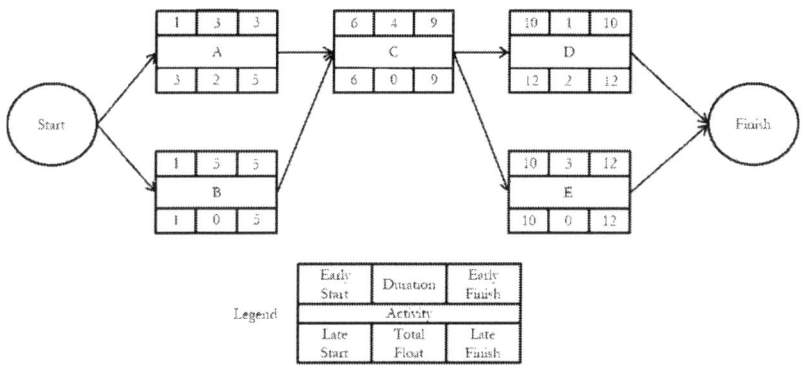

- Use the schedule network in answer 47 for this question. The bolder arrows on a schedule network show the critical path. It is essential to understand what a critical path represents. It is the shortest duration or time required to finish the project.
- Some projects may have multiple critical paths with equal durations. Other projects may have near-critical paths in which the difference in duration between the critical paths is minor.
- For example, the project's critical path has a duration of fifty (50) days, while a near-critical path duration is forty-nine (49) days. Any delay of more than one (1) day on the near-critical path would cause the project to finish late. In these cases, the risk to the project is higher than a project with only a single critical path.
- (PMBOK® Guide – Sixth Edition, page 210)

50. 14 days

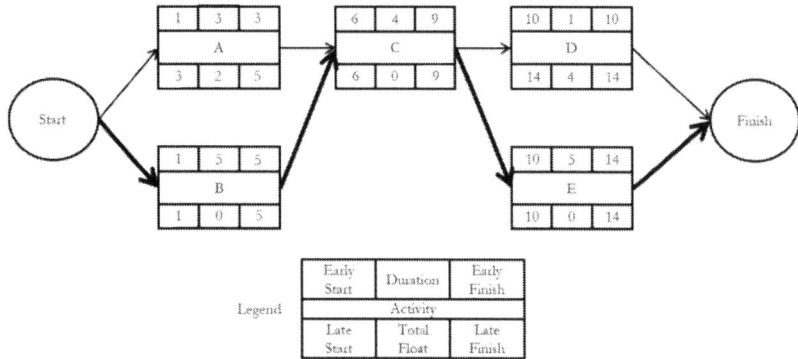

- The critical path or paths determine the longest path and shortest duration. To calculate the shortest duration, add durations from each activity on the critical path. *(PMBOK® Guide – Sixth Edition*, page 210)
51. CPI = 0.8 and the project is over budget
  - The Cost Performance Index (CPI) formula is CPI = EV / AC.
  - CPI = $8,000 / $10,000 = 0.8.
  - The project's CPI is less than 1.0. Therefore the project is over budget. Determining whether a project is over or under budget may be confusing. A CPI of "less" than one (< 1.0) confirms the project is "over" budget for the specified assessment period.
  - Be sure to think through these types of questions, calculate the answer, and then confirm. The team planned to produce $10,000 in Earned Value (EV) during this period. In other words, the earned value of the product, result, or service produced during this period is $10,000. However, the project only earned $8,000 (EV) during this period. The project still needs to produce $2,000 more in value to reach the EV ($10,000). Yet the project's Actual Cost (AC) spent was $10,000. So to create the original EV of $10,000, the project needs to spend an additional $2,000. The Estimate At Completion (EAC) is $10,000 (AC) + $2,000 (Estimate To Complete (ETC)) for total of $12,000. The project is over budget.
  - Don't overthink these questions. What if the project team completed the work but only spent $8,000? What if the

team improved efficiency and now can complete work with less spend? Etc. The question does not state any of this to be true. Neither should you "imply it might be true." If not explicitly stated in the question, then don't consider it on the exam.

- *(PMBOK® Guide – Sixth Edition*, pages 263, 267)

52. A. Project manager
    - The project manager is accountable for the results of the project. This accountability remains true even when other team members, including, in this case, the quality manager, are responsible for the project's quality.
    - The PMBOK® Guide indicates the project manager is "responsible" for project results. The term "accountable," both by general definition and usage in Responsible, Accountable, Consult, and Inform (RACI) matrix, better describes the project manager role. The project manager is the one who needs to justify all project results and decisions. That is the definition of accountable.
    - Often the correct answer on these types of exam questions is the project manager. Whether the question uses the term responsible or accountable.
    - *(PMBOK® Guide – Sixth Edition*, page 552)

53. A. Travel expenses, B. Cultural and C. Team-building
    - Virtual teams typically incur more travel expenses then collocated teams. Virtual teams may travel to participate in team-building, in critical discussions face-to-face, etc.
    - Culturally diverse teams may also be a benefit. Especially when the distribution of the project's product, service, or result is worldwide. Or to leverage critical expertise that resides in another geographical area.
    - *(PMBOK® Guide – Sixth Edition*, page 311)

54. B. Document retention policy
    - All organizations should have retention policies on how long documents (e.g., contracts, emails, letters, etc.). This policy is commonly known as the organization's document retention policy.
    - The project manager must ensure the project team adheres to all organizational policies, including the document retention policy. Policies are Organizational Process Assets (OPAs) since they may be unique to each organization.
    - *(PMBOK® Guide – Sixth Edition*, page 39)

55. A. Project risk
- Project risks are part of every discussion and on every meeting agenda. Project risks are very dynamic. As a result, the focus is always on changing project risks.
- Did the project manager report to stakeholders the project is on schedule? Then is the project's risk, the probability of occurrence, or impact on the project finishing on time now the same or less? Stakeholders will want to know. Did a team member tell the project manager they needed tomorrow off? Did this change the risk of that team member completing their activities on time?
- (PMBOK® Guide – Sixth Edition, page 395)

56. C. Statement of Work (SOW)
- The scope baseline contains all the project scope. This baseline includes both product and project scope.
- The SOW contains the portion of the scope baseline that the buyer will ask the seller to perform. The seller responds with a Request for Proposal (RFP), etc. as appropriate.
- (PMBOK® Guide – Sixth Edition, page 469)

57. D. Assess seller contract terms & conditions performance
- Monitoring and controlling processes compare the plan or expected outcome to actual results. In this case, Control Procurement determines if both the buyer and seller are performing according to the legal contract.
- It is important to note that monitoring and controlling procurement assesses both the buyer and the seller's performance. The assessment is not just the seller's performance.
- Most contracts place legal requirements, such as the specific amount and timing of payments to sellers, on the buyer. Not meeting these buyer legal obligations may lead to a default on the contract by the buyer. The project manager is accountable for ensuring all parties, buyers, and sellers, meet the contract's legal requirements.
- (PMBOK® Guide – Sixth Edition, page 492

58. A. Control Scope
- The Control Scope process ensures the scope baseline remains well defined and maintained. Scope creep would occur without this control. Scope creep by definition is when stakeholders ask the project manager, or an individual team member, to "just add this one important requirement." Soon the project scope is out of control.

- Scope creep may result in missing schedule deadlines, the incurrence of additional costs that were not part of the cost baseline, etc. This impact results in the project team getting demoralized as the project's performance deteriorates – all resulting from the team working on requirements that are not in the scope baseline.
- In this case, the requested requirement is not in the approved project scope baseline. If the stakeholder wants to pursue adding the requirement, the project manager should begin executing the Perform Integrated Change Control and other processes as necessary. This assessment will determine the scope, schedule, and cost baseline impact. If the decision is to include the new requirement, the change must be approved. Then the baselines and other modifications identified by the Perform Integrated Change Control Process are implemented.
- (PMBOK® Guide – Sixth Edition, page 167)

59. A. Work Performance Data

- Many executing processes produce work performance data. This data describes what the team produced. In this question, the percent of work completed.
- It is essential to realize the project manager cannot tell the status of the project with just work performance data. For example, one team member reported they completed ten percent of the activity. Was this completed ten percent the expected completed amount of work? You cannot tell with just work performance data.
- Monitoring and Controlling processes take work performance data and produce work performance information. Information, by definition, has context. For example, if the plan was to complete five percent of the activity during the assessed period, yet the team completed ten percent, then the activity is ahead of schedule.
- It is essential to understand the difference between work performance data, information, and reports. Many Executing processes produce data. Many of the Monitoring and Controlling processes take work performance data as input and produce work performance information. Work performance reports are provided to stakeholders for awareness and may drive actions (e.g., the addition of resources if the project is behind schedule, etc.).
- (PMBOK® Guide – Sixth Edition, page 26)

60. B. Crashing
    - When adding resources to the project, that is known as crashing. In this question, the team added team members in an attempt to bring the schedule back into alignment with the schedule baseline.
    - Adding resources such as equipment, computers, etc. also crashes the project schedule - a form of schedule compression. Very often, crashing adds cost due to the additional resources and may increase risk.
    - Fast-tracking is another form of schedule compression. This technique often adds risk as more activities are done in parallel, increasing the chance for lower quality and the increased need for rework.
    - (*PMBOK® Guide – Sixth Edition*, page 215)

61. D. $1,500,000
    - EAC = AC + ETC ($1,500,000 USD = $500,000 USD+ $1,000,000).
    - This question asks, "What is the Estimate At Completion (EAC)?" Be sure to read these questions carefully. The question did not ask what it would take to finish the project. That would be Estimate To Complete (ETC). ETC in this question would be $1,000,000.
    - A project manager needs to be able to forecast accurately. The sponsor and other stakeholders, while they want to know the current status, are just as or more interested in the future. Accurate forecasting enables the organization as a whole to effectively forecast future resource needs.
    - (*PMBOK® Guide – Sixth Edition*, page 264)

62. C. Manage Quality
    - An audit is an essential tool and technique in the Manage Quality process. Audits assess whether the organization and project policies, procedures, and best practices are effectively and efficiently producing the desired outcome. An audit may find this is not the case and recommend corrective action.
    - The project may have also created a new or improved on an existing best practice. In this case, auditors ensure the rest of the organization is aware and begin leveraging this best practice.
    - It is essential to remember the organization expects a project manager to contribute to the whole organization's

improvement. This contribution may be referred to as lessons learned.

- *(PMBOK® Guide – Sixth Edition*, pages 333, 334)

63. A. Physical resource assignments and C. Resource calendar

- The Acquire Resources process assigns physical and human resources to the project. Physical resources include all equipment, servers, licenses, etc. needed to complete the project.
- Resource calendars are another critical output of the Acquire Resources process. Each resource, bot physical and human, should have an individual calendar. Resource calendars document when the resource is available, including when the resource starts on the project and when the resource will be released. These calendars are essential as the project will not need every resource for the entire duration of the project.
- Resource calendars also document daily availability hours for physical resources and work hours, vacation days, etc. for team members (human resources).
- (PMBOK® Guide – Sixth Edition, pages 333, 334)

64. A. 4

- The key is reading the question carefully. The question asked, ".. how many MORE…?" The easiest way to calculate is to determine the communication channels with four team members, then with five team members and subtract the difference.
- Four team members $N(N-1)/2$ $4(4-1)/2 = 6$
- Five team members $N(N-1)/2$ $5(5-1)/2 = 10$
- $10 - 6 = 4$. Remember, the relationship is not linear. Adding one project member results in more than one additional communication channel. The new project team member and each of the other team members must now communicate with each other.
- *(PMBOK® Guide – Sixth Edition*, page 370)

65. C. Assumptions

- Subject Matter Experts (SMEs), senior management, trade associations, industry leaders, etc. may state assumptions. These sources are collectively known as expert judgment. For example, an expert may say the following assumptions, "The stock market will rise next year." or "Next quarter, the project funding will be available."

- By definition, assumptions are uncertainty "stated as fact." Sources of documented assumptions include the project charter and assumption log. Stakeholders may state new assumptions or change existing assumptions before starting and throughout the project.
- Sometimes documents like the assumption log are not listed separately as inputs or outputs in the PMBOK® Guide. Instead, assumptions are documented along with other materials and listed in the more general term "project documents." This consolidation may lead to confusion. It is essential to understand where each project document is created or updated as outputs and consumed as inputs for the exam.
- (*PMBOK® Guide – Sixth Edition*, page 409)

66. B. Conduct Procurement
   - Often projects today include one or more sellers. This scenario places a premium on a project manager's negotiation skills. This emphasis is true even though a procurement manager may be providing expert judgment on all procurements.
   - Assessing seller's responses, choosing a seller, and negotiating through to a signed contract are all done within the Conduct Procurement process. How well, will have a significant positive or negative impact on the project.
   - (*PMBOK® Guide – Sixth Edition*, page 482)

67. C. Perform Close Project or Phase for each seller and Close Project or Phase once for the project
   - The project manager and team must perform the Close Project or Phase five times. Once for each seller and once for the project. Assessing each seller's contract performance determines if closing the contract is appropriate.
   - Contract terms and conditions must be considered confidential information and should not be discussed with individuals and parties not part of the contract. In this question, since there are four sellers, there must be four individual executions of this process.
   - The project manager must always perform the Close Project or Phase at least once for the project. Completing this process is the final opportunity to document lessons learned.

- Also, the transition of the final product, service, or result occurs during this process. This transition is critical as on-going operations, and support begins during this process. Remember, teams other than the project team often perform on-going support.
- It is easy to "get lost" in all the exam material. But knowing which process transitions the project deliverables to the customer or on-going operations, post-project, is a critical understanding.
- (PMBOK® Guide – Sixth Edition, page 121)

68. B. Project Charter

- There are four project baselines, scope, cost, schedule, and performance measurement baselines (integrated scope-cost-schedule baseline plan to assess project performance). These baselines, once approved, set the expectations of the project. The team uses each baseline to evaluate the project's expected to actual results as defined by these baselines.
- The primary components of the scope baseline are the project scope statement, WBS, and WBS dictionary.
- (PMBOK® Guide – Sixth Edition, pages 88, 161)

69. B. Organizational Process Assets

- The previous project manager made a risk register template available for future projects. It is expected every project manager increases the knowledge of the whole organization. The former project manager in the question illustrates this expectation by providing a new template. Templates are considered Organizational Process Assets. (PMBOK® Guide – Sixth Edition, page 39)

70. D Schedule baseline

- One should understand on exams what is implied by an approved baseline. By definition, any exam question that states the project is in the executing, monitoring, controlling, or closing phase means all baselines are approved, including the schedule baseline.
- The project team and manager created a project schedule considering all the project's requirements, resources, both physical and human, resource calendars, budgets, etc. At this point, the team has modeled the project schedule. However, once the sponsor and other key stakeholders review and approve the model project schedule, it becomes the approved schedule baseline. Executing the Perform

Integrated Change Control process is then required to change the schedule baseline.

- The team will use the approved schedule baseline to assess actual schedule results to determine if the project is on, ahead, or behind schedule.

- For exams, remember unless clearly stated in the question, project schedules, costs, etc. are accurate and realistic. The project manager would only propose a project schedule to stakeholders that have sufficient resources, budgets, etc. to complete the project per the schedule. Adequate means resources, yet no more resources than needed. "In the real-world", as the project manager or a team member, you may have worked on projects without sufficient resources and an unrealistic schedule. Do not consider this type of real-world experience when answering exam questions.

- (*PMBOK® Guide – Sixth Edition*, page 217)

71. D. TCPI

- To Complete Performance Index (TCPI) is used to determine the efficiency or Cost Performance Index (CPI) the team must achieve to complete the project per the budget.

- Let's say a team has completed half of a project with a $20,000 cost baseline. The CPI at the halfway point is 0.90. The project is over budget. It has only earned 90% of the expected value (CPI = EV / AC, 0.90 = $9,000/ $10,000).

- The project must earn $11,000, with the remaining $10,000 of the $20,000 budget. Therefore, the CPI for the second half must be 1.1 (1.1 = $11,000 / $10,000). The project team will have to be more efficient during the second half of the project, or the project will finish over budget.

- You get the same result (1.1) using the TCPI formula with this same example. TCPI = (BAC – EV) / (BAC – AC) 1.1 = ($20,000 - $9,000) / ($20,000 - $10,000).

- The project manager must be able to forecast future performance. TCPI values greater than one (1.0) predicts it will be harder for the team to complete the project per the cost baseline. Think about this. The project is over budget at the halfway point (CPI = 0.90). Therefore the project must be under budget for the remainder of the project (CPI = 1.1).

- The project manager must assess and understand how the team can indeed perform at a 1.1 efficiency for the rest of the project. Understanding this is critical. If the team is unable to perform at 1.1, the project manager must work with stakeholders to adjust the schedule, scope, or cost baselines.

- (PMBOK® *Guide – Sixth Edition*, page 266)

72. B. Testing the population is a type of gold plating

- Gold plating, a form of scope creep, is a term used to describe providing a deliverable that exceeds the customer's requirement. Surveying the population meets the requirement. Collecting data from the entire population exceeds the requirement.

- Be sure you can identify gold plating on the exam. The project manager and team should never allow gold plating. The schedule, scope, and cost baseline are only sufficient to meet the requirements. These baselines, by definition, are not inflated to produce deliverables that exceed the customer's requirements. Even if the extra features are perceived to increase customer satisfaction.

- (PMBOK® *Guide – Sixth Edition*, page 168)

73. D. Forming, Storming, Norming, Performing, and Adjourning

- All teams go through what is known as Tuckman's ladder or stages. Every team must pass through these stages if the team is to grow, find solutions, plan work, and deliver results. More mediocre performing teams may not get through all these phases. Some teams may not even get through storming.

- Therefore the project manager must assess how well the team is doing. The project manager may need to use team-building, conflict management, and other tools and techniques to help the team.

- It is essential to understand that adding a new team member or assigning new roles may result in the team moving "back" one or more stages. In these cases, a performing team may revert to norming or storming as the team adjusts to the new team member or roles.

- (PMBOK® Guide – Sixth Edition, page 338)

74. A. Urgency, C. Ease of use and D. Sensitivity and confidentiality

- The team must consider each of these when choosing the appropriate communication technology. Choosing the best communication technology is typically a tradeoff between urgency, ease of use, sensitivity and confidentiality, and other factors.

- Urgency is how fast the information must be received or understood. If urgency is high, a phone call may be a better choice than email or perhaps even text.
- Is the receiver of the communication comfortable using the technology? Some team members may not be familiar with certain social media apps or the latest team collaboration software.
- Sensitivity and confidentiality. These communications are typically not appropriate for free email, etc. These free email apps may not be secured. Sensitive and confidential information, such as contracts, individual performance reviews, etc. would be best sent through a secured corporate email. Do you see this conflict? Corporate email may not be as easy to use as Gmail but maybe a better choice for sensitive and confidential communications
- (PMBOK® Guide – Sixth Edition, page 370)

75. B. Risk register
    - The team tracks all information about each risk in the risk register. The risk register is one of several documents that is an input to many processes and updated as output by many others. Therefore it is essential to understand.
    - The risk register is updated, beginning with the identification of the risk as part of the Identify Risks process. Other processes then update the probability of occurrence, impact, selected risk strategy, risk owner, response plan, etc. for each risk. The risk register is used as input to determine the scope, schedule, and cost for the project.
    - (PMBOK® Guide – Sixth Edition, page 417)

76. A. An offer, acceptance, consideration, legal capacity and legal purpose
    - The PMBOK® Guide – Sixth Edition may use the term agreement in place of contract. This is not quite right. An agreement is an understanding, while a contract is a particular type of agreement. A contract is a legally binding agreement enforceable by law. Agreements, other than contracts, may not be enforceable by law.
    - The answer lists each component of a legally binding contract. If any component is missing, it is not a legal contract.

- Offer. A party to the contract must make an offer. For example, "ABC Software will develop the app according to the requirements for $1,000,000."
- Acceptance. The party receiving the offer must accept it. In the previous ABC Software example, the party receiving the app must accept it. Just because an offer is made does not result in an agreement or contract.
- Consideration. The exchange of something of value. In this example, the party pays the other $1,000,000 for the app.
- Legal capacity. The person who can enter into a contract. The project manager may not have the capacity or authority to enter into a contract. Often in an organization, only the procurement manager has the capacity and authority. So it is essential when working with other parties on a contract to understand who has the legal capacity.
- Legal purpose. The reason for entering the contract must be lawful. Parties cannot enter into a legal contract to conduct illegal activities.
- (*PMBOK® Guide – Sixth Edition*, page 489)

77. A. Perform Integrated Change Control
    - It is essential to understand when to execute the Perform Integrated Change Control process. The team must complete this process for any change after the approval of the scope, schedule, and cost baselines. However, any project work before approval of the baselines does not require the execution of the Perform Integrated Change Control process.
    - The purpose of Perform Integrated Change Control is to ensure the team and organization considers all the impacts to a change before approving the change. For example, the team was working based on approved baselines when a stakeholder asked for a new requirement. Will this requirement change the scope? No. By definition, there are no excess resources on the project. Therefore, adding a requirement would also take more time and additional costs. This change may also change both the schedule and cost baselines, not just the scope baseline. Plus requirements documentation, traceability matrix, communications, quality metrics, etc. may all require updating.
    - The project is under budget and ahead of schedule, so the team agrees to implement a change because they can still

meet the original plan. Does Perform Integrated Change Control need to be executed? Yes. The project team does not decide how to use excess budget and time. Instead, they should return any excess budget, time, and resources to the organization. On the other hand, the sponsor and key stakeholders may determine during executing Performing Integrated Change Control that it is best to apply these excess resources on the project.

- (*PMBOK® Guide – Sixth Edition*, page 113)

78. C. Project Management Plan
    - The project management plan describes how the team will do the
    - executing, monitoring and controlling, and closing process groups. The project management plan includes all the individual knowledge area management plans, baselines, and other components to complete the project.
    - Remember, a project may not require performing every *PMBOK® Guide* process, tool, or technique. A critical skill of the project manager is to tailor which components in the project management plan are needed to complete the project.
    - (*PMBOK® Guide – Sixth Edition*, page 86)

79. D. Over budget and on schedule
    - It is essential to understand a project's status based on the Cost Performance Index (CPI) and Schedule Performance Index (SPI). A CPI of less than 1.0 indicates the project is overbudget. The earned value (EV) is less than the actual cost (AC) incurred during the selected period. An SPI or CPI, equal to 1.0, indicates the project is on schedule or budget.
    - (*PMBOK® Guide – Sixth Edition*, page 267)

80. C. Validate Scope
    - Knowing the difference between verified and accepted deliverables is critical. The project team verifies the deliverable meets all requirements as part of the Control Quality process. The verified deliverable is an input to the Validate Scope process where the customer accepts or validates that the deliverable meets expectations.
    - Even though both the team and customer agree the deliverable met the requirements, it may not meet the customer's needs. This discrepancy may be due to several reasons. Perhaps the customer needs have changed, market

conditions changed, the deliverable no longer competitive in the marketplace, etc.

- The project manager must determine how often to perform Validate Scope to ensure the customer accepts each deliverable. Discovering that a deliverable is unacceptable early is critical to avoiding or minimizing project delays, unnecessary expenses, or even project cancelation.
- PMBOK® Guide – Sixth Edition uses the term accepted deliverables. Prior versions used the term validated deliverables.
- (*PMBOK® Guide – Sixth Edition*, page 163)

81. C. Performing

- During the performing phase, the team focuses on achieving the goal, making decisions without intervention by leaders, working autonomously, etc. The team has progressed through the forming, storming, and norming phases of Tuckman's stages or ladder. However, the team has not yet accomplished the goal, so the team is not in the adjourning stage.
- It is essential to realize it is natural for a performing team, or any team, to return to one of the previous stages if new team members join the team, existing team members leave, or roles change.
- (*PMBOK® Guide – Sixth Edition*, page 338)

82. B. Receiver

- Who is responsible may be confusing. Often the sender is believed to be responsible that the message is understood. That is not the case. The sender is responsible for transmitting a clear message and confirming it was received, correctly interpreted, acknowledged, or responded to appropriately. Understanding the entire message and confirming that understanding is the responsibility of the receiver. (PMBOK® Guide – Sixth Edition, page 372)

83. A. SWOT

- A team may use Strengths, Weaknesses, Opportunities, and Threats (SWOT) technique to assess an organization, project, or product. A SWOT assessment is done by creating a four-quadrant diagram and listing in separate quadrants the strengths, weaknesses, opportunities, or threats. A team may use a SWOT to compare one option to another option, a product against a competitor's product, etc. (*PMBOK® Guide – Sixth Edition*, page 415)

84. B. Material Breach
    - In this question, the seller did not provide a deliverable with a critical requirement. The result is a breach of the contract. However, since the project cannot continue, the severity or significance makes this a material breach.
    - Based on the contract terms, the buyer may either terminate the contract or force compliance. Confirming both the buyer and seller is meeting the terms and conditions of agreements or contracts, is a function of the Control Procurement process.
    - (*PMBOK® Guide – Sixth Edition*, page 492)

85. D. Review scope baseline
    - The scope baseline includes the WBS and scope statement. Two of the other possible answers. The WBS dictionary is also part of the scope baseline. Verifying the deliverable meets the requirements, as defined by the approved scope baseline, before meeting with the customer is always a good practice.
    - This question is a common type of exam question. One should always consider the best answer to be the one that includes one or more of the other answers. In some cases, WBS or project scope statement might be acceptable answers. But in this case, the best answer is scope baseline as it includes both.
    - (*PMBOK® Guide – Sixth Edition*, page 161)

86. B. Constraint
    - Something that restricts or limits the ability to complete a task, project, or produce a deliverable is a constraint. For example, the question states engineers are not available until July. The team must consider this constraint in the project's schedule and risk analysis. Examples of other constraints include having a fixed budget, a limited number of developers, etc.
    - A constraint is a statement that is proven to be true, and therefore, not an assumption. An assumption is stated as a fact when it has not validated as true. Had the functional manager said, "I doubt if any engineers are available until July," that would be an assumption. The project manager should then seek confirmation that engineers are not

available until July. If true, this assumption then becomes a fact or constraint.

- *(PMBOK® Guide – Sixth Edition*, page 415)

87. C. What is in-scope and out-of-scope for the scope

- The project scope statement describes the major deliverables, assumptions, and constraints, along with a description of the project scope. The project scope, in this case, includes both the project and product scope.
- What is in-scope is what the project will deliver. But often, it is just as important to describe what is not in the project scope. Stating what is out-of-scope helps clarify to the stakeholders what is in-scope. Identifying out-of-scope deliverables promotes communication among stakeholders. This discussion ensures understanding of the project scope before the stakeholders approving the scope baseline.
- *(PMBOK® Guide – Sixth Edition*, page 154)

88. A. Moderate to high

- Matrix teams work across areas of expertise or functions (IT, accounting, production, marketing, etc.) to deliver a product, service, or result.
- Matrix organizational structure types range from strong to balanced to weak. Whether the structure type is strong, balanced, or weak depends on the project manager's authority, engaged full or part-time, is typically full time, manages the budget, etc.
- *(PMBOK® Guide – Sixth Edition*, page 47)

89. A. Manage closely

- A stakeholder with a high level of authority (power) and great concern (interest) in the project is one whom the project manager will want to manage carefully.
- The project manager should assess each stakeholder's power, interest, influence (active involvement in the project), and impact (ability to impact the project planning or execution). The project manager may plot key stakeholders on a power/interest, power/influence, or impact/influence grid. A stakeholder's power, interest, influence, and impact may vary during different phases of the project.
- *(PMBOK® Guide – Sixth Edition*, page 512)

90. D. Decomposing

- Decomposing is a technique that takes a higher level of deliverable or work and further defines it. Decomposition is an iterative process where each iteration adds more clarity or detail. Decomposition continues until the team can estimate the effort, duration, resources, and cost needed to produce the deliverable. Decomposition is a critical technique in the Create WBS process. *(PMBOK® Guide – Sixth Edition*, page 158)

91. C. 5 years

- The payback period is a financial analysis tool used to assess two or more options. The payback period is one method to identify which project or opportunity has a more favorable financials. Make or by decisions may also calculate the payback period. Other decision analysis tools, return on investment (ROI), net present value (NPV), etc. may also be used along with the payback period to decide the best option.

- Payback period = total cost per period / revenue per period. $10,000 / $2,000 = 5. Since the cost and revenue are in years, the answer is five years. After five years, the cost ($10,000) will be recover.

- *(PMBOK® Guide – Sixth Edition*, page 34)

92. C. The output continues to diminish until the additional cost exceeds the benefit

- This answer is the definition of the Law of Diminishing returns. As resources, people, equipment, money, etc. are added to the project, the cost-benefit analysis changes. Initially, the benefit of additional resources may exceed the cost.

- However, at some point, the additional benefit value equals the cost. At this point, there is no benefit to adding more resources. After this point, each additional resource produces less benefit than the cost of that additional resource. The project schedule and cost become increasingly less efficient.

- Calculating the communication channels is a simple example of the Law of Diminishing returns. Remember the number of communication channels formula N(N-1)/2? A team of two has one communication channel. A team of four has six communication channels. A team of eight has twenty-eight communication channels. At some point, the benefit of more team members is less than the additional cost of communicating and coordinating those additional resources.

- The Law of Diminishing returns is one reason Agile recommends teams to be between three and nine developers. Do some projects have much larger teams? Yes. The cost-benefit varies with the project. But the Law of Diminishing returns holds true for all projects. At some point, the cost of adding more resources exceeds the value of the benefit.
- (PMBOK® Guide – Sixth Edition, page 197)

93. A. Sunk cost
- An essential concept of analyzing decisions is sunk costs. The project so far has spent $1M. Should the $1M be considered in the decision analysis to invest more in the project? No. All past project spend, $1M, in this case, is sunk cost. There is no option at this point that can recover this project's previous spending.
- The project team must consider various options as to what it would take, Estimate to Complete (ETC), the project. Then the team chooses the best option without considering the sunk cost. The best option may be to stop the project.
- One principle of Agile is to deliver business value early and often. This principle enables, even in the case when the decision is to stop the project prematurely, to potentially deliver value from the sunk costs. Stopping predictive projects that deliver business value at the very end may not produce any business value.
- (PMBOK® Guide – Sixth Edition, page 671)

94. D. WBS
- The Work Breakdown Structure (WBS) is a hierarchical view of the project's deliverable(s). The WBS includes only in-scope deliverables. The team decomposes the WBS until the lowest level enables accurate estimating by the team. (PMBOK® Guide – Sixth Edition, page 158)

95. A. Scope baseline
- The project scope statement, WBS, and WBS dictionary together comprise the scope baseline. While the team is creating the project scope statement, WBS, and WBS dictionary, one may refer to them collectively as the scope baseline.
- Remember, the scope baseline is unapproved during this effort. Once approved, the project team is committed to delivering the scope. Any changes to the scope will require executing the Perform Integrated Change Control process.

- The scope baseline only includes these three components. It may be confusing as sometimes other components, such as work or planning packages, may be listed as part of the scope baseline. These are specific components of a WBS. Therefore, by definition stating the WBS is part of the scope baseline, includes both work and planning packages.
- (*PMBOK® Guide – Sixth Edition*, page 161)

96. A. At the end of the phase or interim deliverable
- The team should perform validation with the customer who is receiving the project deliverables often. The customer may reject the deliverable even if it meets all the project requirements. This reason for rejecting may be due to changing customer needs, market place conditions, etc. Therefore, it is critical to confirm frequently through the Validate Scope process that the deliverables still meet the customer's needs.
- In Agile, validating deliverables occurs at the end of every sprint. Typically every two to four weeks. Although called a sprint review, it is, in essence, executing the Validate Scope process. This example is one of many where leveraging the concepts of Validate Scope with Sprint Reviews would benefit both traditional and agile projects.
- (*PMBOK® Guide – Sixth Edition*, page 163)

97. B. Direct and Manage Project Work
- It is essential while preparing for an exam not to get "lost" in all the processes, input, outputs, and tools and techniques. The purpose of all projects is to produce one or more deliverables. Either a product, service, or result. But what process does that? The Direct and Manage Project Work process produces deliverables. This process is where the team does the work to produce the project's deliverable(s).
- It is essential to understand the flow of deliverables throughout the project. This flow begins with the Direct and Manage Project Work process that produces the deliverables. The Control Quality process takes those deliverables and produces verified deliverables. Which, in turn, is an input to Validate Scope, which produces validated deliverables. Finally, the transition of validated deliverables to the customer or support organization occurs during the Close Project or Phase process.
- (*PMBOK® Guide – Sixth Edition*, page 90)

98. D. The project manager should seek mentoring to acquire more skills before tailoring

- Skill acquisition is a process that goes through phases. The Shu-Ha-Ri model describes these phases. First, the person learning must follow the rules, process procedures, or standards. This phase is the Shu phase.
- Once they learn the procedure or standard, then the learner may start to make minor changes. This phase is known as the Ha phase. The project manager, in this case, may start tailoring once they reach the Ha phase. Tailoring includes modifying what sections may be in the project charter, project management plan, etc. to align with the project needs. The final phase, Ri, is where the learner creates new processes after considerable learning.
- Since this is the first project for the manager, they are in the Shu phase. They should use the process as is or seek mentoring before tailoring. They should continue to seek mentoring even in the Ha phase were more tailoring may be done.
- (*PMBOK® Guide – Sixth Edition*, pages 28, 679)

99. C. Agile

- The Agile life-cycle is preferred when it is known or expected that requirements will change throughout the project. Frequent sprint retrospectives and reprioritizing the product backlog, plus other Agile concepts, support customer changes to requirements. (*PMBOK® Guide – Sixth Edition*, page 666)

100. B. Variable sampling

- By definition, determining the degree of conformance based on a continuous scale is variable sampling.
- For example, does the thermostat keep the temperature at 68 +/- 2 degrees (Fahrenheit)? In this example, the sampling readings are 68.5, 67.3, 69.1, etc. and the thermostat would pass.
- Attribute sampling assesses an item for discrete attributes. This conformance assessment is either a "yes" or "no" (pass/fail, true/false). Does the thermostat turn on the heat? Cooling? The answer to each is either yes or no.

ABOUT THE AUTHOR

Tom Schoen, President of 1411Consulting, LLC, has over thirty years of results-based leadership experience at a Fortune 100 global company. Tom has held supervisory leadership roles across infrastructure and software application development and support teams plus service desk teams. Tom has also led multiple projects across the entire technology and process stacks. Also, Tom has led commercial software and vendor capability and contract assessment projects based on defined business requirements.

Tom has taught graduate and undergraduate technology and project management courses at Bradley University, Illinois Central College, and the local Project Management Institute (PMI)® chapter.

Tom is a certified Six Sigma Black Belt, a certified Project Management Professional (PMP)®, and a PMI-Agile Certified Practitioner (PMI-ACP)® and a SAFe® 4 Certified Agilist.

You will find free online learning materials to help prepare you for the (PMP)® and (PMI-ACP)® exams at 1411Consulting.com.

Printed in Great Britain
by Amazon